To: Sue,

This story to me to New

Enjoy!

MILES TO GO BEFORE I SLEEP

A Survivor's Story of Life
After a Terrorist Hijacking

JACKIE NINK PFLUG

With Peter J. Kizilos

■ **HAZELDEN**®

Hazelden
Center City, Minnesota 55012-0176

09 08 07 06   8 7 6 5

Unless indicated otherwise, all photographs are courtesy of Jackie Nink Pflug.

Library of Congress Cataloging-in-Publication Data
Nink Pflug, Jackie.
    Miles to go before I sleep : a survivor's story of life after a terrorist hijacking / by Jackie
Nink Pflug, with Peter J. Kizilos.
        p.   cm.
    Includes bibliographical references and index.
    ISBN 1-56838-837-3 (pbk.)
    1. Nink Pflug, Jackie.   2. Victims of terrorism—United States—Biography.
3. Hostages—United States—Biography.   4. Hijacking of aircraft—Egypt.
I. Kizilos, Peter. II. Title.
    HE9882.7.Z7H56   1995
    362.88—dc20
    [B]   95-18989
                                                                                              CIP

The cloth printing of this book contains the subtitle *My Grateful Journey Back from the
Hijacking of EgyptAir Flight 648.* The original subtitle was changed to *A Survivor's Story of
Life After a Terrorist Hijacking* for the paperback release in November 2001.

THIS BOOK IS DEDICATED TO

Scarlett Rogencamp and Nitzan Mendelson—
the two women cold-bloodedly executed
by the hijackers of EgyptAir Flight 648.

The forty-nine other passengers—
from Israel, Canada, Australia, Belgium, Egypt, France, Ghana,
Greece, Mexico, Morocco, the Philippines, Spain, and Tunisia—
killed during the storming of the plane.

The eight children
who spent their last hours as hostages
aboard the plane.

And to the thirty-five men and women who survived:
My prayer is that you found the gift behind the tragedy.

*The day you can be grateful for every single trifle in your life,
for the moving train, for the water that runs down a tap
when you open it, for the light that comes on when you press
a switch, for clean sheets on your bed. . . . your heart will be filled
with a deep contentment and with almost continuous joy.
The secret of being always joyful is to be always grateful.*
—ANTHONY DE MELLO
SADHANA: A WAY TO GOD

CONTENTS

PREFACE

THE TERRORIST ATTACK ON THE WORLD TRADE CENTER and the Pentagon on September 11, 2001, in New York City has shaken and saddened the very soul of America. It has caused shock waves of fear that most people have never before experienced. Reports of heightened anxiety, depression, and inability to sleep or concentrate at work abound. People have cancelled vacations and have even turned in rage and fear on their neighbors who do not look like them. I recognize the terror. It is a terror I personally experienced sixteen years ago when EgyptAir Flight 648 was hijacked and I was shot in the head at point-blank range, dumped from the airplane, and left for dead on the tarmac.

The recent suicide attacks resurrected my fear briefly, and then the difficult lessons I learned from my own tragedy reasserted themselves. In my long and difficult journey back from my own encounter with terrorism and death, I discovered that there is always Divine Good in what appears to be only bad. The seeds of healing and growth are buried in the rubble of tragedies. Although hard to see and even harder to believe, the hand of Divine Good is present in this horrific, unimaginable act. It is visible in the outpouring of help to the survivors—the prayers and food and money and clothing and time. It is visible in the renewed sense of life, commitment, and unity that this horrific act engendered.

We can respond to this and other tragedies, from individual to global ones, in ways that help us to live fuller lives and move the world closer to peace and fullness. We can heal. I know.

When the hijacked airliners, two in New York, one in Washington, D.C., and one in Pennsylvania, exploded in flames with 266 passengers and crew members, I felt an overwhelming sadness. I didn't actually know the men, women, and children who died in the crashes, but I know what they went through: the shock, the disbelief, the confusion about who to believe, the fear that they may not be alive in the next hour, the sadness, wishing they had time to do all the things they love, time to say "I love you," time to give hugs, time to say good-bye. I felt close to them all. Scarlett Rogencamp sat next to me on EgyptAir 648, and we comforted each other mostly without words, by touching, and by a visceral and transcendent knowledge of what we were feeling. The hijacker's bullet killed Scarlett, and though I never met her before I boarded that airplane, I still miss her. On a beautiful day I will walk outside into the sunshine and think, Scarlett would have loved this day. I feel that kind of connection to the people who died in those planes and am filled with sadness.

I feel a connection, too, to the survivors, the people who fled the towers, and to the family and friends of the survivors and victims of the suicide terrorists. Beyond that, I feel a connection to all the people in our country and others who watched the events unfold on television and suffer the shock of a world turned upside down. What touched me, my friends and family who cared for me sixteen years ago is now touching America on that same level. People are asking questions. Why did this happen to us? What do we do now? What does my life mean? Why are we here on earth?

In the aftermath of the recent attacks, millions of people find themselves filled with fear. I hope my story can help them in their struggles. After my own encounter with death and paralyzing fear and after years of work toward healing, I have been compelled to share my story. God's voice, or what some people call an inner voice, higher power, or goodness of being, has said to me repeatedly that my purpose on earth now is to tell my story of healing and hope. I believe it can help people who have to face all kinds of difficulties from stress to illness to catastrophes to look for the Divine Good in the difficulty. At some point, everyone has to heal. Everyone goes through the same healing process. This is a book about healing.

In the months after I was left for dead on the tarmac, I was filled with fear. I was afraid to go outside my house, to the grocery store, a movie, or use a public restroom. I was afraid I would be hunted and gunned down. I struggled to get back on an airplane. Each time I got on, I walked down the aisle sneaking glances at laps to see if they were holding packages that could be guns or grenades. This fear gripped me and wouldn't let me grow. I went through severe depression and lived with an overpowering anger for years. Ultimately I learned to forgive.

I don't use the word *forgiveness* glibly; it is a word that gets thrown around way too much. It took me eleven years to forgive the hijackers of

EgyptAir 648, eleven years of doing something every day, whether consciously or not. I started with hatred and anger. You cannot forgive if you're still angry. I cried. I grieved. I raged. I hung in there, kept my faith, worked with a therapist, and finally was able to let go. I'm so glad I did. Forgiving does not condone what the hijackers did. Rather, forgiveness is a release, a letting go so that the person no longer has a hold on you. For a long time, I had to make sure that the man who shot me, who was held in a Malta jail, was not a happy man. I wanted him as miserable as I was. Little by little, I began to accept what had happened, who this person was, and stop hungering for his punishment.

I had, and still have, physical challenges. My vision is fractured. I see only parts of things, so I have had to learn to walk again without bumping into walls or trees. I have had to learn to read again. I suffer memory loss and seizures. I lost my career, income, and marriage. I lost my dream of living in other countries among other peoples, including the Arab people in Egypt who I loved and continue to love so much. But I was given a gift as well. The hijacking was a wake-up call for me to slow down, cherish life, and pay attention. It forced me to deal with a reality that I would have postponed until my dying day. I learned to look past the obstacles that get in my way and focus on what really matters in life. I tend to worry a lot about little things, but if I am paying attention and self aware, I don't let myself do that anymore. I live in the moment, and I'm fine. I'm great. I have lost a lot of my vision, but I'm light now.

I talk to God a lot, and in the weeks since that sad, unforgettable Tuesday morning in September, I keep hearing God's voice saying everything is going to be okay. I know this voice does not mean that I will be able to see well again, or read more easily, or that my epilepsy will disappear. It does not mean that I will never have my heart in my throat as I round a dark corner or board an airplane, or that no one will be paralyzed or die. But it means we can make good happen by this. We have no guarantee about what will happen to our bodies, but we can be assured and guaranteed that our spirits will be okay, that who we really are will be okay.

When I was shot in the head, I was awakened to life. I try every day to remember that I already have what I need and be thankful on a daily basis. I try to remain alert every moment of every day, alert to the sunshine and the rain, alert to the pain and pleasures of my fellows and family, alert to opportunities to be the kind of friend to others that I would like to have as a friend.

Each of us can make a profound difference in the world by paying attention to what happens in our own personal spheres of influence. We live in an increasingly violent world. I believe there is a way, through reconciliation, love, acceptance, and understanding that each of us—individually and collectively—can truly make a difference in the world. We can reach out and stop the cycle of violence and hatred.

We can make a difference by slowing down, noticing the moment we live in, extending ourselves to others, living with integrity, and telling ours mates, children, friends, and family that we love them. Ask, why am I here on earth? Am I doing my part? Am I committed to forgiving others and healing the hurts in our relationships? Do I expect and give thanks for the everyday miracles I see all around me? Am I letting my spirit sing while I'm here?

I am immensely saddened by the terrorist attacks that took so many lives and spawned so much understandable fear and rage. The sadness is with me every day. The sadness has been with me every day for the last sixteen years, an unavoidable recognition of pain and hurt. But I am still hopeful that we are moving forward toward peace here on earth. As in every tragedy, whether it is an act of terrorism, a life threatened by cancer or AIDS, an accident that leaves one disabled, a separation from a loved one, we can know that Divine Good is always present and that our spirits will heal.

ACKNOWLEDGMENTS

THIS BOOK WOULD NOT HAVE BEEN POSSIBLE without the generous and loving help and support Peter and I received from so many people.

We'd like to thank Irene Getz, Ph.D., for reading early drafts of the work; Cheryl Haraseth, for her incredible diligence in transcribing hours and hours of taped interviews; and Bill and Marcia Behring, my business partners, for all their help and hard work during many wonderful years of working together.

Others who helped Peter and me and deserve recognition include my mother and father, Rylma and Eugene Nink; Scott Pflug; June and Greg Pflug; Barbara and Wayne Wilson; Debbie Reno Wells; my sister Mary Nink and my nephew Michael Nink; my sister Gloria Beaver; Mr. E. C. Woods; Cindy Carter; Anne Moen; Ellie Hyatt; Roger Brunner; Mark and Betsy Gathercole; Kathy MacPherson; Ursula Lommen; Barbara Zimbeck Garland; Brenda Schaeffer; Mark Lyso; Don George; Stephen Boehlke; Paul and Rina Kizilos; Tolly and Betty Kizilos; Michael and Meg Adamovich; Jack Orth; George Cleveland; Rudy Ruettiger; and Ken Schelper.

We also wish to thank Rebecca Post, our editor at Hazelden, for her insightful and incredibly skillful advice and help in shaping this book. We'd like to thank everyone at Hazelden who helped make this book possible—including sales and marketing staff, graphic designers, manuscript editors, and proofreaders.

Many thanks to other friends and supporters who offered their critical comments, encouragement, moral support, and love throughout the project—especially Jim Olsen and Nancy Clift.

Finally, I'd like to thank my Inner Voice for urging me to share my story—even when I didn't seem to listen.

INTRODUCTION

THE HIJACKING OF EGYPTAIR FLIGHT 648 was a terrifying drama that sent shock waves around the world.

For an entire week in late November 1985, it was the lead story in the *New York Times*, the *Washington Post*, the *Los Angeles Times*, and on television network news broadcasts worldwide. Millions of concerned readers and viewers followed the fate of passengers from fourteen nations who were left to the mercy of three cold-blooded killers.

I was a thirty-year-old special education teacher, and one of three U.S. citizens on the plane when it was forced to land on a darkened, desert airstrip on the tiny Mediterranean island of Malta. Along with the ninety-four other men, women, and children, I waited nervously as the international community considered its response.

President Ronald Reagan and U.S. Secretary of State George Shultz joined the Maltese, Egyptian, and other world leaders in seeking to negotiate a peaceful end to the siege. When the terrorists' demand for fuel was refused, they threatened to start executing one passenger every fifteen minutes—starting with Israelis and Americans—until they got what they wanted. The world watched in horror as the terrorists carried out their plan.

I was the fifth person shot in the head at pointblank range, shoved out of the plane and onto the tarmac, and left for dead.

When negotiations finally broke down, Maltese and Egyptian government officials decided to storm the plane in a desperate effort to rescue the remaining hostages. There was plenty of second-guessing and finger-pointing after that strategy failed. At the same time, tensions in the Middle East flared as Egypt braced itself for a possible attack by Libya. The United States issued a strong condemnation of terrorism and vowed to hunt down terrorists everywhere and bring them to justice.

As time passed and the immediate crisis faded, the story of the hijacking of EgyptAir Flight 648 slowly drifted to the back pages—and, eventually, disappeared.

Yet the bullet's impact on my life continued to grow and grow. In addition to vision and memory loss, I struggled to cope with a severe learning disability, a strange numbness in my left side, epileptic seizures, post-traumatic stress disorder (PTSD), and clinical depression. The long, uphill struggle to heal from these wounds and their emotional consequences wreaked havoc on my marriage and other relationships. There were times when despair closed in around me and life didn't seem worth living.

For me, the real drama of the hijacking begins after the cameras stopped rolling and the front-page stories were filed and forgotten. The "story behind the story" starts in the quiet and lonely place where I come face-to-face with the fear, anger, sadness, and grief stirred by the hijacking. It starts on the long road to recovery. It starts when I begin to own my bitterness, pain, and many losses. It starts when I asked myself the question: What am I going to do about it now?

There were two obvious choices: I could slip into self-pity and blame, and see myself as a victim for the rest of my life. Or I could choose to accept total responsibility for my responses to a terrible tragedy. Either way, I came to realize that the decision was up to me.

Choosing the second option, to reclaim my life and my dreams, would require years of slow and painful work. It would take every ounce of strength, every bit of courage, persistence, and determination I could muster. I'd have to be willing to probe deep inside, to explore a murky world of hidden emotions. I'd have to apply everything I knew about teaching learning disabled children to myself. I'd have to become more patient with myself, become thankful for the small things, and learn to trust my gut for answers.

I had to rely more on my Inner Voice—my words for what others call the Christ Within, God, intuition, insight, a Higher Power, or Higher Consciousness. Listening closely to my Inner Voice helped me solve many problems I could never have handled alone.

I had three major goals after the hijacking: to raise my reading level, drive again, and go back to work. I was determined to do everything in my power to come back strong.

It's taken me ten years to feel ready to share the lessons I've learned in my recovery and rehabilitation—ten years of slow, and often tedious, progress. It's been a long road, but, unbelievable as it may sound, I can honestly say I wouldn't trade any of my experiences. Through them all, I've continued to grow and learn and find new things to be thankful for—even in the midst of sorrow.

After speaking to a group of foster parents in Minneapolis, a woman raised her hand to ask me a question. "Are you healed?" she asked. I had to pause a moment to think about it. "No, not yet," I said. "Healing is a process that is never fully completed. We wouldn't still be on earth if we were completely healed."

Be good to yourself. Take care of yourself. Be true to yourself and, above all—love yourself. That's where it all begins.

TERROR IN THE SKY

MY LIFE COULDN'T HAVE BEEN GOING BETTER. After years of feeling stuck, I'd finally freed up my spirit to pursue dreams that once seemed far too distant for a young girl growing up in Pasadena, Texas.

The notion of becoming a teacher had at first sounded like a lofty, unattainable goal. Yet now, with discipline, and years of study and hard work, I was teaching learning disabled children and enjoying the thrill of seeing them grow.

I'd dreamed of visiting strange and exotic lands, meeting interesting people, and living in a place where it snowed. These visions, too, seemed worlds away from the "meat and potatoes" part of south Texas where I was raised. Yet I'd found a way to make those fantasies also come true.

I had quit my secure job as a special education teacher and school psychologist in suburban Houston and spent the last two years teaching overseas in Stavanger, Norway and Cairo, Egypt. I'd grown up a lot by traveling overseas and immersing myself in other cultures. I had found my niche in life, my reason for being—and it felt great! My heart's desires were being fulfilled. Nothing was holding me back.

Then came a thunderbolt from out of the blue—and it was all over.

It all happened so quickly, in the time it takes to draw in a deep breath and slowly let it out.

One minute I was in a safe, predictable world governed by civilized rules that I knew and understood. I was happy-go-lucky Jackie Pflug, a fireball who had the world by the tail.

The next minute, I was immersed in a fearsome world of human evil, cruelty, and insanity. All of my hard-won efforts to take charge of my life and future suddenly turned to dust in the terrifying series of events to follow.

On that fateful Thanksgiving weekend in November 1985, I was returning home to Cairo, Egypt, after spending three days with my husband, Scott Pflug, in Athens, Greece. For Scott, the trip was a mixture of business and pleasure. In addition to teaching physical education at the Cairo American College (CAC), a K–12 school in the suburb of Maadi, he coached the girls' volleyball team. The girls did well enough that season to be invited to Athens to compete in an international tournament. Scott would be coach and chaperone to the twelve high school girls who made the trip.

I was excited for the girls. I'd attended every one of their home games that fall and many of their practices. Scott and I had the team over for pizza several times. We both loved traveling and being involved in sports. I arranged to meet Scott and the team a day after they arrived in Athens. I was looking forward to exploring another new city.

In Cairo, I'd certainly indulged my passion for adventure. I took full advantage of living in Egypt to explore museums, the great Pyramids, the Sphinx, and other exotic and historic sites.

Scott and I lived only a mile and a half from CAC, so we could easily walk or bike to the marketplace and softball fields. We took cabs into Cairo, which was about fifteen minutes away, and rode buses for longer trips outside the city. As a frequent passenger, I got to know some of the cab drivers well. They got a kick out of shuttling a curious, talkative, young American woman around.

Every Wednesday after school, I walked or biked to the market to do my grocery shopping. The Egyptian people in the marketplace, especially at the vegetable and fruit stands, were always very friendly and helpful. I soon made friends with several shopkeepers. They often gave me extra bananas, loading them into my bag until I said, "Stop!" They were so sweet. I'd load up the basket on my bicycle with local delicacies: vegetables, yogurt, grape leaves stuffed with lentils.

Walking back home through the crowded, colorful streets of Cairo was a cultural experience in itself. The Old World and the New existed side by side. The peasant men and women I met in the streets and marketplace wore *gallabeyyas*, traditional Egyptian clothing resembling a long nightshirt. The men usually wore white or gray, while the women's version was more decorative. Some Egyptians wore Western-style suits or dresses. Walking down a busy street in the middle of the day, I'd see dusty new Mercedes Benz automobiles parked alongside mule-driven street carts laden with garbage, fresh fruit, or pots and pans.

The Egyptians I met on my excursions around Maadi and Cairo were warm and welcoming. Their Texas-style openness made me feel right at home.

Scott and I chartered old, rickety, vintage 1930s sailboats—the same "boat taxis" that shuttled Egyptian commuters back and forth across the Nile every day—and went sailing on the Nile. Two barefoot Egyptian guides, wearing long robes and turbans, sailed the boats. Their skin was dark and leathery from constant exposure to the desert sun.

One weekend, I flew to Luxor, Egypt, with a group of women from CAC. We rode donkeys through the countryside and took a leisurely tour of ancient tombs buried deep in the mountainside of a small village in the back country of upper Egypt. In Luxor, we were invited into a family's home for tea—a great honor in Egypt. We were a bit naive about the intentions of our young male guides, however; after showing us around, they became a bit *too* friendly.

Another time, I joined friends and co-workers for an excursion into the Sahara Desert. I felt like Lawrence of Arabia riding on my camel with the Pyramids in the foreground. After pitching camp on the edge of the desert, we sat on a blanket in the sand and watched the setting sun. Our Egyptian guides looked so majestic with their white turbans and gallabeyyas glowing in the dying light. At night, we sat near our camels, in small circles around the campfire. I had the sense of being on a movie set or of being pushed back in time.

Two weeks before going to Greece, I signed up for Arabic classes to improve my ability to communicate with the people I met. I'd already learned a few simple phrases. One of my favorite was "In Sha Allah," which means, "If God so wills," "It's in God's hands," or "Whatever God wants."

Instead of saying "Have a good day!" the Egyptians said, "In Sha Allah!" when greeting me or bidding me good-bye.

As much as I loved the romance and adventure of living in Cairo, I was really looking forward to visiting Greece. Though I'd never been there, I knew Greece was more modern and Westernized, that it would feel more like "home." I was ready for a change of pace.

In Cairo, the tasks of daily living took up a lot of energy. Because there was so much dust from the surrounding desert—it coated everything—it was hard enough just to keep clean. We had to dust our apartment every day—even if we kept the windows shut.

When I got home from grocery shopping, I had to spend three to four hours scrubbing ground-in dirt off the vegetables, soaking them in bleach for twenty minutes, and then putting them in boiled water to kill any remaining bacteria. Any meat we bought had to be frozen for the same reason.

Laundry was a big chore too. Like most teachers, we didn't have a washer or dryer, so we sent our clothes out with an Egyptian woman who lived nearby. She'd scrub our clothes with stones and hang them out to dry in the sandy air. They always came back stiff and faded. Scott and I often laughed at the way they looked and smelled.

Scavenging for simple housewares, like curtains, was a major headache. We couldn't just walk into a WalMart to get what we needed. To get curtains, we had to know somebody who knew somebody's brother who might be able to find fabric to make the curtains. I didn't give up though. Days before going to Greece, I had some curtains made. I was excited to finally have them up three days before we left and was looking forward to enjoying them when we got back.

I was saddened by the depth of poverty all around me. Most people in Egypt live at the poverty level. For example, the caretakers in our apartment building, a family of eight (including two parents, four kids, and two grandparents) lived in an abandoned elevator shaft in our building. It was a small space with no roof. It almost never rained in Cairo, but when it did, the rain fell on their one piece of furniture: a couch with a tattered plastic covering.

When we went down to the marketplace on Fridays and Saturdays—our weekends—we'd see mothers holding their half-naked babies in the streets, begging for food. The women were dressed in black, some with black veils hiding their faces. Begging was the only job they could get to survive.

There were frequent reminders that we were living in a tense and often unpredictable part of the world. Egyptian security police frequently patrolled the streets with machine guns in hand. There was often bitter infighting between Egypt's political leaders and Muslim fundamentalists who wanted Islamic law and codes of behavior to replace the nation's constitutional government. The rival groups were constantly at war. The government often cracked down on Muslim leaders by making mass arrests.

On August 15, 1985, the same day Scott and I arrived in Egypt, Israeli diplomat Albert Artakchi was murdered in a machine-gun slaying at the Israeli embassy in Maadi—only a few blocks from our apartment. On August 20, a group called "The Egypt Revolution" released a letter claiming responsibility for the attack. The assassins—from Lebanon, Tunisia, and Egypt—were linked to Libyan President Moammar Khaddafy and the infamous Abu Nidhal, the most notorious terrorist leader in the world.

The group vowed to carry out more attacks "until the Israeli colonialists leave the country." It attacked Egyptian President Hosni Mubarak for keeping troops on the border with Libya but not Israel. The letter claimed that the group included Egyptian military officers who were angry because they were posted on the Libyan border.

Though we often heard news like this on the radio, it didn't greatly concern us. We felt safe.

I put in a normal day of teaching on Thursday, November 21, and went home that afternoon to pack the big blue-and-gray suitcase I bought in Baytown, Texas. I brought a sweater—the weather was supposed to be cooler in Greece—some short-sleeve shirts, and my favorite pair of blue jeans, the ones with the thin white pinstripes that fit just right, and my Pentax camera.

I packed light because friends wanted me to bring back canned goods and other items that were hard to find in Cairo.

I took a cab to the airport in Cairo and then headed to check my luggage and present my round-trip ticket on EgyptAir, Egypt's national airline. It was a routine, two-hour flight. I sat in the front of the plane and met a businessman from Sydney, Australia.

He was a good-looking, sandy-haired fellow. I'd never met anyone from Australia before, so I was interested to find out more about his life. It just so happened that he'd lived in Houston for a while and planned to go back to do some work. We talked about our jobs, our spouses, and our lives. He seemed really happy.

Before we got off the plane in Athens, I turned to him and said, "If you want someone to show you around or you want some company when you're in Houston, I can give you my parents' number."

"Sure," he said.

I wrote down my parents' phone number on a sheet of paper and handed it to him. He thanked me, and we went our separate ways.

My Athens adventure began with an exhilarating taxi ride from Greece's Hellinikon International Airport to the Athens American School, site of the volleyball tournament.

If you've never ridden in a Greek taxicab, let me tell you, it's quite an experience. We zipped through the narrow, congested streets of Athens during rush hour, searching for the school. The driver didn't know where we were going and didn't speak English. My sign language directions failed miserably. Finally, we stopped to ask for help at the American embassy, where I found someone who spoke both English and Greek. They didn't know where the school was either. The cabbie stopped at a hotel while I ran in and found an English-speaking clerk who knew how to get there.

I was relieved when I finally reached the gym where the girls were playing volleyball. Scott came over to greet me and gave me a big hug and a kiss.

While I watched the game, I got to talking with a woman who coached the Kuwaiti girls' volleyball team. She was about my age and was from Minneapolis, Minnesota—Scott's hometown. She was teaching in Kuwait and described her life and work there. I was curious, because I'd gotten a job offer to teach in Kuwait too. As she described her life there, however, I had no regrets. It sounded too restricting.

Late that first evening in Athens, Scott and I sat out on the balcony of our hotel room overlooking a small park and a restaurant or, as the Greeks call it, a *taverna*. As we ate, we listened to the muffled sounds of the city below. It felt so great just being together, doing nothing. In Cairo, we were always so busy.

We'd only been married three months and were still basking in the glow of our honeymoon period. I'd met Scott the year before when I was teaching at the American School in Stavanger, Norway. The tall, dark, and handsome stranger from Minnesota immediately caught my eye. One year from the beginning of our whirlwind courtship and engagement, here we were in one of the most romantic settings I could ever imagine. It felt wonderful to have finally found someone who really shared my hopes, dreams, and passions.

The next day, Friday, I watched Scott and the team rack up victory after victory in the volleyball tournament. I watched most of their games, and in between matches I slipped away to do some shopping. The streets of Athens were busy and crowded. The little shops were filled with modern wares that were hard to find in Cairo. Most of the Greek shopkeepers spoke English and were very friendly and willing to help me.

I racked up a healthy Visa card bill on my shopping sprees. I bought a new skirt and a nice royal blue top, which I planned to wear at a big Christmas party put on by CAC. I also scored a special prize: a tape of Bruce Springsteen's "Born in the USA."

I also went to a supermarket in Athens to buy canned foods, some chocolates, and Mexican ingredients to make Mexican food. I wanted to stock up for a Mexican dinner party I was planning to host in Cairo. The taste reminded me so much of home. In Cairo, I'd been living on a lot of care packages—which included refried beans, tortillas, salsa, chips, and so on—sent by my friends Barb Wilson and Debbie Reno in Texas.

When I got back to the gym on Friday afternoon, Scott had good news:

our girls beat a team from the American School in London to qualify for the finals!

❦

I'll never forget our last night in Athens. In the afternoon, Scott and I took the girls out for an early dinner at a fun, little Mexican restaurant to celebrate their success in the tournament.

After dinner, we all strolled through the ancient city's streets together, not far from the Parthenon and other famous Greek ruins. I was glad I'd brought a sweater to protect me from the chill in the air. Eventually, we wound up near the University of Athens and the Acropol Hotel where we were all staying.

My original plan had been to fly back by myself on Saturday afternoon. Scott and the girls were booked on a Sunday morning flight. But now that the girls had a shot at the championship, I wanted to stay longer to cheer them on.

That night at the hotel, I called the Athens airport to see if I could change my ticket. It was no problem to cancel my reservation and book a later flight.

Before going to bed, I sat down at the table in our room and wrote out some postcards to my friends back home and my parents.

"You may be getting a call from a man who is from Sydney, Australia," I wrote in my card to Mom.

❦

The next day, Saturday, we anxiously and excitedly waited to see who our opponent would be in the finals.

We waited and waited. The other girls' teams were so good that their games kept going into overtime.

That afternoon, I called to cancel my ticket a second time—and reserve a still later flight to Cairo. The last flight out, EgyptAir Flight 648, was scheduled to depart at 9 P.M.

At 7 P.M. we were still sitting on the edge of our seats waiting to play. I could feel the anticipation and excitement in the air. I'd been hoping to be in the bleachers for the championship game, but it didn't look like that was going to happen.

I had classes to teach the next day—Egypt is a mostly Muslim country, where people worship on Saturday and work on Sunday. If I missed the last plane out, I wouldn't make it back in time.

I kissed Scott good-bye, wished him and the team good luck, and took a taxi back to the Acropol Hotel. In our room, I packed my suitcase with canned goods and other presents I'd bought for friends. I turned in my key at the front desk and went outside to catch a cab for the airport.

It was a chilly, rainy night as I stood shivering on the corner. I was lightly dressed in an oversized, plain white T-shirt tucked inside my favorite blue jeans. Normally, I avoided wearing larger sizes (they made me look bulky), but this was the only T-shirt I'd brought that went with my pinstriped jeans.

When a taxi finally came, I handed the driver a note that someone had hastily written in Greek. It said, "Please take me to the airport."

After checking in at the airport ticket counter, I walked to the terminal gate. I was surprised to see so many airport security guards toting guns.

The heightened security was one of the many small reminders Scott and I often got that we were living in a "year of terror"—a year that shocked the world with an unprecedented string of terrorist bombings and shootings, including the hijacking of TWA Flight 847 from Athens to Rome on June 14, 1985, and the hijacking of the Italian cruise ship *Achille Lauro* near Port Said, Egypt, on October 7, 1985.

It was especially dangerous for Americans traveling abroad. For the first time, average American citizens were being singled out as victims of bombings, hijackings, shootings, and other acts of terror. The Ayatollah Khomeini, ruler of Iran, declared open season on Americans, and much of the Arab world followed suit. U.S. support for Israel enraged extremist groups claiming to represent Palestinian interests.

In the TWA hijacking, PLO terrorists forced the pilot to land in Algeria. For the next three days, the hijackers ordered the plane back and forth between Algeria and Lebanon and murdered U.S. Navy Diver Robert Stetham. Eventually, about seventy hostages—including thirty-nine

Americans—were taken from the plane and held for fourteen days in various Beirut locations by Amal, a Shiite Muslim militia. They demanded the release of more than seven hundred Shiites jailed by Israel to end their siege.

PLO terrorists on the *Achille Lauro* shot and killed Leon Klinghoffer, a sixty-nine-year-old wheelchair-bound retiree from Garden City, New Jersey, and threw him overboard.

In the United States, security was stepped up at many government and military installations. Air traffic to Europe slowed to a trickle as thousands of Americans canceled or postponed vacations and business trips, deciding it was just too dangerous to risk going abroad.

Many friends warned me not to go to the Middle East.

Before starting the 1985–86 school year, I'd flown back to Houston to plan my wedding with Scott. I was sitting in Barb Wilson's kitchen, writing out wedding invitations, when news of the TWA hijacking flashed on the screen.

"Jackie, look at this," Barb said.

I looked up from what I was doing and focused on the television.

For a couple of minutes, we silently stared at the screen and listened to the voices of TWA Capt. John Tesstrake and the hijackers who were pointing a loaded gun at his head.

"Jackie, you know if you go overseas, that's a real possibility," Barb said, with concern.

I said, "Oh, Barb, don't be ridiculous. That kind of stuff doesn't happen to people we know—and it sure isn't going to happen to me." I assured her everything would be okay.

I was determined not to live my life in fear. That's exactly what the terrorists wanted to accomplish by randomly terrorizing average Americans. They wanted to inject fear into all of our hearts—to make us pull back and retreat from our involvement in the world.

I never really thought much about terrorism when I was living overseas. I never would have considered letting the fear of terrorists stop me from fully living my life or pursuing my dreams.

Yet I couldn't very well close my eyes and pretend that we weren't living in a war zone. While we were living in Egypt, Scott was a daily reader of newspapers that were filled with stories of conflict and tension in the Middle East. He closely followed the TWA hijacking and other activities by terrorists. Hijackings and terrorist acts were everyday occurrences in this part of the world.

One afternoon in late October, I was walking through downtown Cairo when I saw a small crowd of Western-looking people gathered outside the American embassy. A shopkeeper told me they were survivors from the *Achille Lauro* hijacking getting ready to return to the United States.

My curiosity was piqued by these men and women. I'd never talked to someone who had been hijacked. *Wow,* I thought, *that must be exciting.* I wanted to hear their stories.

🖋

The Athens airport was an international hot spot all that summer and fall. On June 18, four days after the TWA hijacking, the U.S. State Department issued a travel advisory warning American travelers to avoid the Athens airport. But the advisory was lifted on July 22—four months before I flew into Athens—after careful inspections by the International Air Transport Association and the Federal Aviation Administration led to tighter security. Both agencies ultimately labeled the Hellinikon one of the world's "best guarded" terminals.

Extra security had been added recently. On November 20, the day Scott and the girls arrived in Athens, sixty people were injured, including twenty police officers, in an ugly street riot. Radical student protesters who blamed the United States for supporting a military dictatorship in their country from 1965 to 1971 tried to firebomb the American embassy in Athens.

Walking through the airport, I noticed that the number of security guards had been tripled or quadrupled from just two days earlier, when I flew into Athens from Cairo. I could feel the tension and fear of terrorism in the air and see it in people's eyes.

Before boarding my flight back to Cairo, I stood in a long line to have my bags checked for guns or explosive devices. The airport security guards made us put our suitcases on a long metal table and open them for inspection. As I watched them sifting through other people's bags by hand, I thought, *I could have a gun in my bag and no one would know it.* I was irritated and concerned by the sloppy way that the guards were pawing through our luggage.

My thoughts were interrupted when two Greek men cut right in front of me in line. I bristled with anger. Who did these jokers think they were? Whatever happened to common courtesy? I wanted to tell them off, then decided not to bother.

After walking through the airport metal detector, I looked down at my watch to check the time: it was 8:27 P.M. My mind drifted back to the volleyball tournament. The girls must be playing by now. . . . I wondered how they were doing. . . .

My irritation at the two Greek men soon faded as I settled in a long line waiting to board the plane. As I looked around, I noticed a group of beautiful Arab children laughing and playing in the terminal. This group of eight to ten year olds was a joy to behold. Their little faces and dark shining eyes were glowing with positive, hopeful energy. Their proud parents stood close by, talking with one another while keeping a watchful eye on the kids.

My love for children is what led me into teaching. In Cairo, I taught special education classes for children this same age. One of the kids in this group reminded me of a little girl I taught at CAC. She had the same wonderful, infectious smile and the same glowing tan skin as my student Alysha.

"Passengers on EgyptAir Flight 648 nonstop service to Cairo may now begin boarding," a Greek man's voice crackled over the loudspeaker. Finally, the line was moving. I began talking to a Canadian woman who was traveling with her baby. I helped her carry the baby carriage down the stairs to where the plane was waiting.

I shivered slightly in the blowing wind as we climbed up the stairs leading to the front door of the plane.

After stepping into the plane, I quickly found my third row aisle seat. I liked being near the front of the plane, closer to the center of action.

I reached up to stow my carry-on bag in the overhead bin. As I turned back to sit down, my gaze fixed on a passenger sitting across the aisle.

I found myself staring into the piercing blue eyes of a young, curly-haired man. He wore a well-tailored sport coat and tie, and looked like a businessman. He was attractive, solidly built, with finely chiseled Semitic features. A good-looking man.

Two very attractive, refined, well-dressed women were sitting next to the handsome stranger. The women both had dark hair and dark eyes. One of them looked at the man with a little extra interest.

But something was wrong. The curly-haired man seemed agitated or upset. He didn't talk to the two women. Instead, he clutched his briefcase tightly and was dripping with sweat. He looked very controlled, as if he was determined to do something and nothing was going to stop him. He kept shifting his eyes from the front to the rear of the plane. I felt the fear in his eyes, and thought maybe it was his first time flying.

A flight attendant approached our seats and then stopped. She looked down at the floor and pointed to a black briefcase blocking the aisle. "Whose briefcase is this?" she asked a male passenger.

"It's not his! Leave it alone!" the curly-haired man yelled back at her and snatched the briefcase.

It seemed odd. *Was he on drugs?* I quickly dismissed the thought and settled back in my seat.

As I flipped through the pages of my magazine, flight attendants at the front of the plane demonstrated how to use the life jackets under our seats in case we had to make an emergency landing. They also showed us how to fasten our seatbelts and use the oxygen masks, should the cabin suddenly depressurize.

I looked up briefly, then returned to my reading. *What's the big deal?* I thought. How hard can it be to use one of these things? You just stick it over your mouth and breathe.

My mind was already back in Cairo as we taxied for takeoff. I was glad to be going home. I was thinking about my students and classes the next day and the Thanksgiving dinner that friends were preparing for my arrival. I felt so grown up and "civilized." Here I was, Jackie Nink Pflug, from Pasadena, Texas, jetting back and forth between two of the world's most ancient civilizations—the center of so much culture, philosophy, art, and science. What a trip! My dreams were coming true.

We were cleared for takeoff shortly after 9 P.M. As the engines roared, I plopped the new Springsteen cassette into my Sony Walkman. "Born in the USA" was blaring in my earphones as we lifted off the ground and steadily ascended to cruising altitude.

As the "Fasten Seatbelt" signs went off, I lowered my seat back to a comfortable position and took off my headphones. Since I love making new friends, I offered some caramels to an older Egyptian man sitting next to me. We chatted a while. He was curious about why I'd come to live and work in Cairo. I told him about my love for children and travel and asked about his family. Egyptians are very family oriented and love talking about their children and spouses. My new friend was delighted when I asked to see pictures of his wife and two handsome young sons.

After talking a while and listening to more music, I caught the smell of deli sandwiches drifting my way. The flight attendants were moving up and down the aisle, passing out dinner trays. I hadn't eaten much before we left, so I was looking forward to the in-flight meal. As the flight attendant edged toward my seat, I heard some commotion behind me.

When I turned around, I couldn't believe my eyes.

The curly-haired man who had been sitting across the aisle from me was now standing in the aisle with a gun in one hand and two grenades in the other. He was tugging at the safety pin of one of the grenades with his teeth, but couldn't remove it.

The two pretty women who were sitting next to him looked terrified. The one who was sitting in the middle seat, right next to the hijacker, had a look of terror and hysteria on her face. She leaned toward her friend, trying to get away from the curly-haired man.

This can't be! This can't be happening. Why isn't somebody doing something? Why are we all just sitting around? We have to do something!

I was seized with fear and panic. It was the worst feeling of my life.

I turned around again to confirm the terrible scene, desperately hoping

I'd imagined it. But it was no mirage. The curly-haired man was still there, grimacing with fear and anger. The nightmare was real. We were being hijacked.

People panicked and started getting up out of their seats and reaching into the overhead bins to check their money or carry-on bags.

"Sit down and shut up! Get back in your seats!" the hijacker screamed at a group of Filipinos sitting in the back.

We froze from the horror of it all.

"Are we going to be okay?" I asked my Egyptian seatmate, desperate for reassurance. His head was bowed in prayer, and he said nothing.

Time seemed to stand still. It was as if I had entered a completely different type of reality—my worst nightmare was being played out right in front of my eyes.

"Don't move!" the curly-haired hijacker shouted in Arabic and English.

To protect myself, I instinctively leaned forward and covered my face with my hands and silently whispered, "Oh, my God!" *This is it*, I thought, *I'm going to die*. My whole life was suddenly and unexpectedly about to end.

In quick succession, two sharp blows landed on my head. Slowly, I lifted my head. The curly-haired man was standing over me, digging the cold, hard steel of his six-shooter revolver into my skull.

"Are you scared, lady?" he asked in a mocking tone.

I held my breath, trying to control my quavering voice and shaking hands.

"No, I'm not," I gulped.

On that cue, my Egyptian friend snapped out of prayer and began shouting at the hijacker in Arabic. The hijacker yelled back in Arabic. I didn't understand what they were saying, but knew the old Egyptian was trying to protect me.

With the gun still at my temple, I put my hand on the Egyptian's knee. "It will be okay. Don't do this," I said.

In my mind, I saw the hijacker saying, "Look buddy, don't argue with me"—then Bang! The curly-haired hijacker left my side when the old Egyptian stopped arguing and returned to prayer.

A second hijacker with straight hair stood up and forced his way into the cockpit and confronted the EgyptAir copilot, Imad Bahi-El-Din. At first, Bahi-El-Din thought it was a prank. He half smiled at the hijacker—his entrance was so theatrical. On taking a second glance at the grenade in his left hand and the pistol in his right, however, the copilot knew this was no joke.

The group hijacking the plane called itself the "Egypt Revolution." They ordered the pilot to change course for Libya. But the captain, Hani Galal, warned there wasn't enough fuel to make it.

The captain radioed several countries, asking permission to change course and land—but every request was refused.

The situation was desperate. Galal and his copilot warned the hijackers that the plane would crash into the sea unless it landed on the Mediterranean island of Malta, a tiny country about the size of Rhode Island, between Sicily and North Africa. He radioed Malta and was initially denied permission to land. After explaining our dangerous position and pleading with Maltese officials, they reluctantly gave in.

In the main cabin, one of the hijackers ordered a flight attendant to translate his instructions. "Nobody does anything but what I say," the hijacker's helper told us. "Do what I tell you, and nobody gets hurt."

On our way to Malta, the hijackers donned black masks and moved passengers sitting in the front of the plane to the rear of the plane. I was the last passenger from the front section to change seats, and I was moved to the last row aisle seat, next to another hijacker. I could see he had glasses on underneath the mask.

From my new position, I could see some of the children standing up in their seats and facing toward the back of the plane. These sweet, innocent little faces staring back at me were the same ones I'd seen in the airport terminal just a few minutes ago.

I looked over and saw two attractive women sitting right across the aisle from me—the pair appeared to be a mother and her daughter. I later learned that Mrs. Guadelupe Palla de Ortiz De Pinedo and her daughter, also called Guadelupe, were two very popular and famous actresses who had appeared in numerous Mexican film, television, and stage productions. They were ending a two-month European holiday which had taken them to Britain, France, Spain, Switzerland, Belgium, Italy, and Greece.

After we were settled in our new seats, the hijackers began rounding up our passports. In shock and stunned silence, we raised our hands over our heads as ordered.

One hijacker forced a crew member to assist him in collecting our passports. In twos, they systematically approached each of us. The hijacker held a gun to our bodies while the flight attendant frisked us for possible weapons. They threw each passport into a briefcase.

I sensed a sinister purpose behind this move and considered ways to disguise my citizenship. I remembered the earlier conversation I'd heard between the two Mexican women. Maybe I could pretend to be Spanish. I had short, black, curly hair, a dark tan, and, in Texas, people often mistook me for Mexican. I studied Spanish in elementary and high school and remembered a few basic words and phrases. It might work.

My appearance might fool the hijackers. Yet my Levi jeans and Nike running shoes pegged me as distinctly American. . . .

The hijackers approached a well-dressed, broad-shouldered man near the front of the plane and demanded his passport. He reached into his jacket pocket—and pulled out a gun. He was a plainclothes EgyptAir security guard assigned to our flight as a safety precaution.

Bang! The first shot rang out. More followed. In the chaos and confusion, twenty-two bullets were fired; some hit the passengers and the aircraft, others ricocheted in all directions. I hid behind the seat in front of me to escape the hailstorm. The bullets badly damaged the plane's cabin and fuselage, and, in a matter of seconds, we dropped like a rock, losing twenty thousand feet of altitude. This caused the cabin to depressurize and left us gasping for air. It was pure pandemonium. Passengers were screaming and shouting amid total chaos.

During the descent, there was a sudden swoosh as the orange oxygen masks dropped from above. I pulled mine over my face, but no air came out. I couldn't get it to work—and I was suffocating. I kept hitting the thing, desperately trying to make it work. The hijacker wearing glasses underneath his mask was standing beside me. He saw me hitting my mask, coughing, and suffocating because I couldn't get any air.

Because I hadn't been listening to the flight attendant's instructions, I didn't know that you have to yank the cord to get air flowing through the mask.

The hijacker hit the male EgyptAir flight attendant sitting next to me on the shoulder and muttered something in Arabic. A week before, I'd started learning Arabic, but I didn't understand what he was saying. Instantly, the Egyptian man gave me his oxygen mask and I could now breathe. The hijacker had ordered him to help me. The two of us shared the mask from then on.

I turned to thank the hijacker. He said nothing.

In the blaze of gunfire exchanged by the hijackers and guards, several passengers were wounded. One of the hijackers, the curly-haired man I'd noticed shortly before takeoff, was killed in the gunfire; the EgyptAir security guard lay bleeding near the front of the plane. It turned out that there were three other security guards on board, but they were not able to get to guns that were stowed in the overhead compartments.

Our pilot brought the aircraft to an altitude where breathing was possible. And when the smoke cleared, the terrorists had total control of the aircraft. They continued confiscating our passports. Since I was sitting way in the back, I was the last passenger on the plane to surrender my passport. I was scared and trembling when they approached me.

To retrieve my passport, I'd have to get out of my seat and walk all the way down to the front of the plane. It was packed away in the carry-on bag I'd stowed above my assigned seat. I was terrified of being shot if I made the slightest false move.

I stood up, shaky, and took one step forward toward the third row. Then I felt a sudden lurching of the plane and stopped dead in my tracks. "We're about to land," I said. I quickly returned to my seat and buckled my seatbelt.

The hijackers were also caught off guard by the sudden, rough landing.

Although they had given us permission to land, Malta still hoped to avoid hosting a hijacking on their soil, so they turned off all the runway lights at Luqa Airport in Valletta, Malta, the nation's capital. Captain Galal managed a rough emergency landing, guided only by the faint lights of another plane. The pilot of the grounded plane had seen us coming in and, on realizing we had no landing lights, positioned his plane to illuminate part of the runway.

At the time, of course, none of us passengers knew where we were. All I knew was that it wasn't Egypt.

After the plane rolled to a stop, I still had to get my passport. I was so scared my hands and my whole body shook as I walked down the aisle to the front of the plane. On my way, I stepped through splattered food and garbage, and—worst of all—had to climb over the dead body of the curly-haired hijacker, the man who had rapped me on the head with his gun.

My hands were trembling as I fished the passport out of my carry-on bag. I was still afraid that if I made the slightest wrong move, I'd be killed.

"Are you scared, lady?"

The hijacker's words still haunted me. He could have pulled the trigger. Maybe next time I wouldn't be so lucky. . . .

Don't draw any attention to yourself. Don't even look at the hijackers. Keep your head down. Don't make eye contact.

I handed my passport to one of the hijackers. He looked at the blue cover with the embossed silver eagle, the Great Seal of the United States of America, then, staring me straight in the face, spat out the letters, "U-S-A," with obvious disgust.

The hijackers made me get up and change seats again. This time, they moved me from the rear of the plane to an aisle seat near the middle of the plane. Scarlett Marie Rogencamp, the other American woman on board, sat next to me in the middle seat. Alfons DeLaet, a Belgian man, sat by the window.

Scarlett told us she was working as a civilian employee at a U.S. military base in Athens. I overheard her tell Alfons that she was worried about the money in her purse. By that time, my thought was, *They don't care about our money. We're not going to be alive very long—who cares about money?*

Scarlett and I didn't talk much. Most of the time, I kept to myself. I focused on every little detail of what was happening around us. Though I was strapped into my seat, my body was always moving. I kept hoping to spot a chance to escape.

We were all in a state of shock.

As I looked around the plane, it was clear that people were coping with the tragedy in different ways. One young man sitting a few rows back just sat and stared out the window. A Palestinian woman tried to comfort her three young children. She slowly rocked her baby back and forth in her arms. She was softly singing. Every few minutes, she wiped the tears from her eyes.

I turned to Scarlett.

"Do you have any idea where we are?" I asked.

"Someone said something about Malta," she replied.

While Scarlett and Alfons continued quietly talking, I found a map of Malta in the seat pocket in front of me and studied it carefully.

Shortly after landing, the hijackers opened communication with the airport control tower. By this time, Maltese Prime Minister Carmelo Mifsud Bonnici and members of his cabinet were assembled there. The hijackers demanded enough fuel to reach Libya, an ambulance, and a doctor. The government agreed to the medical requests but refused to provide fuel unless the passengers were released.

At first, there was reason for hope. The hijackers released two wounded flight attendants and eleven women—three Egyptians and eight members of a Filipino dance troupe.

Again, the hijackers demanded extra fuel. But the Maltese government remained steadfast in its refusal to provide any fuel unless *all* passengers were released.

In response, the terrorists threatened to kill one hostage every fifteen minutes until Malta agreed to their terms. They'd start with the Israelis and Americans and work their way through the Canadians and Europeans. They had our passports so they knew who we were.

What if something happens to us and my friends don't get all the food I bought with their money? I thought to myself. Then I remembered the glass bottles in my suitcase. *I hope they don't break.*

TAKE THE WINDOW SEAT

SEVERAL HOURS WENT BY before the maltese government responded to the hijackers' threat.

It was a strange feeling to realize that the hijackers couldn't care less about our individual lives. They didn't see us as people with feelings, hopes, dreams, mothers, fathers, brothers, sisters, daughters, and sons. They didn't care who we were or why we were on the plane. They didn't care that I loved the Arab people and Arab children. None of that mattered.

When we looked into the hijackers' cold eyes, we saw reflected back an image of ourselves as hated objects, "things" to be used for their own purposes. To the hijackers, we were cattle to be sacrificed in the name of some obscure cause. They tried to strip away our very humanity.

I'd always seen people as individuals. The idea that others could see and treat me as an object—a political symbol—was completely alien to me. It was also terrifying to realize that my dignity and value as a human being mattered nothing to the people who held my life in their hands.

I was absolutely certain that if I lived through this ordeal, I would never forget the pain and hatred I saw in those eyes.

Throughout the hijacking, there was a lot of back and forth negotiating between the hijackers and the Maltese government. Most of it took place in the cockpit, out of sight. As passengers, we knew that our fate depended on the skill of those who were dealing with the two remaining hijackers. I hoped to God that they were good at their jobs.

The United States government sent a crisis negotiation team from Sigonella Air Base in Italy to Malta, carrying a planeload of counter-terrorism equipment to help defuse the crisis. The equipment included eaves-dropping devices that could allow Maltese and Egyptian officials to pinpoint the exact location of the hijackers inside the plane. President Reagan had also dispatched Delta Force, the U.S. Army's crack counter-terrorist unit, to Malta for a possible rescue effort. This elite group of U.S. troops was on its way.

The two hijackers waited several tense hours for Malta to respond to their threat. They seemed very agitated as they waited.

The hijacker who seemed to be in charge kept going into the cockpit, returning nervously, then going back in.

The hijacker exchanged some words with one of the flight attendants. Acting as an interpreter, the attendant asked if any Greek women were on board.

A voice from somewhere said, "How about a Greek baby?"

There was no response from the two hijackers.

More time passed before the hijackers received Malta's reply to their threat: There would be no agreement until all hostages were released.

The hijackers yelled out an Israeli woman's name—Tamar Artzi—then took her up to the front and opened the door. We all thought Tamar was being released—like the Filipino and Egyptian women who had been released earlier. Tamar did too. She got up from her seat willingly.

As she was descending the stairs, however, the straight-haired hijacker pointed his pistol at her and shot her in the back of the head. The awful sound that broke our hearts and confirmed our worst fears was followed by the sick-ening and unmistakable sound of a body thumping down the stairway.

"They've shot her!" someone gasped.

There was a collective gasp and the sound of wailing. A woman in the back screamed something in a language I didn't understand. A hijacker yelled something back.

My God, how can this be happening! I had been sure they were going to let Tamar go or maybe threaten her to convince the Maltese government that they were serious.

Then came another shock. Tamar was alive! Alfons DeLaet, the Belgian man sitting next to Scarlett, saw her move on the tarmac. *Play dead,* I thought to myself. *Why isn't she playing dead?*

The hijacker who was acting as executioner saw her move too. When he did, he stood at the top of the metal staircase and shot directly at Tamar's quivering body. He fired again, and again, and again—until she didn't move anymore.

Words can't describe the horror we felt.

Five minutes later, the hijackers forced one of the EgyptAir security guards to call for the second Israeli passenger on board. There was no reply. Again, he asked for the other Israeli to come forward. There was still no answer.

At gunpoint, the security guard was forced to sort through the passports in the briefcase and pick out the green Israeli document.

The guard opened the passport and stared at Nitzan Mendelson's picture. The hijackers grabbed the passport out of his hand and quickly scanned the rows of seats until they found her.

"Another passenger is being prepared for execution," Captain Galal told helpless officials assembled in the Luqa Airport's control tower. "I demand fuel," he said. "I do not want more bloodshed. I am responsible for the safety of the passengers and crew. I hold you responsible for any more killings."

Nitzan screamed and resisted every step of the way as the two hijackers dragged her to the front door and put the gun to her head.

"He is killing another one," Captain Galal said desperately.

Two loud gunshots rang out. The hijackers wanted to make sure each of their victims died. Following the gun blasts, we heard the same dreadful sound of a body thumping down the staircase.

There was more shouting, soft whimpering, and crying among the surviving passengers—then an eerie quiet.

Some of the passengers closed their eyes. Others gently rocked back and forth in their seats. I heard a woman two rows back softly saying her prayers.

I couldn't watch or listen anymore. It was too horrible. I closed my eyes and put my hands over my ears whenever it was someone's turn to die. I had to block it out.

After shooting the two Israeli women, the two hijackers forced the security guards to help identify the American passengers. The three of us were Patrick Scott Baker, 28, of White Salmon, Washington; Scarlett Marie Rogencamp, 38, of Oceanside, California; and myself.

As the two helpers approached each one of us, the hijacker at the back of the plane pointed a gun at us and signaled us to stand up. The helpers then walked us to the front of the plane and tied our hands behind our backs with neckties.

"I'm sorry," I heard the reluctant accomplice whisper in Patrick's ear.

We stepped past the body of the hijacker killed in the midair gun battle which had been laid over some seats.

They shoved Patrick in the aisle seat. Then, because I had been sitting behind Patrick, they pushed me toward the middle seat.

I was going to take the middle seat, but something inside me said, *Take the window seat.* I didn't understand. Why the window seat? Though it made no sense, I listened.

Patrick was in the aisle seat, Scarlett in the middle, and I sat by the window. During the next few hours the three of us waited on death row. Patrick, Scarlett, and I became close to each other in a way few people ever do. It was a short, but very intense period in our lives. We didn't say much, but I felt a deep, deep connection with their spirits. *It's too bad,* I thought, *but it often takes a shared tragedy to really share our hearts with others.*

Scarlett was a tall, beautiful woman with striking red hair. She told me she was from California and had been living in Athens for the last year. She was visiting Cairo on vacation, planning to see the Pyramids and other historic sites. Scarlett was a fairly quiet and reserved woman. I liked her. She reminded me of my sister Gloria with her sense of vulnerability mixed with strength.

Patrick was someone I really identified with. He was a tall, thin, energetic young man with a dapper, dark mustache. A real live wire. Patrick was out to see the world and pursue his passion for photography. I could tell he'd be lots of fun, that I'd enjoy knowing him under different circumstances.

I was glad when Patrick offered some comic relief after the three of us were seated. "I'm Patrick Baker," he said, introducing himself. "So, where are you ladies from?"

"What a thing to say at a time like this!" Scarlett said.

I laughed, grateful for the opportunity to release some of my nervous tension.

Scarlett was terrified, as was I, but she let more of her feelings show. I could sense her deep, deep despair. She didn't say much. At one point, she complained that her hands were tied too tightly. She wanted the hijackers to untie the rope so it wouldn't hurt so much.

They don't give a darn about whether your hands hurt, I thought to myself. I worried that Scarlett was drawing too much attention to herself. "Work with it a little bit," I advised. "Maybe if you play with it a little bit, you'll loosen it up."

My hands were tight, but they weren't hurting like Scarlett's. The way I saw it, they had to be tight for the hijackers to do what they were doing.

Scarlett continued to cry softly. I wanted to cry, too, but I just couldn't. I felt numb inside. I was in a state of shock. For the first time in my life, I didn't have a choice about whether I lived or died. There were other firsts.

I saw a gun used in a gruesome murder. I saw a grenade. I saw a dead body and was, eventually, forced to sit across the aisle from it. My hands were tied behind my back and I was told, "Do this—and if you don't, you're going to be killed." We waited for them to come and get us. We just waited.

They came for Patrick first. One of the EgyptAir security guards who was forced to help the two hijackers approached Patrick and lifted him up out of his seat. The helper walked Patrick to the front door of the aircraft and out onto the platform. At that point, a hijacker stepped forward and pressed his gun to Patrick's head.

There was a loud *Bang!* followed by the sound of Patrick's body thumping down the staircase.

Again, I closed my eyes and turned away, trying desperately to deny the awful reality of the scene. Since I was in the front, I could see and hear everything.

The procedure was always the same. Every fifteen minutes, the hijackers' helper came to lift us out of our seats and walk us down the aisle to the front door of the plane. Then the executioner placed his .38 caliber revolver to our head and squeezed the trigger. After he shot us, he pushed us twenty-five feet down the metal steps to the tarmac.

After Patrick was shot, Scarlett and I were alone. Who would be next?

Every few minutes, the executioner came out of the cockpit to the passenger section to check on his prey. He seemed like a crazy person to me. I could see in his eyes that something was wrong with him. He stationed himself at the front of the plane and, once when I looked up, he was staring coldly back at me.

What's the point? I thought to myself. *We're not going anywhere.*

Whenever I heard the sound of the door opening, my head went down. I didn't want to look at the hijacker.

"He keeps looking at me," Scarlett said frantically. "Every time he comes out, he's looking right at me."

"Don't look at him," I said. "Just keep your head down. Whatever you do, don't look at him."

"It's those eyes," Scarlett said, sobbing, "those eyes."

"Don't look at him," I repeated, firmly. "Don't make eye contact."

My strategy was to avoid eye contact with the hijackers at all times. Whenever one of them looked at me, I turned away. I didn't want to draw any attention to myself. I wanted to be as invisible as I could be.

I leaned my head up against the window and prayed. I didn't know what else to do.

Faith was an important part of my home life growing up. My parents, my two sisters, Gloria and Mary, and I regularly attended a Catholic church. My Roman Catholic upbringing gave me a strong faith and belief in a loving God. I learned that our souls never die, that we all go somewhere after death. I also learned that we can ask other people to pray for us. I learned about angels and that we can call on angels to comfort and protect us.

My parents taught me that life was a gift, that I shouldn't misuse it. Maybe that's why, as a child, I was always talking to people and making new friends. Life was so precious to me that I wanted to enjoy it with others.

At one point, Scarlett nudged over to me. "What are you doing?" she asked through her tears.

"I'm praying," I said.

"Would you say some prayers for me?" she asked.

"Yes," I answered.

"Would you say the 'Hail Mary'?" she asked.

I hadn't said it in years, but I remembered every word.

Scarlett and I squeezed our bodies together. Our hands were tied, so we couldn't hold each other. Our faces were right next to each other. I was close enough to hear her slow, regular breathing.

> *Hail Mary, full of grace, the Lord is with thee.*
> *Blessed art thou among women, and*
> *Blessed is the fruit of thy womb, Jesus*
> *Holy Mary, Mother of God,*
> *Pray for us sinners,*
> *Now and at the hour of our death,*
> *Amen.*

There were tears in both our eyes as we sat huddled together. It's impossible to communicate the feelings we both had in those precious moments we spent preparing to die. Scarlett would be the last person to see me alive. And I would be the last person to see Scarlett alive. A few hours ago, we were perfect strangers. Now the bond between us was strong and deep.

I said the prayer again.

Then I said the "Lord's Prayer" to myself:

> *Our Father Who Art in Heaven*
> *Hallowed Be Thy Name*
> *Thy Kingdom Come*
> *Thy Will Be Done*
> *On Earth as it is in Heaven*

Give us this day our daily bread
And forgive us our trespasses
As we forgive those who trespass against us.
And lead us not into temptation,
But deliver us from evil
For Thine is the kingdom
And the power, and the glory forever.
Amen.

After praying, I continued to steel myself, determined not to give in to the hijacker's terror and intimidation. I wanted to comfort Scarlett more, but I didn't dare. If I let myself become emotionally involved, I might break down. I leaned my head up against the window again and just sat there and waited.

Be strong. Don't break down. Don't show your fear or weakness. Be aware.

A few minutes later, the hijacker who was shooting everyone came toward us, waving my passport. I assumed I was next.

Instead, they took Scarlett.

It was about 5 or 6 A.M. when the two hijackers lifted Scarlett out of her seat and walked her a few paces to the front door. The straight-haired man with the gun hummed and sang as he pressed the revolver to her head.

He fired a single shot at point-blank range and Scarlett died instantly. As her body went limp, he pushed her out the door, and her body thumped down the metal staircase onto the tarmac.

I was next. There were tears in my eyes. I looked at my wedding ring and prayed that, by some miracle, I'd see Scott again.

For some reason I'll never know, there was an unexpected pause in the shootings. I kept looking out the window for some sign of hope.

There wasn't much to see. Captain Galal had pulled the plane onto a deserted stretch of Luqa Airport, to reduce the risk to other passengers and airport personnel.

In the haze, I could barely make out a few big military trucks with tarps on top in the distance. These dark trucks looked like military vehicles I'd seen in the movies. I hoped to see someone step out of one of these trucks and silently mouth the reassuring words, "Everything's going to be okay." Or I wanted to see a small troop of men with guns slithering on the ground, out of the hijackers' sight.

But I didn't see a soul. The trucks looked deserted.

I was totally alone now, with no one to comfort or distract me from my agony. *I'm going to die*, I thought, *and neither Scott nor my students will ever know what happened to me. I'll never get to say good-bye.*

I looked across the aisle and saw the dead hijacker's body lying over some seats. The hijacker's helper came over and scrunched the hijacker's legs into his body. I could tell that rigor mortis had already set in by the effort it took to bend the stiffened limbs and the loud cracking sound it made. The helper looked over to me and smiled, as if to say, "Can you believe his legs just did that?"

About nine hours had passed since we left Athens, and some people raised their hands and asked for permission to use the toilet. The hijacker in the back of the plane, the one with the glasses, signaled to people, one at a time, to get up and go. I had to go to the bathroom so badly, but I didn't dare raise my hand. I still didn't want to draw any attention to myself. . . . I didn't want the hijackers to know anything more about me than they already did.

Minutes stretched into hours as I continued waiting to die. I knew there would be little or no warning when the time came. Each breath might be my last.

At one point, the hijackers allowed food to be distributed among the passengers. A heavyset woman with long dark hair, the chief flight attendant on the plane, walked up and down the aisle passing out deli sandwiches wrapped in clear plastic. Many of us hadn't eaten for twenty-four hours and were famished.

The flight attendant tossed a deli sandwich on the seat next to me, where Scarlett had been sitting.

"I can't eat that," I said.

I couldn't pick it up because my hands were tied behind my back.

The flight attendant didn't hear me and just kept walking.

Another flight attendant, much younger, saw the sandwich sitting on the seat. She came over to me and said, "Would you like to eat?"

"Yes," I said.

She picked up the sandwich and fed it to me in little bites. The younger flight attendant had dark hair and was very pretty. She looked Egyptian.

"Are you thirsty?" she asked me.

"Yeah," I said.

"Would you like some water?"

"That sounds good."

She went and filled a cup with some water and held it up to my mouth so I could drink.

As I waited my turn to die, I reflected on the meaning and direction my life had taken. This was no idle exercise. It was time to be totally honest with myself.

Did I like the life I had been leading?

Continuing to review my life, I felt that the answer was yes. I was especially proud of all the work I'd done to free my spirit in the previous two years. After years of self-doubt and second-guessing myself, I had acted on my lifelong dream of living in a foreign country.

In February 1984, I'd finally gotten up the nerve to attend a job fair in New York City for teachers interested in working overseas.

I sure seemed to be in the right place at the right time. Many schools at the job fair were just starting special education programs and were looking to hire someone with my background in education and diagnostics. Everything was working out better than I could have ever hoped or planned.

A few weeks after flying back to Houston, the job offers started rolling in. Eventually, I accepted a position with the American School in Stavanger, Norway. In August 1984, my long-postponed dreams were coming true: I was going to live overseas and in a place where it snowed.

I remember talking with my dad out in the garage after my bags were all packed. "Are you sure you want to do this?" Dad asked.

I said, "Yeah, Dad, this is what I really want to do. I have to do this. I have to go out and see the world. It's what I have been dreaming about. I don't know what I'm after, but I have to do it."

He saw the excitement and commitment in my eyes. "I know how you feel," he said. "When I joined the navy after high school, I loved traveling around and seeing all those places. Sometimes, I wish I'd had a chance to travel more."

My dad is a man of few words, but I knew he'd just given me his blessing.

Once I made the decision to follow my dream of going overseas, I experienced a major personal growth spurt. I started erasing some of the old tapes from childhood that had been blocking me from doing the things I really wanted to do. For the first time in my life, I was deciding what was right for me. I wasn't letting others' opinions and beliefs about who I was control me.

Living in Norway was the first time I'd ever really lived away from home for an extended period. I'd set up the school's first special education program. I'd gone hiking in the fjords near Oslo, cross-country skiing near Stavanger, and spent Christmas break downhill skiing on the slopes of Innsbruck, Austria.

The world was opening up to me and I was drinking it all in.

I felt stronger and more mature after braving the hardships of daily life in Cairo. I'd also gone through a lot of changes in the past few months: I'd started a new job, adjusted to a new country and culture, gotten married, and made new friends. Making it in a country so different from my own did wonders for my confidence and self-esteem. I was growing a lot and had lots to be thankful for: a new husband, a great job, students I really loved, and the chance to travel.

Then I suddenly recalled the two Greek men who had forced their way to the head of the line at the Athens airport. At the time, I was really burned up about it. But from my new vantage point, it all seemed so trivial. *What was the big deal?* I could have chosen to let it bounce off me instead of getting mad. How pointless it is to get mad about things we can't control. . . .

I thought about other ways that I'd let little things get in the way of really experiencing life. Before the hijacking, I'd been just as caught up in looking good and worrying about other people's opinions of me as anyone else. I'd defined success as having a good job, a nice house, and a relationship with a man.

I realized that none of these were bad to want, but that there was so much more to life than trudging off to work every morning, wearing the right clothes, and driving the right car. I realized how pointless it was to let others' opinions determine how I lived my life.

As death drew near, a strange, unfamiliar feeling rushed through me: I felt a strong, surging desire to live. I wanted to see my students, spend more time getting to know Scott, and keep learning and growing. I felt grateful that at least I'd followed my heart for two years. But there was so much more I wanted to do! I wanted to see my hair turn gray. I wanted to live to see my grandchildren some day. . . .

If only I had more time.

For the first twelve hours of the hijacking, I stayed keenly alert, devoting all my mental and physical energy to planning a possible escape. During the night, I managed to work my hands free of the tie that bound them.

If I'm going to be shot, I kept thinking, *I hope it's at night. Maybe I can crawl away in the dark. Or somehow knock the gun out of his hands and make a run down the stairs.* But they had guns and grenades. Maybe there were more bad guys around the corner that I didn't see—with more guns and grenades. And I was so tired. . . .

I wanted to live so much, but it wasn't under my control. I did the only thing I could think of. I prayed the "Lord's Prayer" again.

One hour, then two hours went by. I kept praying.

Looking out the window, through the faint glare of headlights from the trucks surrounding our plane, I saw rain coming down in sheets. It was storming outside. Every now and then, lightning lit the sky.

Dear, God, I want to live. I put my life in Your hands.

All of a sudden, a bolt of lightning lit up the sky like I'd never seen before. Tears were pouring down my face as the rain poured down.

I suddenly knew I was going to be safe. I didn't know whether I was going to live or die; I just knew I was going to be safe. A wonderful, warm sensation flooded my body—and I felt safe. Nobody could hurt me. The hijackers could do whatever they wanted to my body, but I'm going to still feel safe.

I smiled and said, "Thanks, God." As I said this, I no longer heard the noise of the plane's engines or children crying.

Whatever happens, happens, I thought. *If I live, I'll be okay and if I die, I'll be okay.* That's what the safe feeling meant to me.

I'd never practiced meditation, but I entered that same calm, centered state of being. I turned all my worry and anxiety over to God. I stopped thinking about ways to escape. I let go of any attempt to control my destiny. I felt that either I was going to continue living on earth or I was moving on to another life. In either case, I was going to be all right.

I thanked God for my life, and I thanked God for the people that I got to share it with. I said good-bye to everyone in spirit—my parents, my friends, Scott, and my students.

More time passed. Soon, it was mid-morning. No one had been shot for at least four hours.

Maybe, just maybe, I'd be spared. I had prayed so hard. Maybe I was going to live. Maybe the hijackers negotiated an agreement to release us. A long break in the shootings gave me hope.

I briefly glanced behind me and saw the old Egyptian man I'd befriended early in the flight. "You're going to make it," he whispered.

"It's not over yet," I said quietly. "If you make it back to Cairo, go to the American School and get a message to my husband, Scott Pflug. Tell him I love him."

🌿

It was about 10 A.M. on Sunday morning, Malta time, when the executioner and his helpers came marching down the aisle, straight to my seat. The endless hours of waiting were over.

I still felt calm and centered. I was actually feeling sorry for the hijackers, that they had to do something like this to get their message across—one that I didn't even understand. I knew I was caught in the middle of something much bigger than me or the other passengers on the plane. And I was helpless to do anything about it.

My hands were still free, but I kept the tie wrapped around them. Again, I thought briefly about shoving the hijacker aside or kicking him in the groin and making a run for it down the staircase. But that thought disappeared quickly.

But it didn't matter anymore. I felt such an odd safeness, a sense that I didn't need to resist or control what was happening.

They picked me up out of my seat and walked me a few feet to the front of the plane. They positioned me so I was facing the door. I knew what was next.

Forgive them, Father, for they know not what they do. That's crazy. Who do I think I am?

One of the hijackers opened the door of the plane and I looked out onto the runway. The morning light stung my eyes. This was to be the last thing I'd ever see on earth.

The hijacker nudged me out onto the platform of the movable staircase pressed up against the plane. I felt the cold steel of a .38 caliber revolver dig into the back of my skull. I still felt safe.

In the control tower, Maltese officials heard our captain describe the chilling scene. "He is killing her now," Captain Galal said. "Do something. . . . He is outside shooting her now. . . . I am the captain. You are wasting life; you are wasting life."

The executioner squeezed the trigger. I felt an awful pressure in my ears, as my world exploded. I heard the hijackers speaking in Arabic. But it seemed to be coming from another world. I was leaving this one.

"He is killing her," Captain Galal said. "He has killed her already, and in a few minutes he will kill another."

CHAPTER 3

GOD, I NEED THIS RAIN TO STOP

A BANG, A FLASH, AND DOWN I WENT. It all happened so fast. Tumbling and floating, floating and tumbling. I was moving in a slow motion haze. It felt as if a massive surge of electricity was jolting through my skull. Splashes of light and color, a strange feeling of heaviness, a hazy numbness. It felt as though my eyes were pushed into the back of my head.

Then I was going down, down, down—into what?

I never heard the sound of my body crashing down the metal staircase like I had when the passengers before me were shot, but I knew I was falling.

Then it stopped.

Where am I? Is this heaven? Is heaven hard?

I was lying on a gray slab of concrete. I didn't feel anything as I fell twenty-five feet down the metal stairs onto the tarmac. Yet I was still conscious when my head hit the ground.

I don't know how much time went by, but I eventually opened my eyes—ever so slowly. I looked up and saw white, puffy clouds. I thought, *How strange this is all happening on such a beautiful day.*

Then I quickly shut my eyes again. *I'm not dead, am I? How could this be? Am I hurt? How bad? I don't know.*

I was disappointed to find myself still on earth. I was physically, mentally, and emotionally exhausted. I hadn't slept for so long, keenly aware that each hour might be my last.

I'm so tired. I thought this was going to be over. I just want to sleep. How much longer do I have to hang on?

I was sprawled facedown on the airport tarmac in Malta with a bullet in my head, my blood slowly draining onto the cement. My head was facing left, my left arm was under my chest, and my right arm was free and extended over my head. I was lying with my head sideways, at the foot of the metal staircase, so I could see the wheel of the plane through one eye. I felt a dull ache in my head and heard an irritating, high-pitched sound coming from the plane.

The first thing I had to do was keep myself from swallowing my tongue, because I kept trying to do that. I had to pee real bad, too. On the plane, I had decided it was just too risky to ask the hijackers for permission to use the bathroom. I couldn't hold it in any longer. Yet I was afraid the hijackers might notice the wet spot on my pants and the concrete and realize that I was still alive. I had to risk it. . . .

Stay calm, just stay calm. Think. That's right, think. What do I do? Don't move. Whatever you do, don't move. Remember what happened to the Israeli woman. She moved, and she's dead.

Bang! Bang! Bang! One of the hijackers had pumped her quivering body full of lead. The metallic ring still echoed in my ears.

Keep your head down on the cement. Don't look up. Play dead and you'll live. Keep calm. Keep perfectly still. Don't move a muscle. Shallow breaths. Stay cool.

I was grateful that I was wearing an extra-large sized T-shirt. It meant that the hijackers couldn't tell my chest was moving while I breathed in and out.

My body was shutting down, my mind starting to fade. I was slipping away. The bullet in my head must have gone in too deep. I wasn't going to make it. I couldn't focus or think straight. I was losing control. Thoughts were drifting by.

For the next few hours I kept passing in and out of consciousness and sleep. I was so tired. Every time I came to, I expected to wake up in a new world. My thoughts were *Okay, God, you can take me. I'm ready to go.*

The next thing I knew, a bright whiteness was all around me. It was my paternal grandmother, Grandma Nora Nink. I didn't speak. She was a whiteness to me, but I knew it was her. Grandma didn't use earth words to communicate, but I knew what she was saying. "Come, Jackie. It's time." She was calling me to join her. As she did, I felt my spirit leaving my body. I saw my body lying facedown on the tarmac. The roaring jet engines were suddenly silent.

Grandma Nink was one of the people I most loved and looked up to in the world. Grandma was a small, thin-boned, German woman. Her head was slightly bent from osteoporosis, but her eyes sparkled with life. She was lots of fun to be with. She was so calm and patient with me. That made a real difference. At home, I always felt jumpy and nervous, afraid of spilling milk or knocking things over. Mom always said I was accident prone.

When I was with Grandma, I didn't get that jittery feeling. I settled down. I wasn't afraid of making mistakes. I loved helping Grandma cook. She patiently showed me how to do things such as cut cucumbers with a big kitchen knife. And she didn't hover over me while I learned. She showed me how to do one cucumber, then let me do the rest.

I was so sad when she died, two years ago, at the age of ninety-three. But when she died, I wasn't worried. I knew she was going to a beautiful place.

Now, we were together again. . . .

Grandma and I were pure spirits without bodies. She was a whiteness to me. I moved toward her. I felt the edge of our spirits softly merge, as if we were touching fingertips. The two of us gently floated through a long dark passage—like a tunnel—toward a shimmering bright light. I knew what was happening: I was leaving earth.

It feels so good being here, in the light, with Grandma. I was so sad when she died. Now I know she is okay. I want to go with her.

Being in the light was a tremendous feeling. I was wrapped in a blanket of perfect love, perfect joy, and perfect peace. I was surrounded and filled with perfect knowledge. I knew all things. When I was in my body earlier, I felt alone, afraid, sad, and mad. But when I left my body, all emotions and feelings attached to the world left.

This must be heaven.

I stopped.

I wanted to go further, but something held me back. I didn't use words, but there was a clear "knowingness" about what I needed to do.

"I love you," my spirit was saying, "but it's not time to go yet."

Grandma didn't try to stop me or change my mind. She didn't look sad or disappointed. Instead, her spirit just continued drifting toward the light. I quickly found myself back in my body.

I startled at the roar of the jet engines and felt the hardness of the tarmac pressing against my head. *Why am I here?* I thought. Then I remembered. I was in a hijacking and I was shot in the head. The dull, heavy feeling reminded me. If you're shot in the head, I knew, either you don't live or you don't live normally. *Either way,* I thought, *I'll take it.* The important thing is not to get shot again, like the Israeli woman was when she moved.

Stay calm. Don't move. Play dead.

Though I felt weak and alone, I kept feeling something else—a flow of energy and a voice inside saying, *Be still, you're going to be okay, just be still.*

When I was in my body, I was full of worry, fear, concern. When I left it, all that went away. I was no longer attached to a body that could feel that. I remembered the feeling of deep peace.

My left hand, still underneath my body, hurt after bearing my weight for so long. I was afraid to move it, afraid that the hijackers would see me. Eventually, I moved my hand and nobody saw it.

I continued to drift in and out of consciousness and sleep.

It must have been mid-afternoon when it started to rain again. I felt a sharp, throbbing pain in my head as a cold, unpleasant drizzle seeped into my bullet wound. The pain was so intense that I didn't think I could stand to lie there without moving if it continued.

I started talking to God again. *God, I need this rain to stop. It will be difficult to lie here, still, with the rain.*

Almost instantly, the rain stopped.

This only happens in the movies! I thought. I fought hard not to smile or let the tears of joy flow from the knowledge that I was being protected.

At some point, I heard something coming toward me. It was faint at first, then grew louder. *What's that noise? It sounds like a truck. What is it?*

I was really curious about the vehicle. Very gently, very carefully, I opened my eyes. All I could see were black shoes scurrying around me. I quickly shut my eyes again.

The color black was very significant to me. The hijackers were wearing black shoes, slacks, and masks over their faces.

Oh my God, it's the hijackers! They're going to kill me. Stay calm. Don't move. Keep playing dead. It's your only chance.

"Okay, pick that one up!" I heard a man yell, as if through a far-off megaphone.

Suddenly, two men lifted me up by the armpits and started dragging my body across the runway. I made sure my body was dead weight, so the hijackers would keep thinking I was dead. I didn't dare open my eyes to see who they were or where we were going. My only chance was to keep playing dead and wait for the right moment to make a break. Little did I realize that I couldn't walk, much less run, from my attackers. But it was my only chance.

Keep still. Keep still. Keep playing dead.

They dragged me about thirty feet, then stopped. "Let's do this one right," one of the men said. "One!—two!—three!"

The two men lifted me up and slammed me facedown on a metal bed. It had ridges on it and they were filled with water. I remember thinking, *this is really rude laying me in all this water.* They didn't know I was alive. I just lay there trying not to breathe.

They lifted me up on the metal bed and shoved me inside a van. The doors closed and we started moving. I thought I was still with the hijackers.

What now? What do I do? Where are they taking me? How do I get out of here? Please, God, I need Your help.

I kept hearing, *Be still. You're going to be okay, but just be still.*

I was lying facedown, with my bullet wound exposed. The man riding in back with me, on my right side, didn't like looking at the gaping hole in my head. So he took my body and flipped me over.

When he did, I gasped for air.

"She's alive! She's alive!" he screamed.

Dear God, I thought, *they know I'm alive. Now they'll finish me off.*

I waited for the final gunshot to end my life.

Nothing happened.

More screaming and yelling.

Terrified, I slowly opened my eyes. But I couldn't see anything.

"Are you guys the good guys or the bad guys?" I softly cried.

"Honey, we're the medics," the young man said. "You're going to be okay."

The van was heading to the morgue. Now, I felt the vehicle spin quickly around as the driver made a beeline back to the airport control tower and a waiting ambulance.

I heard men talking but couldn't see their faces.

My dark skin and bruises made it hard for the rescuers to identify me. "She's Filipino," one said.

"No, I'm American," I said, hoarsely. "I'm Jackie Pflug."

Near the control tower, I was briefly examined by a Dr. A. J. Psaila, an American trained surgeon and head of surgery at St. Luke's Hospital in G'mangia, Malta. Medics rushed me to the emergency room at St. Luke's.

I was so tired, but so relieved. My prayer was answered. I was going to live. I thanked God.

CHAPTER 4

ALIVE, BUT WHAT KIND OF LIFE?

SCOTT AND THE GIRLS' VOLLEYBALL TEAM were still in Athens while I was being hijacked on Saturday night. They won the tournament that night, a few hours after I left for Cairo. Their victory celebration extended late into the night. Before going to bed, they planned to meet at the Acropolis at eight the next morning. From there, they'd board a tour bus to do some last-minute sightseeing before flying back to Cairo that afternoon.

Scott arrived at the rendezvous point early, about 7:45 A.M., to greet the tired girls as they straggled in. About half the team had arrived at the checkpoint when Tonya Smith, an eleventh grader at CAC, pulled up in a cab where Scott was waiting.

Tonya walked up to Scott and jokingly said, "Well, we don't have to worry about getting hijacked. An EgyptAir plane was hijacked last night."

Hijackings were so common in the Middle East that year that people often joked about the possibility of being in one.

"What!" Scott said, in stunned disbelief.

"EgyptAir was hijacked last night," she repeated.

This time the incredible news sank in.

"Jackie was on EgyptAir!" he shouted.

Scott knew right away that it was my flight that had been hijacked. I'd changed my reservations so many times, but he'd remembered that I was on the last EgyptAir flight leaving Athens on Saturday night.

"I'm out of here," Scott told Peter, the other CAC chaperone in Athens.

Scott hailed a cab to the EgyptAir office at the Athens airport. On the way to the airport, he listened to a British Broadcasting Corporation (BBC) news report on the hijacking:

> *Late last evening at 9:37 P.M., EgyptAir Flight 648 was hijacked by members of a terrorist group calling themselves "The Egypt Revolution." The hijackers' original destination was said to be Libya, but the plane was low on fuel and was forced to land at Malta's Luqa Airport.*
>
> *The hijackers demanded fuel to be able to continue on to Libya. They threatened to begin executing passengers every fifteen minutes until their demands were met. Two Israeli women were shot and thrown from the plane. One apparently managed to survive.*
>
> *An American, Patrick Baker, was also shot. His condition remains unknown. Two American women are also on board: Scarlett Rogencamp, of Oceanside, California, and Jackie Nink Pflug, of Pasadena, Texas. Negotiations for the release of the ninety-eight hostages continue. . . .*

When Scott arrived at the EgyptAir office, they were expecting him. He spent several frustrating hours at the EgyptAir counter, waiting for more news but learning nothing new. The only thing EgyptAir could verify was that I was on the flight. They didn't know any details beyond that.

Scott hung out there for two or three hours, then got fed up and left. Before leaving, he heard news reports that I'd been shot in the face and had a broken nose. It was still very sketchy.

The early hours of the hijacking were hard on my family and friends back home. My parents learned of the hijacking from the Saturday night news.

My mom had a sinking feeling as she watched the images on her TV screen. I'd written a week earlier to tell them I'd be in Greece with Scott and the girls' volleyball team that Thanksgiving weekend.

"Oh, my God, I think Jackie is on that plane!" she said.

During the first few hours of the crisis, information was incomplete. There was confusion about exactly what happened. From the early news accounts, they still didn't know if I was, indeed, a passenger on the plane.

No one in my family knew exactly who to call for more information on the hijacking. Gloria called Channel 2 and said, "I think my sister is on that plane."

"Where do your parents live?" the Channel 2 reporter asked, smelling a news story in the making.

"I can't tell you that," Gloria said.

A reporter from Channel 2 called back to say that I was on the plane. The reporter also contacted the U.S. State Department and, from then on, the State Department stayed in close contact with my family.

Barb Wilson called my friend Debbie Reno to ask if she was watching television. "You might want to turn on CNN," Barb said. "They have something about Jackie on."

"What?" Debbie said.

"The plane Jackie was on was hijacked," Barb reported, "and she has been shot. They think she might be dead."

When Debbie got off the phone, she called a prayer hot line at her church to pray for me.

Mom and Dad only got an hour's sleep on Saturday night. A spokesperson from the State Department called every thirty minutes with updates on the hijacking.

The early news offered little comfort.

At about 2 A.M., the phone rang again. My dad answered.

"I'm sorry to have to tell you this," the State Department spokesperson said, "but your daughter is dead."

"What does she look like?" Dad asked.

"She's blonde," he answered.

"No, she's not," he said, "Jackie is dark."

On further checking, the State Department discovered it had confused me with Scarlett Rogencamp, who had light hair.

For my parents, the ordeal was far from over. The news kept changing so quickly. My parents went from hearing that I was dead, to hearing that I might have just broken my nose, to hearing that I was okay and on my way to the hospital.

❧

Scott didn't believe the early reports because, in his mind, the officials didn't seem confident about the accuracy of their information. Someone at the airport offered Scott a ride to the American embassy. His goal was to somehow reach Malta and be near me while the drama unfolded. Scott knew that the American embassy was the place to go for help in a situation like this.

The embassy was already on top security alert. All vehicles entering the embassy compound were checked for bombs by security guards.

At first, it appeared that Scott couldn't get to Malta. Embassy officials told him that Malta's tiny airport would be closed until the hijacking was over. He might have to watch the drama unfold on television.

Embassy officials continued to pass on any information they had about the hijacking. The red tape, bureaucratic nonsense, and frustration were getting to Scott. He lost his cool and shouted at one embassy secretary. Soon after, things started to change. A down-to-earth, straight-shooting embassy official read the anguish on Scott's face and calmly introduced himself.

"One way or another, we'll get you to Malta," he told Scott. "Don't worry about it. We've got the ambassador's jet on standby."

Though Edwin Beffel, a first secretary at the embassy, was powerless to speed up the time frame of when Scott could leave, Scott felt better now that he was finally dealing with someone who acted like a human being.

Scott continued to get reports on the Maltese government's lack of progress in negotiating with the hijackers. Information about the fate of individual passengers, however, remained sketchy. Scott, and the rest of the world, couldn't know what was going on inside the plane.

Scott spent Sunday afternoon restlessly pacing back and forth in a hotel room a couple of blocks from the American embassy, waiting, hoping, and praying that I'd be okay. He continued listening to a stream of news reports, including some reporting that I was dead.

Late that afternoon, Scott collapsed on the bed for a few hours of fitful sleep. Fearing the worst, he tossed and turned, and prayed for my life.

Suddenly, a loud crack of thunder—the loudest he'd ever heard—jolted him awake. He saw the brightest flash of lightning he'd ever seen.

Seconds later, the phone rang. It was Beffel. He had a report that I'd just been shot in the face and pushed out of the plane. That report seemed to jibe with what EgyptAir officials had told him earlier. *Maybe they had gotten it right after all,* Scott thought. . . .

Beffel told him to head over to the embassy as fast as he could.

The loud crack of thunder and lightning coinciding with the call from Beffel seemed to confirm Scott's worst fear: I was dead. Scott thought his role now would be to help with the process of identifying my body and bringing it home for burial.

Scott's first thought was to call his parents in Hopkins, Minnesota. His mom and dad, June and Greg Pflug, were both on the line. They'd been watching the news on television and tried to support Scott.

"I just got a call from the embassy," he said. "They told me Jackie has been shot in the face. I don't know if she's alive or dead."

"Oh my God," June Pflug said. Then she started to cry.

Scott couldn't talk long; he had to get to the embassy.

At the embassy, however, there wasn't much more anyone could do. A few hours later, State Department officials were less clear about who was actually shot. It might have been one of the Israeli women or Scarlett Rogencamp.

Scott was miffed about the confusion. He was angry at the embassy personnel for planting in his mind the thought that I was dead.

Beffel was doing everything he could to get Scott to Malta. He was pushing hard to get a plane, but no one could land in Malta until the hijacking was over. There was also some bad weather.

There wasn't much more Scott could do. He had to sit tight and wait. Scott was helped by a woman who was vice-consul at the American embassy. She was a real caretaker and sweetheart, encouraging and sympathizing, just like a mom would be. She also helped Scott find a place to stay on Sunday night while he anxiously waited for a flight to Malta. She introduced Scott to a gunnery sergeant employed at the embassy who generously opened his home to Scott.

☙

Early on Sunday morning U.S. time, the phone rang again at my parents' house in suburban Houston. My parents felt a mixture of dread and relief. Would this call inform them that I was dead or alive? My father answered. It was the State Department.

"Another woman was just shot, but we don't know who it is," the U.S. government official reported.

A few minutes later, the State Department called back to confirm that I was shot in the head and taken to St. Luke's.

On Sunday afternoon there was a knock at their door. A reporter from Channel 26 stood at the door, asking to come in and shoot some footage of my family sitting down for Sunday dinner.

"No," Mom said. "We'd like to be together just as a family. We'd like to say our prayers for Jackie in private."

To her credit, the reporter understood and left.

My sister Gloria's husband said a simple prayer. "Lord, we just pray that Jackie will come through the hijacking okay and that we can hear from her soon. Bring her back to us safe. Amen."

Debbie and Barb came over to my parents' house to help answer the telephone, field the reporters, and provide support.

☙

After I gasped for breath in the van, and the van reversed course for St. Luke's, the medics immediately began cutting off my blood-stained blue jeans and T-shirt. I couldn't see what they were doing, but I heard the sound of ripping fabric.

Darn, there go my favorite blue jeans! was the last thought I had before everything went blank. I must have passed out, because I don't remember riding to the hospital.

When I came to again, in the emergency room at St. Luke's, I was lying on a metal hospital bed. I was dressed in a hospital gown. Medical technicians were sticking needles in my arm.

I closed my eyes briefly and, when I opened them again, I was staring into a pair of soft brown eyes.

A young man, about my age, hovered over me, wielding an electric razor. "I've got to shave your hair," he said, simply.

He pressed the buzzing instrument to my head and started shearing my dark brown curls. The sound was almost soothing until, suddenly, I jumped.

"Ow! That hurts!" I winced. I was really out of it—just barely able to hold a conversation. He'd run the rotating blades over my bullet wound. "You have to be careful."

"I'm sorry, but I have to go over it. I have to get the hair around it," he said, apologetically. "I'll try to go easier. You're going into surgery, and we need to shave your head to reduce the chance of infection."

Every few seconds, he'd stop shaving and let me take a breath. Then he'd announce, "Okay, I'm going back over it again."

My muscles tightened as I braced myself for more pain.

After the young man finished, another medical aide came in to finish the job with a smaller razor. He also gave me some shots to calm me down and reduce my pain.

A serious man with glasses who looked like a doctor walked over to my bedside. He put his hand on my shoulder and said, "I'm Dr. Lawrence Zrinzo. You're going to be all right. We just need you to sign something."

"What?"

"It's a release giving your consent to the operation, relieving the hospital of liability."

I felt dazed and out of it, but the humor of the situation didn't escape me. "Here I am with a bullet in my head and you want me to sign something?" I laughed.

He nodded.

"Well, I can't see well," I informed him.

"That's okay. We'll just hold it for you."

The doctor put a pen in my hand, and I asked him to steer my hand to the spot where he wanted me to sign. My pen contacted the hard surface of a clipboard and I moved it in broad strokes through the air, like I used to write my name with sparklers on the Fourth of July.

I could only see pieces of the doctor's face, but I felt his reassuring hand on my shoulder. I sensed his positive energy and could tell he was a very sweet, caring man.

I had lost some blood, Dr. Zrinzo reported, but not enough to require a transfusion. He assured me that I was going to be okay. In a few minutes, I started feeling the effects of the anesthesia I'd been given.

The doctor and nurse walked on opposite sides of my bed as they wheeled me into surgery.

"And to think, we just got our equipment last week!" the nurse said, laughing.

What does she mean by that? I wondered, just before passing out.

The doctors at St. Luke's didn't know my medical history. They didn't know that I had a rare allergic reaction to succinylcholine chloride—a muscle relaxant commonly used along with surgical anesthesia. When I had my appendix out as a little girl, the doctors had given me succinylcholine and I had stopped breathing. If they gave it to me again, I could die.

My mom knew my medical history. When she heard that I'd been shot, she immediately thought about the danger of an allergic reaction. She asked my sister Mary to call Pasadena Bayshore Medical Center and tell them to forward my medical records to Malta.

Thanks to Mom and Mary, doctors in Malta used the right anesthesia.

On Monday morning, November 25, Scott was still in Athens waiting to fly to Malta. Embassy officials were in constant contact with ground observers and officials in Malta who would be able to report exactly when Egypt's crack team of "Thunderbolt" commandos stormed the plane.

At about 8 P.M. Sunday night, the commandos were ordered to strike. Less than an hour later, the hijacking was over. The personal ordeal for survivors and family members who had lost loved ones, however, was just beginning.

Some time after the storming of the plane, the U.S. military attaché in Greece was cleared to fly Scott to Malta. Capt. William Nordeen, the U.S. naval and defense attaché at the embassy, drove Scott in a sleek, black bullet-proof limousine to the Athens airport, where the U.S. ambassador's twelve-passenger jet was ready and waiting.

A former navy pilot who had just begun his assignment in Athens that August, Captain Nordeen, like Scott, was from Minnesota. Nordeen and the other crew member were like big brothers to Scott, as they helped calm his nerves with some small talk.

On the way to Malta, Scott rode up near the cockpit.

It was a dangerous mission. There was no time to submit a flight plan for approval, so the pilots risked colliding with scheduled air traffic. To lower the odds of a midair crash, they skimmed the ground—over the water, but under the radar—all the way to Malta.

There wasn't a lot of talking during the flight. Most of the time, Scott sat quietly, wondering what he should be getting ready for. The details on my situation were still sketchy.

"I didn't know if Jackie was alive or dead, whether she'd been shot in the face or had broken bones in her face. I didn't know what to expect," Scott said.

By the time Scott landed in Valletta late Monday morning, I was in surgery at St. Luke's. Scott was cleared by Maltese authorities and assigned a local official to escort him to the hospital. By this time, the atmosphere at the airport had calmed down. It wasn't a three-ring circus.

Officials from the U.S. embassy in Malta and the Federal Bureau of Investigation (FBI) later debriefed us on what happened during the hijacking and rescue effort.

Malta had refused to let the U.S counter-terrorist experts land at Luqa airport. Delta Force, the military's crack antiterrorist commando team, never made it to Malta, either; three of its planes broke down on the way.

The hijackers had agreed to let medics pick up my body (they presumed I was dead) in exchange for food.

The final minutes of the drama unfolded while I was on my way to the hospital and in surgery. Egyptian President Hosni Mubarak ordered twenty-five Egyptian commandos to storm the aircraft. The U.S.-trained team used grenades to blow a hole in the rear of the plane, where the hijackers put most of the Arab passengers, touching off a fierce gun battle. The spray of bullets struck one of the plane's fuel tanks, causing it to explode. This sent a fireball blazing through the cabin, which was still filled with hostages.

While surgeons hovered over my body, doing their best to remove the bullet in my head and skull fragments from my brain, smoke and flames engulfed the runway in a dark, brooding cloud of human misery.

Fifty-eight people perished in the smoke and flames, including eight Palestinian children and their parents, and the hijacker who wore glasses. Everyone at the front of the plane, where I had been seated, died in the fire. The huge death toll made ours the deadliest hijacking and rescue in aviation history. The prevailing opinion was that the commandos used too much force in storming the plane. Not so many people needed to die.

By a strange quirk of fate, only two of the five passengers shot in the head actually died from their wounds. Patrick Baker, Tamar Artzi (the Israeli woman who didn't play dead), and I all lived, while Nitzan Mendelson and Scarlett Rogencamp died. It didn't make any sense. We were all shot in the head at point-blank range. How could anyone have lived through that?

"What kind of bullets were these?" Scott asked a U.S. embassy official in Malta.

"The bullets were homemade; the hijackers packed their own rounds," the official said. "They were regular bullets, but they packed their own gunpowder in them. Some were stronger and better packed than others. Nitzan and Scarlett got good ones." The bullet I got was strong enough to do damage, but not strong enough to kill me.

The hijackers had also been poor shots. The bullet they fired at Patrick only grazed the top of his head. The same happened with Tamar, who had a lot of hair at the time.

Yet Tamar had been shot several times. How did she escape death? Tamar received only flesh wounds from the hijacker's bullets. After being shot several times, she managed to roll underneath the plane. A few minutes later, she got up and ran to safety.

Three Maltese secret service agents greeted Scott at the hospital. They ushered him to the front desk where a nurse briefly explained that I'd been in surgery and would be unconscious for a while—but that he could come in and see me.

The hospital staff was on overload, struggling to deal with the massive number of dead and injured passengers from the plane. St. Luke's was not equipped to handle that many people. Doctors set up makeshift intensive care units in the hallways to take care of survivors.

Secret service agents directed Scott into the regular intensive care unit at St. Luke's, past a line of hospital carts with the sheet-covered bodies of those who died in the failed rescue effort. Intensive care was a small room with only eleven or twelve beds. Most of them were filled with other hijacking survivors.

Scott was in for several shocks. I was laid out on a bed with my head shaved and swathed in bandages; tubes were running in and out of my body. He expected to see my face all bruised up and was pleasantly surprised to see that I looked basically okay.

Scott looked back at the Maltese agents still standing behind him. One of the agents pointed to the adjacent bed and said, "That's the guy who shot your wife. He's the only hijacker who made it out alive."

The straight-haired hijacker who shot each of us was lying in the bed next to me. His chest was bandaged and he was on a respirator. Capt. Hani Galal, our pilot, had hit him with a fire ax when the Egyptian commandos began their assault, and he was further wounded by bullets in the chest.

Malta is a small country with only one hospital near the main airport. All survivors of the hijacking, including the terrorist who murdered Scarlett Rogencamp and Nitzan Mendelson, had to be brought to St. Luke's.

The Maltese official raised his eyebrow and, together with the other agents, left the room. Standing alone in the intensive care unit with me and the hijacker, Scott knew what the official had meant. To emphasize the point, they all bolted from the room at the same time and said, "If there's anything you need—*anything*—just let us know."

"In my mind, he was saying it was okay for me to kill the guy," Scott later recalled. "I hadn't even thought of that when I walked into the room. I had been so focused on Jackie's condition that I wasn't even mad that the hijacker was in the same room with Jackie. But when he gave me that weird look, he planted the thought in my mind.

"I knew Malta didn't want him to live. They didn't want to have to deal with the political pressures of jailing a worldwide terrorist and the hassle of making a prisoner exchange.

"I made a decision. If Jackie woke up as a vegetable, he was going to die. I was going to kill him. I had a plan. I was going to go over to him and rip the bandages off his chest and take out his heart. That was my plan. There was no doubt in my mind that that's what I would have done too."

These thoughts were troubling to Scott. He'd never hit anyone in his life, and now he was preparing to commit a cold-blooded, premeditated murder. It weighed heavily on him. "I felt almost pressured to do it if Jackie didn't come through okay," he said. "I couldn't let anybody get away with that."

That same Monday morning, the media descended on my parents' house in suburban Houston. Reporters from CBS, ABC, NBC, and CNN clamored for my parents' reaction to the hijacking. It was a circus in the front yard as reporters shoved microphones in my parents' faces and fired questions. News producers from New York wanted to bring Dan Rather's news team in the house to film. But it was so crowded with reporters that my mom said no.

She remembered what had happened that previous summer when TWA Flight 847 from Athens to Rome was hijacked. Allyn Conwell, a businessman from Houston and one of the passengers, gained worldwide notoriety as a spokesperson for the hostages during that ordeal. His parents' house in Houston was trashed by reporters covering the story. (Coincidentally, I had taught Allyn and his wife country western dancing when they lived in Cairo.) My mom didn't want that to happen to her home.

She warned any reporters who did come inside to watch themselves. "I don't want anything disturbed in here or moved around or anything," she said.

There was no letup in media interest. Since the hijacking took place on Thanksgiving weekend, my story was especially poignant to the press. That same weekend, terrorists detonated a bomb that wounded thirty-four people just outside a crowded U.S. military complex in northern Frankfurt, Germany. It was the latest in a string of attacks against American military installations around the world.

The media was intrigued by another angle. It turned out that our red, white, and yellow EgyptAir jetliner with the call letters SU-AYK was the same plane that U.S. Navy F-14 Tomcats had intercepted two months earlier when it was carrying the four terrorists responsible for the *Achille Lauro* hijacking. This plane was also hijacked in August 1976 by gunmen believed to be Libyan agents en route from Cairo to Luxor, Egypt. The plane was stormed by Egyptian "Leatherneck" commandos who rescued the passengers.

When I woke up after seven hours in surgery, Scott was standing by my bed in the intensive care unit, holding my hand.

"Hi, babe. Can you believe this happened?" I whispered.

He smiled and bent down to hug me.

I passed out again.

My condition was a big relief to Scott. I wasn't drooling out of one side of my mouth or in some kind of hallucinogenic fog. And I wasn't blind, as the doctors expected me to be. I seemed basically normal and alert.

I can deal with this, Scott thought to himself. He wouldn't have to kill the hijacker after all.

Scott's face was blurry when I looked up at him. But there was more to it; pieces of my visual field were also missing. I could only see straight ahead and to the right. Up, down, and to the left were blank. I figured the vision problem would clear up when my parents sent a new pair of contact lenses to replace those I'd lost in the hijacking. I rested and waited to hear from the doctors about the extent of my brain damage.

Over the next few days, several doctors came in to check on my progress. It took a while for them to get to me. The small hospital was overwhelmed with the magnitude of the tragedy they were suddenly dealing with. In addition to treating people who survived the storming of the plane, they had to perform autopsies on those who died of smoke inhalation, burns, and bullet wounds caused by the commando assault.

Eventually, Dr. Zrinzo, the surgeon who operated on me in Malta came in to explain my situation. He said there was an obvious entry wound in the right side of my head, about one-quarter inch in diameter, and the impact had blown a hole in my skull five inches wide. By some miracle he couldn't explain, however, the bullet that broke through my skull hadn't penetrated my brain. Instead, it had lodged in the skull and pushed skull fragments into my brain. During surgery, Dr. Zrinzo and the other doctors had cleaned out the wound and removed the bullet, along with skull fragments and brain tissue. Doctors grafted skin tissue from my right thigh to cover the gap in my head.

They really didn't know what to expect when I woke up. The bullet destroyed much of the tissue in my brain that controls vision, and doctors thought I might wake up blind. If the bullet had moved a half inch either way in my head, I would have been paralyzed, Dr. Zrinzo said. In the hospital, they gave me a series of eye tests that confirmed what the doctors already suspected: I'd lost my left peripheral vision, my peripheral vision up, and my peripheral vision down in both eyes. If I wanted to see anything in those three places, the doctor said I'd have to look to my left, look up, and look down.

I also suffered from extremely painful headaches, like migraines, anytime I shifted positions. A neurologist explained that a layer of protective gel inside our heads normally provides a soft cushion, or buffer, between the brain and the skull. In my case, the fluid had drained out the bullet hole in my head. That meant that whenever I moved, my brain pressed directly against my skull, causing the shooting pain.

As I gained the strength to sit up in bed and walk around, I had problems with my hearing. I was shot by my right ear and the surrounding brain tissue was swollen. Any loud sound, such as the closing of a door or the flushing of a toilet, was extremely painful. I felt a sharp, throbbing ache in both ears. When I flushed the toilet, I had to quickly put my hands over my ears and run out the door—or ask someone to flush for me. I couldn't stand the noise. I had suffered a concussion to the middle ear, Dr. Zrinzo explained. For about a year, I often had to ask people to speak softly because loud voices hurt too.

I had other hearing difficulties. Doctors discovered that I'd lost some of my ability to hear high-pitched frequencies. Since speaking voices and most other sounds are transmitted at lower frequencies, it wasn't a major problem.

Speaking was hard for me too. My jaw smashed hard against the tarmac when I was thrown from the plane. The force of the impact flowed from my head down into my neck. As a result, my jaw was partially locked. I could open it enough to eat, but not all the way. At first, I mostly drank liquids in the hospital.

I had torn ligaments in my neck from falling onto the tarmac and some black and blue marks, but no fractured arms or legs.

The full impact of all these injuries on my life was yet to be known. I felt lucky to be alive, but what kind of life would it be?

Scott handled all the telephone communications with my parents while I was still pretty out of it. He kept them informed of what was going on and what the doctors were telling him. My mom wanted to know how she and my dad could get to Malta. They both wanted to be by my side, but I didn't want them to come. I was too tired and didn't feel like having a lot of people around me. I didn't want to see the hurt in their eyes. I needed some space—peace and quiet—to sort out what had happened. The doctors felt the same way.

As a special education teacher, I knew something was seriously wrong with my sight, hearing, and memory. In the hospital, I had to ask Scott, the doctors, and the nurses to speak slowly, one word at a time—and to repeat themselves—when they spoke to me. If someone said, "Go mow the lawn," I heard, "Go row the tawn." I'd think, *Why would you want me to go row the tawn?*

I remember one nurse saying, "Go brush your teeth."

I heard, "Go trush your teeth." I didn't get it. What did that mean?

"Say it again," I said, "one word at a time."

She said, "Go."

I processed "go"—what does "go" mean?

"Brush."

What does "brush" mean?

"Your."

I tried to remember what "your" was.

"Teeth."

What's "teeth"?

For crying out loud, this was hard!

Like many people who have had head injuries, strokes, or learning disabilities, I had memory problems and problems understanding simple spoken and written words. My long-term memory was just fine. I recalled my childhood, education, friends, places I'd been, books I'd read, every detail of the hijacking. But my short-term memory, the ability to hold on to things that are happening right now, like this sentence, wasn't working.

Nurses and other aides in the hospital were very kind to me. They did everything they could to make me feel comfortable. Toward the end of my five-day stay in Malta, I was able to start eating some solid foods.

One time, they asked what I wanted to eat. Since I felt like I'd missed out on Thanksgiving Dinner, I asked for some turkey and dressing.

"We don't celebrate Thanksgiving," the nurse said in broken English. "Can you think of anything else you'd like?"

Hmm, I thought, *what's like turkey and dressing?*

"Do you have any chicken and mashed potatoes?"

Her eyes lit up. "Yes! We can get you that."

For lunch that day, the nurse brought in a plate of chicken, mashed potatoes, and gravy. I was so excited. I smiled and laughed. "Thank you," I said. "This is really great!"

Seeing how much I appreciated the meal, that it brought a smile to my face, the nurses brought me chicken and mashed potatoes for dinner. They started serving me chicken and mashed potatoes around the clock—at every meal except breakfast. They'd come in and say, in broken English, "We got you chicken and mashed potatoes!" And their faces would just light up.

"Honey, you've got to say something," Scott said.

I didn't have the heart to tell them that I ate other foods too. "I'll just eat chicken and mashed potatoes," I said.

This went on for about three days.

Before leaving the hospital in Malta and being transferred to a U.S. Veterans Administration (VA) hospital in Landstuhl, Germany, I had to tell officials my story of what happened on the plane. I didn't know why they needed it— they had reports from Patrick Baker and other passengers, but the Maltese police wouldn't release me until they had mine as well. They wrote down everything I said.

Shortly after, they wheeled me out of the hospital. It was great to see the pretty blue sky again. Malta looked like a beautiful country. I wished that I'd been able to enjoy it under different circumstances. Scott and the U.S. ambassador to Malta, Gary Matthews, looked on as medical attendants hoisted me into the plane.

On the flight to Germany, Scott and I were the sole passengers on a USAF C-9 "Nightingale" transport plane, normally used to evacuate wartime casualties. I lay flat on a bed dangling from the ceiling in the cargo bay. I was so tired from the hijacking and the surgery that I slept much of the flight.

At one point, the copilot came back to visit with me. She looked so young, and I asked her when she started flying.

"I've been doing it a long time, ever since I was a little girl," she said. "My father flew. Would you like to come up to the front?"

She led me to the cockpit and let me sit down in her seat and look out. When I started feeling weak, she helped me get back to my bed in the back.

❦

We were en route to the second General Hospital in Landstuhl, Germany, but a snowstorm forced the pilot to divert us to Rhein-Main Air Force Base in Frankfurt and the ninety-seventh General Hospital (the one that Captain Tesstrake and the TWA hostages flew into exactly five months earlier), where we stayed overnight.

The next morning, we continued on to Landstuhl, where I was admitted on the neurosurgery service.

The U.S. military took good care of us in Germany. They put Scott up in a barracks-style hotel on the base, near the hospital. After living in constant worry for nearly a week, and not sleeping for more than a few minutes at a time, Scott could finally slow down enough to feel. The doctors had assured us that I was going to be okay. Scott and I had talked long enough so that he felt happy and confident that I wasn't going to be a vegetable.

He sat on a chair in his room, closed his eyes, and cried. After crying, Scott fell fast asleep. His body had released all the tension and worry.

The next morning when he came to the hospital, I could see that something in his eyes had changed. "What is it honey? What's wrong? Is everything okay?" I asked.

"Everything's going to be okay," he said. "I had a good cry last night, that's all."

I was still numb. I hadn't cried about what happened to me yet. Obviously, there was another side to the story. I'd barely survived a horrible tragedy and was in a state of mental and emotional shock. During the hijacking, I stuffed down my emotions to cope with the trauma. I tried to close my eyes and ears to the horror of what was happening. It was too awful to watch.

In Germany, some of the nurses wondered why I was in such a good mood, why I was laughing so much. I was just plain excited to be alive.

I shared a room with a woman named Susan Joyce, and it turned out she was originally from Minnesota, where Scott was from. She and her husband,

Pat, were living in London, England, where he served in the air force.

Susan was in the hospital for surgery to remove cancerous growths in her brain. She'd already had several operations, but the tumors kept reappearing in different places. She was partially deaf from the surgeries and, after the next operation, doctors feared she'd also be blind.

Hearing Susan's story made me realize I had nothing to complain about. I remember thinking, *Boy, and I think I have it bad. At least I'm not losing my hearing.*

Besides, I was still overjoyed just to be alive. Early on, I didn't think much about the long-term effects of my injuries. Mostly, I was just glad to be alive. I had expected each hour on the plane to be my last. Now, here I was in a German hospital, with Scott and doctors all around me. I felt so grateful. My prayers were answered. Who wouldn't be happy about that?

Scott and I joked around in the hospital. I asked him to take some pictures of my bald head. I wanted to look good for my homecoming, but I was bald and my face looked bruised and raggedy. Scott went out and bought me a wig.

He came back and said, "This looks just like your hair."

I looked at the wig in his hands and blinked twice. *Who were you married to before?* was my thought. The wig was this wild hair that hung down almost to my waist! Before the hijacking, my hair was cut short—just barely over my ears.

"Scott, I can't wear this!" I said. We both broke out laughing. He took the wig back.

I thought everything was going to be okay. Scott and I would go to live in Minnesota. I'd meet some new friends and eventually get a job. Life would move on and we'd be okay.

One day, shortly after I arrived in Germany, a U.S. Army psychiatrist came into my room. He walked over to my bed and sat down. He seemed like a kind man—something in his eyes told me that. "Sometimes," he said, "people who have been in warlike situations, or gone through rapes, major accidents, criminal assaults, or other traumatic events experience post-traumatic stress disorder [PTSD]," he said.

I'd never heard of PTSD before. "What does that mean exactly?" I asked.

"Sometimes, there's a delayed emotional reaction to the event," he explained. "You may find yourself crying or feeling bad in a few days, weeks, or months."

Before the psychiatrist left, he told me to call him if I needed anything or just wanted to talk.

His words didn't really have much effect on me. I was still so excited to be alive that nothing else mattered. It didn't matter that I didn't have any hair. It didn't matter that I'd gone through a hijacking or that I'd had to leave the place I loved. I was alive!

❦

One day, a speech therapist came into my room to do some tests. The first question she asked was what I did for a living. I couldn't remember. I knew I was a teacher in Cairo, but what kind? I looked at Scott and said, "Why can't I remember what I did?"

"Don't you remember?" he said. "You're a teacher. You're an educational diagnostician. And you tested kids."

When he said it, I thought, *Yeah, that's what I did. I tested kids.*

She asked me another question about teaching and testing.

Again, I couldn't remember the answer. I look at Scott and, again, he said, "Don't you remember? . . ."

I just kept looking at him and saying, "Why can't I remember this?"

No one in the hospital had asked me these kinds of questions before. They had asked for my name and that was about it.

The speech therapist showed me a series of flash cards with different pictures on them. First, she flashed me a black-and-white drawing of a watermelon.

I knew what a watermelon tasted like. I knew it was green on the outside and red on the inside. But I couldn't remember what it was called.

She showed me another picture, this time of a pyramid.

The same thing happened. I could see myself at the Pyramids. In Cairo, I saw them almost every day. Again, I couldn't think of the name for pyramid.

I didn't know it at the time, but I was still in shock. I hadn't come to grips with the magnitude of what I'd just been through.

A few days later, things started to change. I started waking up in the middle of the night from nightmares about the hijacking. I kept seeing the little children, the ones that died. I'd hear them cry in my dreams. I'd see them boarding the plane. They were such beautiful children. When children die at an early age, it really hurts me. I couldn't understand why they had died and I had lived.

As my memories of the hijacking slowly became clearer, I began feeling rage toward the hijackers. For the first time, the full weight of the tragedy was starting to sink in. I realized that my vision was damaged, that my memory was really weak, and that I couldn't express myself. Scott was getting frustrated with me because I couldn't do some of the simple things I did before.

It was very uncomfortable for me to let my feelings out. I didn't want to get angry or cry in front of Scott. Growing up, I'd learned that feelings were private matters best kept to oneself.

Naturally, I didn't want Scott to think anything was wrong. I wanted to protect him from my pain. He'd ask me how I was feeling and I'd say, "It's okay, honey. Everything's going to be okay. We're going to get through this."

Boy, who was I kidding! I was holding it all in.

One day, when the pain got bad enough, I decided to call the army psychiatrist. I was afraid Scott would be mad at me for sharing my feelings with a stranger, so I waited for him to leave. This was hard because he rarely left my bedside. I finally saw my chance when Scott left to eat and pick up a few things at the army store. I asked a nurse to get the psychiatrist.

It was over an hour and the psychiatrist still had not showed up. I was getting a little anxious, because I didn't know when Scott would be coming back. Eventually, the psychiatrist walked into my room. I wanted some privacy, so I told him I wanted to talk in his office.

About a week after my surgery in Malta, I was forced to get up and walk around the halls of the hospital. The doctors thought it would be good therapy for me to get back on my feet. But I tired easily, and when I did,

I'd stop and hold on to the walls until I caught my breath.

The psychiatrist and I walked to his office, and when we arrived, he shut the door and directed me to a chair across from him. It didn't take long for the tears to come.

"I'm feeling really sad and angry about the hijackers and the things they did," I said. "I'm having a lot of nightmares and waking up in the middle of the night. I see the faces of the children who died."

"What would you like to do with the hijackers?" he asked.

"I'd like to hit 'em," I said.

He raised an eyebrow. "*Hit* 'em?"

I said, "Yes, I'd like to hit them."

"Wouldn't you like to *kill* them?" he pressed me.

"Well, I'm not supposed to do that," I said.

I grew up with the idea that I shouldn't have thoughts like that—and if I did, I certainly shouldn't talk about them.

In the midst of our conversation, there was a tapping at the door. The door opened and Scott came walking into the room.

I was startled and afraid he was going to be mad at me for talking to the psychiatrist.

"Are you okay?" he asked.

"We're going to need some more time by ourselves," the psychiatrist said.

"Oh, sure," Scott said and backed out the door. "I'll go wait in your room."

I continued talking to the psychiatrist for a few more minutes. He said it was okay for me to cry.

When we were done, I walked back to my room. Scott was waiting there. "Hi, honey," I greeted him.

I got back into bed and looked over to see how Scott was feeling. I thought he would be mad that I didn't ask to see the psychiatrist when he was there. I wasn't honest with Scott about why I waited for him to leave. I didn't tell him that I didn't want him to see me cry.

"You weren't here and I needed someone to talk to," I said.

"Sometimes, that just happens," he said. "You have to do what you have to do."

I felt better. Scott seemed to understand.

Going to the psychiatrist's office that afternoon was a small step toward naming, accepting, and releasing the pain I'd stuffed down for many years. At that point, however, I had no idea of how much I stuffed and held back— toward the hijackers, Scott, my parents, and others in my life.

Shortly after Scott and I arrived in Germany, a drove of journalists descended on us. They had been working on the story for U.S. and foreign newspapers, magazines, and television stations and were following up on the human interest angle of my story. They were panting for juicy details of my life and the hijacking.

We turned down all the interview requests. I was still in shock and had no desire to meet the press. I needed to focus on recovering in quiet. I spent most of my time sleeping.

Yet one reporter managed to get past the head of army public relations. He claimed to be with a respected daily newspaper in New York City. The reporter offered to pay Scott two thousand dollars for his version of the hijacking story. Scott and I discussed the offer and agreed that Scott would talk to the reporter. We were both concerned about my mounting medical bills; we thought doing the interview would help us meet some of our expenses.

Scott gave the interview, including his chronology of the hijacking and how we had both spent the previous two years in Stavanger, Norway, and Cairo, Egypt.

But the story did not go according to plan. The article appeared in a big, sensationalist tabloid newspaper. And we never saw a dime of the money that was promised.

I was in Germany for about a week. I spent most of that time sleeping, hobbling around the hallways, and slowly starting to realize what I'd been through.

The first days and weeks after the hijacking were hard on my family and friends back home. They felt helpless to do anything but pray for me in those dark hours of the hijacking. I couldn't be reached by telephone for about a week after I was shot.

On Friday afternoon, November 29, my parents got two pieces of news: a letter I'd written from Cairo, telling them about my upcoming trip to Greece and Thanksgiving plans (including a picture of me riding on a camel near the Pyramids) and a phone call informing them of my transfer to Germany.

Then, one day, a phone rang at the nurse's station of the VA hospital. A nurse at the switchboard interrogated the caller asking to speak to me. "Are you a relative?" the nurse said.

"Yeah, this is her sister Barbara," Barb said.

The nurse came to get me out of bed. I got up, dizzy, and she motioned for me to come over to the phone. "It's your sister Barbara," the nurse said.

I don't have a sister named Barbara, I thought to myself. *Who could this be?*

I put the receiver to my ear and heard a familiar voice.

"Hello, Jackie?"

"Barb?"

It was my friend Barbara Wilson. She told the nurse that she was my sister because the hospital was only allowing me to receive calls from immediate family members. I was glad that Barb had exercised a little ingenuity to get around the bureaucracy.

I met Barb shortly after I started teaching special education in the Baytown School district, a few minutes west of Pasadena, Texas, the Houston suburb where I grew up. Barbara was also a teacher, and the two of us hit it off immediately. We hung out with the same crowd, went to the same parties, took trips together, and got to be like sisters to each other.

It was five o'clock in the morning Texas time when Barb found out what hospital I was in. She still didn't know how badly I was hurt and wanted to hear my voice. Barb was thrilled when the nurse said I was walking down the hall to get the phone.

"I thought, *God! She can walk!*" Barb later recalled. "I didn't think Jackie would be able to get out of bed because of the head injuries. It was so good to know she could get around on her own."

For the first few minutes on the phone, we both just cried. Then there was a long silence. We didn't need words to communicate our feelings or how much it meant to hear each other's voices again.

When we finally started talking, I told Barb about my out-of-body experience. I also talked about my vision problems and how I thought they would clear up when I got a new pair of contact lenses.

It was so good to hear Barb's voice. She and her husband, Wayne, wanted to fly to Germany to visit and support me. But the doctors said I'd be leaving in a few days anyway, so I didn't think it was worth the expense. Barb told me that she and Wayne, along with my parents, my friend Debbie Reno, and others had held an around-the-clock vigil for me in the hours and days during and after the hijacking.

Simply talking to Barb gave me a big boost. I didn't feel quite so alone anymore. At least not for a while.

After about a week in Germany, doctors thought I was ready to go home. Before leaving the hospital, a woman gave me a scarf to put over my bald head. Scott put some makeup on my face. I couldn't keep from laughing while he put it on. The makeup looked kind of blotchy, but at that point I really didn't care.

Scott and I flew back to the United States. The government flew me in a huge, old, dark green army transport plane. The plane carried medical equipment and other sick passengers from the VA hospital in Landstuhl. Again, I was lying flat on my back. A kind serviceman came back to visit and check on me, and snuck me some fruit juices.

It felt good to be going back to the states. But the prospect of living in a new place and making new friends was scary.

Our plan was to return to the United States so that I could get the best possible medical care. We still hoped to return to Cairo to teach, yet we didn't know if or when that would happen.

In Germany, Scott called one of our friends at CAC. Scott asked him to get the key to our apartment and pick up about two hundred dollars in cash that we had saved up. Scott directed the friend to take the money and give it to the caretakers of our building, the Egyptian family living in the elevator shaft.

CHAPTER 5

SMASHING INTO WALLS

AFTER AN ELEVEN-HOUR FLIGHT from Germany to the United States, we touched down at Andrews Air Force base in Washington, D.C. It was early December 1985, the first time we'd been back on American soil for four months. Reporters were waiting at the airport to accost us. Fortunately, military and airport officials kept them a safe distance away from us, pressed up against a restraining fence.

It was the first time Scott and I started realizing that we were going to be living in the spotlight for a while. Scott did not trust the media, especially after our experience with the reporter in Germany who lied to us. The way Scott saw it, the media was interested in only one thing: exploiting me. "My whole purpose was to shield you from the media," Scott said, "to be there for you and to keep the media away." I just agreed. I didn't care. We were still relatively protected, however, because we were in the U.S. military's hands.

We spent our first night back home in a Washington, D.C. hospital near the airport. It was the first night since the hijacking that Scott and I laid down on a bed together and just held each other tight.

The next day, we took off again for the Minneapolis/St. Paul airport. We landed at about ten o'clock that night. I was immediately whisked from the plane on a stretcher and carried into an ambulance waiting to take me to the University of Minnesota Hospital.

In the ambulance, paramedics started hooking me up to a heart monitoring machine. I thought this was strange, because I hadn't been hooked up to any machines for two weeks. I told them I didn't think it was necessary, but they insisted on going by the book. They put an oxygen mask over my face and hooked up the heart monitor.

On the way to the hospital, the song "Penny Lane" by the Beatles came over the radio. It brought a smile to my face. This was the first time I really felt like I was back in the states again.

A hungry pack of reporters lay in wait for us at the airport. They followed us to the University of Minnesota Hospital. Camera crews and reporters with their lights had staked out the building, in anticipation of my arrival. Though security tried to protect us from the unwanted exposure, a clever few managed to sneak into the hospital's underground parking garage before the doors shut.

On stepping out of the ambulance, Scott found himself looking down the lens of an enormous television camera. Scott was enraged that the hospital's security staff had done such a poor job of keeping the media away. He told the cameraman to back off, and when he didn't, Scott gave him a push and he fell to the ground. The media left us alone for the rest of our visit at the hospital.

I was exhausted by the long trip. I thought we'd just stop in to rest at the hospital for a few minutes and then be sent home.

A neurosurgeon came into my room to explain my situation. "I have to do some tests," he said.

"Can't we just go home and do the tests tomorrow? I'm really tired."

"What will it look like if you come in and I send you home right away?" the doctor said.

I was angry that he was more concerned about public relations than how I was feeling. But I was so exhausted that I didn't have much fight in me. I was ready to agree to anything. Besides, he was the doctor after all. What was one more night after everything we'd been through?

The doctor left to take care of some other business, and Scott and I were alone. "You have the power to tell him what you want to do. He's going to listen to you," Scott said.

For two hours, I went through a bunch of neurological tests. I was not discharged until about 1 A.M. I was absolutely exhausted. I couldn't put out that kind of energy. I was barely awake while he did the tests.

Scott and I went straight from the hospital to his parents' house. Of course, everyone in the Pflug family wanted to visit. They were gathered around the kitchen table. I could tell they really wanted to talk to us and find out how we were. I wanted to make a good impression on Scott's family, but I was so tired. It was hard for me to say that I just wanted to go to sleep.

Mr. and Mrs. Pflug showed me the room in their basement that Scott and I were going to be staying in—the same room that Scott grew up in. It felt really good to finally crawl into bed and put my head down on the pillow.

I slept very late the next morning. Scott was already up and dressed when I straggled into the kitchen and sat down at the table with him.

"I don't know what all this means," I said. "I don't know what to do with my life. I don't know what's going to happen now."

"I don't know either, honey," Scott said. He was just as confused as I was. "Maybe we weren't supposed to be over there. I just don't know," he said.

We were looking forward to some quiet time to sort through it all, but newspaper reporters practically had the house surrounded. They wanted to get interviews with me for their papers. They took pictures of us through the windows of the Pflugs' house. Every two seconds, the phone rang. It was some reporter working on a story about the hijacking. Scott took the calls and sent them away empty-handed, as I instructed him.

I was trying to weed through it all, but it didn't make any sense.

I had lots of trouble seeing things. Objects in my visual field were floating all over the place: buildings, people, cars, letters and words on a page—everything was floating.

For the first few days, I thought that this problem would be corrected when I got the new pair of contact lenses my parents were sending to Minnesota. My old pair was destroyed when the plane caught fire, and I didn't have a spare pair of glasses. So I was walking around practically blind. My vision is normally 20/400 without correction.

I was excited when my new pair of contacts finally arrived. But when I put them on, I was shocked. I could only see parts of people's faces and bodies! When I tried to read, I could only see parts of each word in a sentence. And I could only read half the letter in each word. A simple written phrase such as "By the way" looked something like "y e y."

With my visual problems, navigating around the Pflugs' house took a major effort. I was always bumping into things around the house—chairs, tables, countertops, walls—because I couldn't judge how far away these objects were from me. Sometimes, when I got lazy and didn't bother to move my head to compensate for my vision loss, I'd get into more trouble.

One time when I went to reach for a bar of soap in the bathroom and didn't look underneath where I was reaching, I hit my curling iron and burned my arm. I had bruises on my left side and shoulder from reaching for something and then smashing into a shelf or other solid object.

Why was I having such problems seeing properly?

I reported my symptoms to my neurologist, hoping he'd be able to tell me what was wrong. He explained that my brain was still swollen from the bullet wound and that this was causing the visual abnormalities.

That Christmas, 1985, my parents flew up from Houston to spend the holidays with Scott and me. It was an emotional reunion. I was tired and worn down, but so glad to see my parents. One of the first things I did was to let my parents feel the soft spot in my head.

Mom was worried that I might bump my exposed head. If anything hit me in the head, it could kill me. It would have gone right into my brain. "You've got to get a plate in your head," she kept telling me.

My problems seemed to build and build. I started to get angry without any obvious reason. My emotions were all over the place: I went from feeling as high as a kite—giggling and laughing uncontrollably—to the depths of despair. And I didn't understand why.

None of my doctors had prepared me for something this bad. No one ever said that this emotional roller coaster is common among persons with a head injury.

I didn't know whether my reactions were the result of the head injury or the emotional trauma I'd just gone through—or maybe both.

One of the bright spots in those initial weeks and months in Minnesota was getting to know Scott's mom and dad. They were sweet and loving people who took me into their arms and treated me as if I were their own daughter. Even though I was far from my family in Houston, I felt adopted by the Pflug family.

June Pflug, Scott's mom, was the first person I came to know and trust in Minnesota. She was very caring and down-to-earth. June knew how to manage a household too. Her husband was a salesman and was on the road five days a week. She had to raise the couple's seven children, five boys and two girls, practically on her own.

She knew the pain of grief and loss too. Her son David was killed in a car accident at age twenty-two. Scott never said much about David, but June told me the two of them had been very close. June could deeply empathize with my pain and often held me when I cried.

June and I spent a lot of time together. She helped me get around when I couldn't drive or do many things for myself. She said things that made me feel better about myself too. "You're so pretty bald, Jackie," she said. "No one could pull that off but you."

I looked in the mirror to see for myself. *I do have a pretty head*, I thought to myself. *It is nicely shaped. There aren't any bumps.*

It took about six months for my hair to grow back; during that time, June offered more compliments. Spiked hairstyles were popular among women that year, and she said I fit right in with my short hair.

It was easy to see the resemblance between Scott and his dad, Greg Pflug, whom we all called "Pops." Pops was a tall, thin man who liked to express his strong opinions. Like Scott, he had a great sense of humor. Pops could always make me laugh, even on some pretty dark days.

It was such a relief to be welcomed into the Pflugs' home, and to have a place to stay while we regrouped. I thought finished basements were pretty neat—we didn't have them in Texas. June helped me navigate around the house whenever I took a wrong turn, as I often did. It was easy for me to get lost in the basement. It seemed as though there were a number of long hallways and, if I missed the right one, I'd end up in the laundry room instead of our bedroom.

When I went up the stairs, I'd constantly smash against the wall. I didn't see it. June couldn't figure out why this kept happening. I saw the wall but didn't know where it was in relationship to my body. If I slowly approached the wall and held on to it, I could avoid running into it. But I always forgot to do that.

I often felt as if I had a brain transplant. My adult brain was gone and, in its place, was the brain of a little child.

June was patient when I floundered. For example, in the morning I'd go into the kitchen to pour myself a bowl of cereal. I'd keep pouring and pouring. . . . Cereal would be spilling out all over the countertop. My vision loss prevented me from seeing how much cereal was in the bowl. Then I'd add the milk, spilling it all over everything. Again, I couldn't see where the milk was going. The same thing happened with orange juice. When I was finished pouring myself a glass, I'd be surprised to see that I'd made a huge mess and start crying. *Why was this happening?*

June was so understanding. She didn't hover over me or get mad when I spilled milk.

And she was wonderful in the kitchen. It freed me from having to cook, which was a big help, too. I was so out of it that I didn't know that if I wanted to cook something, I had to turn on the stove.

One time, Scott, his parents, and I were all sitting at the dinner table. June passed a bowl of spaghetti around and everyone took some. Then she dished some out for me and we all started eating. I finished my spaghetti and was ready for seconds. "Could I have some more?" I asked.

"But Jackie, you still have some spaghetti on your plate," June said.

I looked back down at my plate. I'd eaten the middle and the right side of the spaghetti—the only part I could see. June took my hand and guided it to the upper left side of the plate and down to the bottom. The gaps in my visual field were mirrored in the leftover spaghetti. We all had a good laugh over that one. Yet I was also embarrassed.

For the first three months after the hijacking, while my brain was still swollen, I didn't know if I was full or hungry. My brain wasn't sending me the right messages. I knew that I had to eat breakfast every morning, because it was part of my routine—not because I was hungry. I knew I was done eating when I'd finished the food in front of me—not because I felt full.

Before dinner one evening, Scott said he needed to go get some gas and asked if I wanted to go with. At the station, Scott started filling the tank.

"I want to pay for the gas," I said. I wanted to do something to help. I also wanted to start spreading my wings a little bit and getting back into the world.

He took out his wallet and handed me some money. "I don't really know how much it's going to be," he said. He hadn't finished filling the tank.

I took the money and, just as I opened the glass door to go inside, I heard Scott yell, "Jackie, will you get me a Milky Way bar?"

"Okay," I hollered back.

As I entered the store, my mind suddenly went blank. I looked down and saw all this money in my hand, but didn't know what I was supposed to do with it. *What am I supposed to do with this?* I wondered.

Then I looked outside and saw Scott still filling the car, and I remembered the gas. But there was something else that he just yelled at me. *What was it?*

I opened the door again and yelled out, "What was it you wanted me to get?"

"A Milky Way bar," he shouted back.

Like a mantra, I kept repeating it over and over—gas-Milky Way bar, gas-Milky Way bar, gas-Milky Way bar—as I walked through the store.

I went over to the rack of candy bars. I didn't remember what the Milky Way wrapper looked like, so I had to go through and read each label one by one. Meanwhile, I kept repeating, gas-Milky Way bar, gas-Milky Way bar, gas-Milky Way bar.

It was taking me a long time. Scott had no idea what had happened to me. He had just hopped in the truck and waited.

When I finally found the Milky Way bar, I had to think, *What do*

I do next? The answer wasn't automatic. Then it came to me: Stand in line.

I went over to stand in line to pay for the gas and Milky Way bar. After a few minutes, it was my turn to pay.

"I want to pay for this Milky Way bar and gas," I announced.

"That will be $10.73," she said.

"What is it?" I asked.

"$10.73."

I looked down at the money in my hand, but didn't know what to do with it. I had a fistful of papers with the numbers "5," "10," and "1" on them. This was the first time I'd really looked at money since the hijacking. Whenever we went somewhere, Scott had always paid.

I kept looking at my money, thinking that something was going to click any second and I'd know what to do. But it never did.

In the meantime, people were coming into the store, and it was getting very crowded. A long line had formed behind me and there was only one clerk on duty.

"Oh, just put your money down!" she said with irritation.

I laid my money down on the counter and she counted it for me. She gave me the Milky Way bar and my change and I walked out.

I started sobbing. I felt so humiliated and embarrassed, like a helpless little child. I didn't even know how to count money anymore.

"What's the matter, honey? What happened in there?" Scott asked as I got back in the Bronco.

Between sobs, I said, "Scott, I don't know how to count money. I didn't know what the money was."

"It's going to be okay," Scott tried soothing me. "It's going to be okay."

In my pain, I didn't believe him. I couldn't believe him. I wanted the earth to open up and swallow me whole.

When we got back to the Pflugs' house, where we were still staying, I sat down with June and practiced counting money. We got out a bunch of quarters, nickels, and dimes, and she helped me add them together. "This is a quarter," she'd say. "When you take two quarters and put them together, you have fifty cents."

After a while, I slowly started to catch on. The knowledge that a quarter was equal to twenty-five cents never left me. The part I no longer understood was *What does twenty-five cents* mean? *What do people do with money?*

It was just about impossible for me to add numbers in columns, however. It was just too overwhelming to distinguish the different numerals. They all blurred together. I had to use a calculator to add, subtract, multiply, or divide numbers.

Other abstract concepts, like telling time, were hard for me to grasp. I knew what six o'clock was—that it was an hour in the day—but what did that *mean?* What did people *do* with time?

"At 6 P.M.," June patiently explained, "people are getting off work, starting to come home. In an hour or two, many people eat dinner. . . ."

The fact that there were two six o'clocks—6 A.M. and 6 P.M.—was also confusing.

"At six in the morning" June said, "many people are getting up to go to work. At six in the evening, twelve hours later, people are coming home from work and sitting down to dinner."

June helped me learn more concrete lessons too. I'd point to the arm of a chair and say, "What is this?"

"That's the arm of a chair," she'd say. I'd point to other objects and she'd say, "Those are blinds, that's a couch, that's the seat of a chair."

Life in Minnesota was lonely. The only people I knew were Scott's family and friends. Since I couldn't drive, I had no way to get around and make new friends. For a person who loves meeting and talking to people, and exploration and adventure, this social and physical isolation was particularly limiting. I felt totally dependent on Scott for all my needs. After being so independent all my life, I felt like a helpless child again. It was only when we arrived in Minnesota that I realized how much I needed a solid support system.

Day after day droned on and I felt bored, restless, and useless. I was supposed to heal, but what did that mean? None of the doctors in Malta, Germany, or Minnesota helped me understand all the changes I would be going through or suggested I get rehabilitation or reading help. They essentially stitched me up and cut me loose. I was supposed to figure everything out alone, and I had no clue as to what I was dealing with.

Much of the time, I felt helpless, out of control, and lonely. No one took me by the hand and told me what I needed to do to get on with my life. I was terribly sad, lonely, depressed, and bitter. My emotions fluctuated between happy, giggly highs and tearful, depressed, irritable lows. It was scary because I didn't understand why this was happening—and no one explained it to me. *Was I going crazy?*

In Minnesota, I had to meet with more doctors than I ever knew existed. Every time I turned around, it seemed, I had to see another doctor.

Knowing that our destination was Minnesota, the American doctor in Germany referred me to a prominent neurosurgeon at the University of Minnesota Hospital in Minneapolis. I saw him at least once a week for the first few months after the hijacking. He and other doctors wanted to keep a careful watch over the status of remaining bone fragments lodged in my brain. I had to have regular CAT scans to check on the location of these fragments and make sure there weren't any major changes.

My neurosurgeon reminded me of an old German grandfather: he was all business and very stubborn. I always had the feeling he was in a hurry to get my examination over with so he could move on to his next patient. He had no time for my questions about my treatment or condition. His bedside manner was "Why are you asking questions? Just listen to me, *I'm* the doctor." He was set in his ways, a man who knew everything.

It was hard for me to question his approach. I'd always looked up to doctors as authority figures. As the patient, I thought my job was to accept and do what they told me. In time, I came to appreciate how human they are.

On one visit to see my doctor, maybe three months after the hijacking, I was wearing a wig to cover my bald head—and feeling pretty good. The doctor walked right up to me and said, "Boy do you look good!" He immediately began running his hands through my hair, without giving me a chance to take off my wig. He searched, in vain, for my scar.

Can't he tell that I'm wearing a wig? I wondered. *Can't he feel the little net?*

I looked over at Scott, and he had his hand over his mouth to keep from laughing. The doctor wasn't giving up.

Finally, he said, "Where is your scar?"

"Doctor," I laughed, "I'm wearing a wig!"

I took it off and my hair was just barely growing back—my scar was so obvious.

"Oh, well, your scar is looking pretty good," he said, still stone-faced.

Scott and I cracked up with laughter as we got in the car to leave the hospital.

What troubled me more than my doctor's lack of humor was my sense of not being heard when I talked about my ongoing health concerns. For example, I kept telling him about a problem with my neck. Anytime I moved my neck forward, the whole left side of my body went numb. He put me through some painful x-rays to diagnose the problem, but came up with nothing. He and several other doctors said I'd just have to learn to live with the problem. They said I had a brain dysfunction.

My first doctor had a pessimistic view of my future. He was convinced that I would never be able to work or drive again, or be able to live by myself. "There's no way you can drive with your vision," he said. Though he didn't even know what level I was reading at, he said, "You're not going to be able to read any faster than you do now. What you have right now is what you're going to get."

I wanted to change doctors, but I didn't know if or when I should. It would take time and energy for another doctor to become familiarized with the pages and pages and piles of stuff on my case. *Was it worth the risk of leaving someone who knew my medical history?*

I scheduled an appointment with an educational diagnostician at the University of Minnesota. I wanted to know what my strengths and weaknesses were.

The first test she gave me was the Weschler Adult Intelligence Scale, Revised or WAIS-R. As an educational diagnostician, I'd taken the test before and administered a similar version to hundreds of children in testing for learning disabilities.

A learning disability is a very specific type of learning problem. Before a student can be considered learning disabled (LD), I as a school psychologist had to first rule out the possibility that the child's learning difficulty was not caused by a physical disability (such as deafness or blindness), and/or environmental, cultural, or emotional problems. Students had to have a significant gap between their intellectual scores and reading and/or math achievement to be considered LD. If there's no gap, it may just be that the child is a slow learner.

While ignorant teachers and parents believe LD stands for "Lazy and Dumb," the great irony is that LD kids have higher than average intelligence.

Some LD experts believe that many brilliant historical figures, including Albert Einstein, Thomas Edison, Woodrow Wilson, Socrates, and Leonardo da Vinci, could probably be classified as LD, based on the problems they had with formal schooling.

I went through an extensive two-year training in my master's degree program to be able to administer the WAIS-R. I was completely familiar with all aspects of the test and its scoring.

Under these conditions, there is no way that I could take the WAIS-R and have the results be considered valid. "You really shouldn't give me this test," I objected. "I've given this test many times. It's not going to be valid."

"We'll just see how it comes out anyway," the tester said.

I felt hurt and patronized. I felt she was treating me like a child—not as an equal. Yet I felt helpless to do anything about it.

I went ahead and took the test, hoping the evaluator would still pick up on some of my learning problems. I puzzled over many questions on the WAIS-R. I could tell that my responses to some of the questions were different than they would have been before I was shot.

As I studied the words and pictures on the page, I'd get a sudden flash of insight and think, *Oh my God, I just did something significant. I just did something that was pretty weird.*

I looked up, hoping the evaluator had caught it too. Though evaluators are always supposed to observe persons taking a diagnostic test, my tester wasn't watching me. She was busy scoring my previous test. I felt terrible.

I also saw myself in her. As a school psychologist and diagnostician, I often did the same thing. While kids were taking one test, I was grading the previous one. I wondered if my students felt as frustrated as I now did because nobody was paying attention to them or their learning process.

This testing session was frustrating in other ways. I knew something was wrong with my memory and vision. I couldn't see the words clearly. I was also working at a very slow pace.

I actually did fairly well on parts of a memory test. I was given two words like *dog* and *house*, then asked to recall them. By visualizing a picture of a dog sitting on top of the house, I often answered correctly. I had taught students this mnemonic technique to sharpen their memory. Unfortunately, using the technique now allowed me to mask a deeper problem: I wasn't recalling words; I was remembering pictures—a completely different mental process.

I asked the evaluator to give me another memory test, but she didn't think it was necessary. I was very disappointed. At the end of the testing session, I still didn't know what grade level I was at in reading or math because she didn't test my reading or math comprehension.

Little things that I had always taken for granted were now, suddenly, huge obstacles. Since all of my clothes had been left in Egypt or lost on the plane, June Pflug took me shopping one day to buy some new clothes. It wasn't easy walking around the mall where we went. I had to hold on to my mother-in-law to keep from falling sometimes.

After going to a few stores, June saw a pair of pants that she thought might look good on me. I went into the dressing room to try them on but came out crying.

I couldn't tell what they looked like on me. I only saw pieces of the pants in the mirror.

I knew something was terribly wrong with my ability to process information. I didn't feel any less intelligent than I had before getting shot in the head, but I knew I was slower in understanding things. I thought a lot about my years of teaching learning disabled kids, hoping that, somehow, I could draw upon that knowledge to get a handle on my situation.

Before the hijacking, my second job after college was teaching special education classes to second, third, and fourth graders at Bowie Elementary School in Baytown, Texas. This job taught me a lot more about learning disabilities and the frustrations of LD kids.

LD kids were smart enough, but they had a hard time doing simple things such as finding their way to and from the bathroom. I had to take them by the hand and lead them to the bathroom time and again. After a few times, I'd say, "Okay, do you think you can find the bathroom by yourself?"

They would nod their little heads "yes," so I'd let them try going alone. I remember what happened to little Beth one time. She was a skinny, little girl who was quite a bit slower than the rest. She suffered from a lot of diseases.

I let Beth go to the bathroom by herself one time, but twenty minutes later, she wasn't back. "Now where is Beth? How could she be in the bathroom for twenty minutes?" I was worried.

I went looking, but Beth wasn't in the bathroom. I started roaming the halls. When I found Beth, obviously lost, she was crying. "I couldn't find the bathroom," she said. She'd been wandering the halls all that time, unable to find her way back to the classroom to tell me she was lost.

Sometimes I lost patience with my students. "Why aren't you listening?" I'd ask. "Why aren't you paying attention?"

Oh, the irony.

CHAPTER 6

GOT YOU THIS TIME!

IN JANUARY 1986, LESS THAN TWO MONTHS after the hijacking, I flew down to Houston for the first time since Scott and I were married. I was still too scared to go on a plane by myself, so I arranged to fly to Dallas with Scott's sister Margaret, who had to travel to Dallas-Fort Worth on business. Barb Wilson would fly to Dallas, meet me there, and then we'd fly to Houston.

It was scary being on a plane again. I cried when I sat down in my seat. Almost immediately, I found myself staring at other passengers' laps to check for guns and grenades. Somehow, I managed to settle down after a while.

Barb Wilson was waiting to greet me in Dallas. Together, we got on a commuter flight to Houston's Hobby Airport.

On the drive home from the airport I gazed out the window, watching the familiar landscapes of my youth scrolling by on our way to Pasadena, the Houston suburb where I grew up.

Pasadena has a couple of big claims to fame. It's home to many of the world's largest oil refineries. Driving along Highway 225, between Houston and Deer Park, oil fields and refineries stretch as far as the eye can see. At night, it's quite a sight. The flashing, glowing lights of the refineries create the illusion of strange, ghostly cities out of a science fiction novel.

Before it burned down in 1989, Mickey Gilley's famous country western nightclub was also in Pasadena. Gilley's attracted national attention as the place where *Urban Cowboy*, the 1979 movie starring John Travolta, was filmed. Barb Wilson and I used to go there on Friday nights to ride the famous mechanical bull and practice country western dance steps such as the Cotton-Eyed Joe, the shottish, the polka, and the two-step.

In the daytime, there's nothing romantic about the area immediately west of Houston. It's a sprawling urban mess—a mishmash of residential, commercial, and industrial construction. Houston is the only large American city with no zoning laws, and you can see the results. In Houston, and its suburbs, your next-door neighbor can open an automobile repair shop in his backyard—or a marble and cement mixing operation, for that matter—without a permit. Abandoned oil rigs, like iron dinosaurs from another era, dot the landscape. They stand idly by fast-food restaurants, miniature golf courses, flea markets stocked with velvet paintings and cheap jewelry, gas stations, and motels.

Pasadena is a blue-collar, working-class suburb where southern hospitality still prevails. People drive Ford and Chevy four-by-fours, wear cowboy hats, and enjoy home cooking.

On this first trip back home, I stayed with my parents and with Barb and Wayne part of the time, as I had the previous summer. Outside Barb's house was a big banner that read WELCOME HOME JACKIE. She and my other friends had tied a yellow ribbon around the huge oak tree in her front yard.

It felt good to be home again, surrounded by close friends and family. I spent a lot of time with my mom and dad, in the same house where as a young girl I'd played school with my sisters and neighborhood friends.

My mother, Billie, and my father, Eugene, met in the navy during the Korean War and settled in Pasadena soon after. They were typical of their generation. Dad joined the navy after high school and worked as an aviation electrician. He served on board the Intrepid in the South Pacific and later in Seattle, Washington. After the war, he worked as an operator for Ethyl Oil Corporation for thirty-four years.

My dad's ethnic background is German—and he is known to display the stubbornness which Germans are famous for. My dad also has a very gentle, loving, and sensitive side. His mother's maiden name was Brahms—and she was directly related to the family of the famous composer, Johannes Brahms. The two Brahms brothers came over to America on a ship in the late 1890s.

One decided to stay in Texas; the other, the composer who wrote "Brahms Lullaby," returned to Germany.

Mom's background is French and Irish. She grew up in New Hampshire and, after high school, joined the navy. She later served in the Korean War and was stationed in Seattle, Washington, where she was a chaplain's assistant and met my dad.

When I first arrived at Barb and Wayne's house, I sat in the same kitchen where Barb and I watched the TWA hijacking unfold in June. How different the circumstances were this time!

I was wearing a red scarf and wig to cover my shaved head, and the scar from my bullet wound was still visible. I removed the scarf and wig to let Barb see the soft spot in my head move up and down when I breathed—just like the soft spot on the top of an infant's head. It was pretty scary.

Barb arranged a homecoming party for me that gave me a chance to see all my old friends again. It gave me a big boost to see how much they cared about me. "I was praying for you, Jackie," my friend Debbie said. "We're all so glad you made it through."

About three hours later, after the last person left the party, I went into Barb's bedroom and just broke down. I sobbed and sobbed. I felt as though I had to hold everything in while people were around. Now I could let go and let things out.

Barb must have heard me, for she came in and sat down next to me on the bed. She just held me while I cried. "It's okay, Jackie. It's okay to cry. Just let it all out," Barb said.

"Why am I crying?" I said. "I just get so down."

"The only way to get through it is to let your emotions out, honey."

"But I'm so afraid of letting people down. I want to be strong. But it's so hard."

"Tears are good," Barb said. "If you don't show your emotions, you're going to have a hard time. Don't be afraid to cry."

I was physically and emotionally exhausted most of my time back home.

I was so wiped out that I needed to take a nap every afternoon. I felt completely drained.

One afternoon when Barb was at work, Wayne asked if I wanted to see any of the television coverage of the hijacking that he had taped. I said yes.

Wayne popped the tape into the VCR and I lay on the carpet, watching the terrible event all over again from a strange new perspective. I just lay there on the floor, staring at the painful images flashing across the same screen on which I'd seen the TWA hijacking unfold six months earlier.

Wayne saw the pain on my face as I saw the news coverage of the hijacking for the first time. I felt like I was living through it all over again. Watching the tape gave me a sense of what it was like for people back home.

The two of us didn't say much as we watched. I sensed that Wayne was at a loss for words. I made only one comment.

"That's him," I pointed to the screen. "That's the man who shot me."

The video footage all seemed so strange and unreal.

The next day, I called an old friend who is a clinical psychologist, and asked to meet him for dinner. He was the first person I opened up to about the spiritual questions I was having after the hijacking.

At the restaurant, I asked my friend, "Isn't there more to life than what we're doing? Isn't there more to life than just waking up every morning, weaing the right clothes, and driving the right car? Is there some deeper meaning to life?"

I was searching for the meaning of life and, because my friend was a psychologist, I hoped he could help me answer the questions in my heart, questions like: "Why are we here? Why did the hijacking happen to me? What's going to happen to me now?"

My friend is a very sensitive and thoughtful man. He listened closely before speaking. "It's not unusual for you to have those questions, Jackie," he said, quietly. "I'd be surprised if you didn't. It's probably going to take some time before things make sense again."

I told him more about my perception and memory problems and, on this subject, he had some ideas. He had a friend who was a neuropsychologist—

a doctor who studies and treats the language, perception, memory, and behavior problems often caused by brain damage and brain disorders—who was interested in testing me. I called and made an appointment with him.

When I went in, I took a battery of reading and memory tests, including the Wepman Auditory Discrimination Test, designed to measure how well people can distinguish different sounds. He recited word pairs such as "house-mouse," "red-Fred," then asked me whether the words were the same or different. Time and again, I answered "same" when the words were different. I failed the Wepman test.

Another memory test he gave me was similar to one I'd taken in Minnesota—with one important difference. This test required me to recall pairs of *abstract* words. For example, he presented me with word pairs such as "because-acknowledge." Since I couldn't make a picture of "because" or "acknowledge," I couldn't use a mnemonic technique to hide my learning disability.

The neuropsychologist was hesitant to tell me the results of my reading test. He didn't want to hurt my feelings, but I needed to know. "Your short-term memory is very, very weak, Jackie," he said. "You're reading at a third-grade level and comprehending at a first-grade level."

It was a big relief to finally have my learning problems identified. Now that I knew what I was dealing with, I could do something about them. Before I left the doctor's office, he suggested some techniques that could help strengthen my memory and reading ability.

The Sunday before I went back to Minnesota, I was invited to speak at my church—Trinity Episcopal, in Baytown—to share my story with the congregation. I was pretty nervous about it. What would I say? It had only been a short time since the hijacking. I was still in shock. But I agreed.

The night before, Barb helped me write down what I wanted to say. We sat at the kitchen table and worked on the speech. The next morning, Barb, Wayne, and I went to church together.

It was the first time I had ever publicly shared my story. Before this, I had only talked about what happened with my family, close friends, and people who knew me in Minneapolis. I was very, very scared.

Barb sat in the front row the whole time. There was only one point when I was overwhelmed by the sadness of what I'd been through. The tears started to come.

I stopped and Barb walked up to the podium and gave me a big hug. "I can keep going," I whispered in her ear.

I finished my speech with a quote Barb had hanging on her bedroom wall. I knew right away that it was something I wanted to share with others.

> *I got up early one morning*
> *And rushed right into the day.*
> *I had so much to accomplish*
> *That I didn't have time to pray.*
> *Problems just tumbled about me and heavier came each task.*
> *Why doesn't God help me? I wondered,*
> *He answered, "You didn't ask."*
> *I wanted to see joy and beauty,*
> *But the day toiled on gray and bleak,*
> *I wondered why God didn't show me,*
> *He said, "But you didn't seek."*
> *I tried to come into God's presence,*
> *I tried all my keys at the lock,*
> *God gently and lovingly chided,*
> *"My child, you didn't knock."*
> *I woke up early this morning,*
> *And paused before entering the day.*
> *I had so much to accomplish,*
> *That I had to take time to pray.*

"I want to be in Egypt," I told the audience in closing, "but I can't be in Egypt. People say, 'The U.S. is wonderful, why don't you want to be here?' I love the U.S. and, yes, I'm going to be here and I'm going to love it here. But I want you to understand that, for me, leaving Egypt is hard. I feel the way you might if you were suddenly snatched from your home and loved ones."

I'd been so nervous before giving the speech, but I was excited by people's reactions. They gave me a standing ovation when I was through. It felt great. Afterwards, some people came up to tell me how much it meant to them.

I flew from Hobby Airport back to Dallas-Fort Worth in a first-class seat. Barb Wilson's mom was a travel agent in El Paso, and she had upgraded my ticket from coach to first class.

My friend Suki Fitzgerald was waiting to meet me in Dallas. Suki had trained me as an educational diagnostician in Baytown, and we discovered that we had a lot in common and became good friends. She and her husband had moved to Dallas shortly before I went overseas. I loved the opportunity to catch up with her.

Suki came on board to make sure I got settled safely into my seat for the flight to Minneapolis. I was in for an unpleasant surprise. I'd been bumped from my first-class seat.

"Do you know who this is?" Suki demanded of the flight attendant at the ticket gate. "This is Jackie Pflug; she's the one who was just hijacked a little while ago. She needs special attention."

I smiled. I also got my first-class seat back.

"You take good care of her," Suki advised the flight attendant.

I was really nervous and jittery about being back on board an airplane again. I was shaking and feeling kind of out of it.

A man sitting next to me could tell something was wrong. I told him about being in the hijacking, and he nodded sympathetically.

Early in my recovery, I was reluctant to say much about the hijacking or discuss the details with strangers. When Scott and I went to parties or other social gatherings, people often asked me what it was like. And people often told me what they would have done if they were in my situation: "Well, if I was on the plane, I would have done this, or I would have done that."

I remember doubting myself and thinking, *Gosh, maybe they're right. If I had done that, what would have happened? Maybe I could have saved some children's lives.*

After a while, I didn't want to hear it anymore. I decided to say it was "scary," then change the subject. Or else I'd say, "It's easy for you to say that when you're on safe ground."

There was another reason why I stopped talking about the hijacking. I didn't trust people's motives in asking me about my experience. Were they just out for a good time? I didn't feel like opening my life up to someone drinking a can of beer, distractedly looking off in the distance.

I wasn't interested in telling the story to people who asked, "What's it like to be on a plane that was hijacked?" To me, it seemed as insensitive as approaching a rape victim and eagerly asking, "What's it like to be raped?" I didn't want to be that vulnerable; I didn't want to have to keep reliving the experience with anyone who asked.

I was very hurt by the hijacking. I am a very trusting person by nature, and it hurt to realize that someone could actually kill me without batting an eye. That knowledge does something to you; it changes you. I had to feel very safe before I felt comfortable sharing my story or being that open with someone.

Yet I could understand people's curiosity. I wanted to talk about the experience, but not in a sensational way. I was interested in talking about all the lessons I was learning from the experience.

The hesitation I felt about sharing my story also extended to the national news media. Right after the hijacking, I was swamped with interview requests by producers of *Good Morning America, Today,* and other talk and news shows. You name it and they called. I turned them all down. I didn't feel like I had anything to say. I hardly knew what a toothbrush was; what was I going to tell millions of people on national television?

Besides, I was suspicious of the media's motives. Yet Scott and I took down the names of everyone who called, and we kept the list in a drawer.

A few months later when I finally did start talking to people in the media and giving some interviews, Scott didn't understand it. I felt that sharing my story was a necessary part of my healing process. This later became a source of conflict.

The hijacking and its aftermath was going to severely test our relationship. Scott and I really didn't know each other that well. When we'd met, we both had that twinkle in the eye and the unbounded optimism of youth—and the belief that, with love, anything is possible.

I hadn't dated much in high school—my first date was the senior prom—so I was still amazed that a handsome man saw me as attractive too.

Scott was the first boyfriend whom I knew I'd be afraid to leave. In the past, I'd always been the one to call it quits. It was something I didn't like about myself. I always wondered, *Why is this? Everyone else can stay in a relationship; am I so different?* I wanted to get married and have children.

When Scott and I started getting more serious, I thought, *Wow, this is great!* I was already thirty years old and I thought, *I better grab him, because this may be my only chance to get married.* I did want to have a family and it seemed like the right time to start.

There were many things that attracted me to Scott. We quickly found out that we had a lot in common. We had the same beliefs and wanted the same things out of life. We had the same thoughts about God, life, and our purpose.

I liked that Scott was aggressive and spoke his mind. On the other hand, I often found him intimidating. I was afraid of his reaction when *I* spoke *my* mind. Sometimes, it seemed that my opinions and feelings were less acceptable than his.

At the end of the 1984–85 school year, our teaching contracts in Norway were up. We'd dated about seven months and were now facing a big decision: get married or go our separate ways.

We decided to get married. We both wanted to continue teaching overseas, so we attended a job fair in London for teachers, similar to one I'd attended a year earlier. We both got jobs in Cairo, teaching at the Cairo American School. Scott would be coaching and teaching physical education, while I would be working with learning disabled students in grades four through six.

That summer, Scott and I flew back to the states to spend some time with our families. During that time, I flew to Minneapolis to meet Scott's parents and relatives. In early August, Scott flew to Houston to meet my family and friends for the first time. On August 10, 1985, Scott and I exchanged wedding vows at Trinity Episcopal Church in Baytown. Two days after the wedding, we were on a thirty-six-hour flight from Houston to Cairo.

In Cairo, the bubble began bursting on my fantasies of married life. Scott and I had known each other a whole year, yet we only seemed to communicate on a superficial level. I tried to push away my doubts, hoping things would improve as we settled into our new jobs and apartment. I kept thinking, *it will change. It will be okay; we'll learn to communicate.*

I had no idea what marriage was about. I had this fairy-tale image in my head that we'd have children and everything would be fine and dandy. I knew what I liked and what I didn't, but I really wasn't mature enough to make a solid decision on marriage. I loved Scott and I thought that was all that really mattered—that we could work through anything if we love each other.

Besides, lots of newlyweds second-guess themselves or their partners. I decided to focus on the positive.

Now here we were, a year later, and our real problems were just beginning.

❧

In mid-January 1986, I got a phone call from Cindy Carter, an FBI agent based in Washington, D.C. Carter explained that she was in charge of coordinating the FBI's investigation of the hijacking. In that capacity, she supervised the gathering and analysis of evidence, interviewed witnesses, and followed up on leads throughout the world.

Because Americans were on board the hijacked plane, the FBI was involved in the case right from the start. Agents were on the ground in Malta even as the Egyptian commandos prepared to storm the plane. After the disastrous rescue attempt, the bureau's "Disaster Squad"—a specially trained response team of investigators and technicians—combed the wreckage for evidence that could later be used in court or to help Maltese and Egyptain authorities identify bodies.

At the time of Cindy's call, prosecutors in Malta and the United States were both preparing separate cases against the one surviving hijacker, Omar

Mohammed Ali Rezaq. The FBI was working with Maltese authorities to gather its own evidence in case Malta could not—or would not—prosecute the hijacker. If Malta chose not to prosecute for any reason, the U.S. government would attempt to have Rezaq handed over to the United States for prosecution. Carter asked if I'd be willing to testify in Malta and at a trial in the United States, if one were held. I said yes.

The FBI was rigorously preparing its own case against Rezaq. They had evidence that he took charge of the hijacking after one of his comrades was killed in the midair gun battle. They investigated and documented the evidence in preparing for an indictment.

The FBI had a good relationship with Maltese officials on the case. Maltese technical experts flew to the FBI lab in Washington, D.C.—probably the finest crime lab in the world—to examine evidence. FBI forensic experts conducted ballistics tests on the spent cartridges found in the aircraft, helped with autopsies, and looked for more fingerprints.

Carter asked if I would fly to Washington in mid-April 1986, to testify before a special grand jury convened to handle terrorist attacks against American citizens living or traveling abroad. Congress had passed a special "hostage taking" statute allowing the Justice Department to prosecute terrorists who attacked Americans traveling on board foreign planes and ships. Previously, only American passengers traveling on American carriers were protected under U.S. law.

This grand jury, first convened in October 1985, was the same one that indicted three terrorists for killing Leon Klinghoffer, a passenger on the *Achille Lauro*.

Carter explained a little about what would happen in the event of a trial in Washington, D.C., and why my testimony was important. "This really is a case of identity—that's what the whole trial will be about," she said. "They will say, 'Yes, the defendant was there, but he's not the one who pulled the trigger.' That's probably what it will come down to."

I was an eyewitness to everything that happened. Having the testimony of a victim was important to the prosecutors, and it would appeal to the jury.

I was scared about going on another airplane to testify. Hijackings and terrorist attacks continued to be common occurrences.

I had planned to testify at the hijacker's trial for murder and attempted murder in Malta. As the March 1986 trial date approached, however, I was having second thoughts. I was still deathly afraid of the hijackers, whether they were dead or in jail. Months after the ordeal, I was still afraid that someone would gun me down in the street. I hated being at large gatherings. When I went, I was like a small child. I was afraid of everyone. I trusted no one. I was continually plagued by insomnia and a recurring nightmare. This made it hard to get the rest my mind and body craved so desperately.

In my nightmare, the doorbell rang and Scott went to answer it. He'd come back and say, "It's for you." A tall, dark-haired man stood in the doorway, extending a gift. I said thank-you and started unwrapping the box. I love getting gifts so I eagerly opened the present. Inside were three small boxes within boxes. Inside the last was a note saying, "Ha, ha. Got you this time!"

In my nightmare, I looked up at the man at the door as he reached into his bag, pulled out a gun, and shot me in the head. I fell to the ground and the man ran away. Scott started yelling, "Jackie, are you okay? Are you okay?" There was blood all over the white carpet. I looked Scott in the eyes, said, "I don't think I can make it this time," and fell into his arms.

I knew I was having other nightmares, too, ones that I couldn't remember when I woke up. I knew they were nightmares because I could feel them in my body, and I'd wake up in the middle of the night, crying.

The hijackers haunted me during the day as well. I often thought about the curly-haired hijacker who banged me on the head, the one who died during the midair gun battle. I could feel his body and sense his presence near me. Doctors said I was hallucinating, but that wasn't it.

I didn't hear him speak, but felt him saying, "You're still mine. I still gottcha. You can't get away from me."

I'd fight back, saying, "Leave me alone!"

Shortly before I was scheduled to testify in Malta, I reached a crisis. I was afraid to travel and said I wanted someone to protect me. I was afraid that Rezaq's buddies might show up and kill some of us who were planning to testify.

It wasn't an idle concern. The FBI received a lot of information on the continuing activities of terrorist groups in the region. There was always a concern that Libya or another group might attempt to disrupt the trial. Days before the hijacker was arraigned on charges of murder and attempted murder, a bomb exploded at the Libyan Cultural Institute in Malta, a short distance from the law courts. No injuries were reported, but the blast damaged a library. Nobody claimed responsibility.

Malta guarded Rezaq around the clock, which took a lot of resources for a country with such a small military and police force. According to FBI sources, the Maltese wanted to be rid of him, but they were caught in a political mess: if they handed him over to the United States, they would anger Egypt, Libya, Greece, and several other countries who wanted to try him. In the end, it was politically expedient for Malta to try him there.

I called my contact person at the FBI, and she agreed to assign two bodyguards to protect me. They were all set to meet Scott and me at the Minneapolis airport and fly with us to Malta. As the trial date approached, I felt more and more jittery about going to Malta, even for a few days.

In my head I wanted to go, to make sure justice was done. I wanted to put the guy away. But my body kept saying no. I didn't want to go back and live through the hijacking all over again. I didn't want to see or be in the same room with the man who shot me. I didn't want to look into his eyes.

I knew it was too soon for me to make the trip back to Malta. I was shaking and scared inside. I was terrified by the mere prospect of getting on a plane again.

In February 1986, I called my FBI contact in Washington, D.C. I was crying on the phone. "I can't do it, I just can't," I told her. I felt as though I was letting everybody down by not going to tell my story in court.

"That's okay, Jackie," she said, gently.

I was so glad that she wasn't mad at me for changing my mind.

"I'd like to be able to do something to help you put this guy away. Is there any other way I can help? Could I tell my story here in Minnesota?"

"Sure, we can do something in Minnesota," she said. "You can testify there. We'll have someone take your statement."

Two FBI agents from the Minneapolis bureau, a man and a woman, came to our apartment and escorted me to the federal courthouse in Minneapolis. A prosecuting attorney from Malta and a court-appointed public defender representing the hijacker also flew to Minnesota to be present during my testimony.

I was scared when we entered the large, empty courtroom, but the court officials made me feel safe. They ordered the courtroom cleared except for myself, the attorneys, and the FBI agents. They sat me down in the witness stand, and I took the oath.

"Do you swear to tell the truth, the whole truth, and nothing but the truth?" the clerk asked.

"I do."

The questions began. First, the prosecutor asked me to describe the hijacking step by step—what happened and when. He was a kind man.

Then it was the defense lawyer's turn. I'd been terrified by the prospect of facing the man assigned to defend the hijacker who shot me. But the person in front of me was not to be feared. He was a short, bald man with kind eyes. He obviously was sympathetic to me. He was appointed by the court and was there to do his job.

"Do you remember the man who shot you? Can you describe his physical appearance for the court?" he asked.

"Well, he had straight hair and very piercing eyes," I began. . . .

The lawyers asked me to look at some pictures and see if I could pick out the hijacker who shot me. I did. At the time, however, I wasn't sure if I'd picked out the right man.

CHECK THE ORANGE JUICE

ABOUT THREE MONTHS AFTER THE HIJACKING, in mid-February 1986, Scott and I moved out of his parents house and into a two-bedroom apartment in Minnetonka, a western suburb of Minneapolis. We decided we needed to get a place of our own. Naively, perhaps, I still expected us to settle down quickly and get back to a "normal" married life—whatever that meant. I did my best to get on with life, but it wasn't working.

Scott and I both experienced the frustration of living with a head-injured person. There were plenty of times when we'd be leaving to go somewhere and I'd say, "Wait, I have to brush my teeth"—which I'd just done ten minutes before. One time I told Scott I couldn't find my coat. I began searching the apartment from top to bottom—until Scott pointed out that I was wearing it.

Scott was often frustrated with having to repeat things to me all the time. "I just told you that, Jackie!" he often said.

There were other stresses. The Cairo American College honored our teaching contracts and paid our salaries for the rest of the year, but Scott had trouble finding work in Minnesota. Teaching jobs were scarce, and none of the local school districts needed a physical education teacher. Scott had a letter of reference from U.S. Senator David Durenberger, urging employers to give him an interview and explaining our circumstances, but it didn't seem to help much. He got some interviews at Pillsbury and, at one point, was offered a management trainee position at a fast-food restaurant, but he wasn't interested.

Scott did part-time painting and other odd jobs to help support us, but the work was spotty and low paying. Scott also worked as a caretaker at the Stratford Woods apartment building, which allowed us to live there without paying rent.

Meanwhile, my medical bills were still skyrocketing. How were we going to pay them, plus our regular expenses? The crushing financial pressure was hard to bear.

A few months later, a friend of mine in Baytown, Texas, gave us the name of a lawyer at Kreindler and Kreindler, a New York law firm specializing in personal injury lawsuits for people injured or hurt in airplane crashes, accidents, or hijackings involving airplanes. Frank Fleming, a lawyer at the firm, offered to file a lawsuit against EgyptAir to try and recover some damages to help pay for my hospital bills and compensate us for the pain and suffering I'd gone through.

Fleming took a personal interest in the case. He hoped to change the international treaty covering personal injury cases, which he said was hopelessly outdated. For example, the most a passenger could recover from a plane crash under the Warsaw Pact Treaty, signed in the 1930s, was less than fifteen thousand dollars.

Scott laughed when he heard how low the amount was. "You get almost as much for your luggage and belongings as you do for your life," he said.

Neither of us had much interest in filing a lawsuit, but if we could get some money to pay medical bills and help change the law, it seemed important to pursue.

The endless days of being caged in a small apartment were a special form of torture to me. I'd been out exploring the world, living my great adventure. Now I was trapped within these four walls. And nothing was within walking distance. I was bored and restless. I was supposed to heal, but I continued to wonder, *What did that mean?*

As a child, I'd always been the outgoing, adventurous type. I was curious, upbeat, and active. I loved slipping away to touch and taste the world for myself. I tried to see only the good in people and situations, the possibilities. I was intensely curious about everyone and everything. I wanted to meet and talk to different people and get to know them. I wanted to find out about things. I wanted to break out and have great adventures.

My playful antics in our neighborhood were a continual source of frustration and concern for my mother. It wasn't easy to keep me out of trouble. I started riding a bicycle—without training wheels—when I was four years old. I loved my new mobility and freedom. Though my mom had warned me not to ride in the street, I did anyway.

I rode my bike up and down the sidewalk, flashing a big smile and greeting anyone who crossed my path. Often, I wasn't paying close enough attention to avoid the dangers in my path.

One afternoon, I ventured into the street to talk to a new friend. I was so focused on the other person that I crashed my bike into a parked car. I was shaken up pretty bad, but the very next day I was back on my bike, speeding around as usual.

My uncle used to tell me, "Jackie, I believe you'd fall down in the middle of a desert." Now, it felt as if my uncle's prophecy had come true. I'd fallen down and was now marooned in this strange suburban landscape, a prisoner of circumstances beyond my control. My ability to explore and experience the world for myself, my most precious possession, had been stolen from me.

One day, Scott came home with a surprise to ease some of my loneliness—a dog! To me, this was such a wonderful expression of Scott's love for me. It was a little white poodle and I immediately fell in love with him. I hadn't had a dog since I was a little girl. The one I had then was a dachshund named Tammy.

What should we call our new pet? Scott had a great idea and, in a moment of perverse good humor, suggested "Spike." I liked it too. So we named our little poodle Spike.

At least I had a new friend to keep me company. Yet, most of the time, I had to face my problems on my own.

For a while, I felt a new sense of hopefulness. I was willing to work hard to get the old Jackie back. If I was now like one of my learning disabled students, so be it. I'd use every technique I'd learned as a special education teacher to train myself to read and remember. I'd do my part.

As a special education teacher, I knew that learning disabled kids learned best when their lessons were in the form of a game. When they lost themselves in the fun of the game, their anxiety was lowered and they were better able to learn. Also, they came to see learning as something fun—and not to be feared.

I made up lots of little memory games to train my mind to remember things. Turning simple household activities into games was a way to compensate for my learning disability and short-term memory deficit. These games were the mental equivalent of tying a string around my finger. By "loading" information into my long-term memory files, I slowly taught my brain to compensate for its memory and perception problems.

My short-term memory was so bad that I couldn't remember simple things like how many scoops of coffee I put in the coffeemaker. I'd forget what number I was on right after I dumped some inside. So I got creative. I'd ask someone else to count the scoops for me, or I'd record a hash mark on a notepad after each scoop.

I played the "orange juice game" every morning. Scott and I both drank orange juice every day and stored it in a green pitcher in our refrigerator. Before pouring a glass, I'd look at the pitcher and ask myself, "Okay, how full is this pitcher?"

I'd try to remember the liquid line from the previous day. "Okay it's three-quarters full."

Then I'd pour myself a glass and study the container again, noting where the liquid line was. I'd hide the pitcher in the back of the refrigerator so I wouldn't cheat and look during the day.

The next morning, I'd walk into the kitchen and see a little sign on the refrigerator door: "Check the orange juice." Without the sign, I would have forgotten the game entirely. My memory was that weak.

Sometimes, I guessed right. Sometimes not.

When the orange juice game became too easy, I made up harder ones.

One thing I did was to get more serious about people-watching. I didn't just look at people, I *studied* them.

When one of Scott's friends came over, I'd focus on his clothes—the type of pants, socks, and shoes he was wearing. The next time we got together, I'd tell him what he wore on his last visit. I did the same thing with my women friends, concentrating on their dresses, jewelry, shoes, and perfume. I'd say, "You wore those earrings when I saw you on Monday."

I played Ping-Pong and did other sports to try and improve my motor coordination and visual ability. Ping-Pong was good because I could do it anytime. I knew how to play it before the hijacking and was pretty good at it. That helped.

I trained my eye to see half of the ball and connect it with the part of my paddle I could see. Early on, when I played I saw a white line coming toward me—a trail of white—when someone hit the ball to my side of the table. I played with Scott and Scott's friend, Brian, who had a Ping-Pong table in the basement of his house.

Since I seemed to be making such progress in getting my life together, Scott figured it was time to get his life going too. He saw an ad for a job opening at the Northwest Racquet, Swim & Health Club in the paper.

"That one sounds neat," I said.

Scott applied for the job, got an interview, and was hired on the spot. He came home, all pumped up and excited, carrying some new warm-up clothes and suits with the logo on them.

"I got the job, Jackie!"

I looked at Scott and started to cry. The job would require him to work late evenings and weekends. "Why didn't you tell me before you said yes?" I asked. "What am I going to do all night?"

I was angry that Scott and I didn't discuss the job beforehand, that we hadn't sat down and tried to work something out that would take both of our needs into account. I was also afraid that Scott was going to move on with his life and leave me behind. I was afraid he'd meet new people, stay out late, and leave me all alone.

Scott felt really hurt. He was trying to help out by getting a job, but my negative reaction convinced him that he needed to stay home and take care of me.

"We talked about me getting a job, Jackie. Don't you remember? I was only doing what you wanted. That's all I ever do."

Scott called the health club and told the man who hired him that he couldn't take the job and would return the clothes the next day.

It was the first time I knew Scott felt really angry about the hijacking's effect on him.

For quite a while, Scott didn't work much at all. I think he was scared of what my reaction would be.

I felt angry and bitter about my many losses. I hated the hijackers for what they had done to me, to Scarlett, and to the children who died during the hijacking.

I spent a lot of time feeling sad about leaving my job in Egypt. I'd finally found my niche in teaching overseas. I was doing exactly what I wanted to do and was having a blast. I felt a strong connection with the people in Egypt and my students there. Yet I'd never gotten a chance to say good-bye to the people and place I loved so much.

People would say, "Oh, you just have to get over that."

They didn't get it.

Most people see the Middle East as a backwards, dangerous place. How could I prefer living there to living here? Wasn't I glad to be away from all the danger of that region? The answer was no. I felt no danger. I chose to live in the Middle East, and I liked living there. I didn't get a lot of sympathy for my loss.

Nobody from the U.S. government—or any state or federal agency—stepped forward and offered to help out Scott and me after the hijacking. Once Scott and I landed in Minneapolis, we were completely on our own as far as official Washington was concerned. Even though I'd been shot for being a U.S. citizen, the American government seemed eager to wash its hands of the whole affair.

The eyes of the world were focused on me while I lay dying on the airport tarmac. But now that I was alive and the photographers and television reporters had all gone home, nobody cared how I was doing. I was just another nobody with a problem. Apparently, my pain wasn't real anymore. I felt angry and betrayed that nobody stepped forward to help us put our lives back together.

I was also angry at how the U.S. government treated Scarlett Rogencamp, the only American to die in the hijacking, and her family. Initially, the U.S. Army awarded Scarlett, a civilian employee of the Air Force, the Purple Heart. But then Air Force officials changed their minds, stating that the honor was reserved for persons killed in action defending their country. I thought this was incredibly insensitive. As far as I was concerned, once they gave someone a medal, that took care of it. Taking it back seemed incredibly insensitive to Scarlett's memory and the feelings of her family.

I remember sitting in our apartment in February 1986, reading an article about Barbara Mandrell, the country-western singer. The article described her comeback from a head injury she sustained in a near-fatal car accident. She, and the son she was pregnant with at the time, almost died. In her long recovery, she talked about cussing at her husband and then, minutes later, forgetting that she had. I knew exactly what she was talking about.

There were times when I had fits of anger. I'd leave the house, slamming the door on my way out, completely oblivious as to where I was going. Then I'd stop and look around and wonder, *Where am I? What happened? What led me to be here?*

During Mandrell's recovery, the article noted, President Ronald Reagan wrote to see how she was doing. He told her to let him know if there was anything she needed.

Anything she needed! I thought. I was so angry! Though I was targeted solely for being a U.S. citizen, the U.S. government hadn't asked about my needs. My health insurance covered 80 percent of my medical bills, but the

20 percent I was responsible for amounted to a lot of money. Ronald Reagan hadn't called or written me.

Reagan had gone to Andrews Air Force base to personally welcome home survivors of the TWA Flight 847 hijacking. But I never heard so much as a word from him—and I'd been shot in the head!

I wasn't a celebrity, but I sure needed his help.

I decided to ask for it. I got the White House phone number from information and dialed. A White House operator answered.

"I'd like to speak to Ronald Reagan," I said. I didn't call him "President" because I was mad at him.

"Um, he's not here right now," she said, with bemusement. "He's in California."

"Well, when will he be back?" I persisted.

"I can leave him a message," she said. "Who may I say is calling?"

I gave her my name and phone number, then waited a couple of weeks for a reply. Nothing. I kept checking the mail, hoping for some sign of getting through to the president. There was nothing.

I called the White House again. This time, the operator suggested writing a letter to Mr. Reagan.

I vented a lot of anger and frustration in my letter to the president. Scott helped me write it. In hindsight, I'm embarrassed by the angry, bitter tone of it. Still, it certainly did capture my state of mind at the time. I wasn't thinking rationally. I simply wanted someone to acknowledge what I was going through and offer some help.

The letter read as follows:

March 8, 1986

Dear Mr. Reagan:

As you recall, EgyptAir Flight 648 en route from Athens, Greece to Cairo, Egypt was hijacked by terrorists and forced to land in Malta on November 23, 1985. My name is Jackie Nink Pflug and I was on that plane. I am an American and at that time, I was a teacher at the American School in Cairo. Because I am an American, I was shot point blank in the back right side of my head and thrown down a

20-foot metal staircase. Through God's kindness, I survived. The bullet was surgically removed by a Maltese doctor. Because of the incident, my left perifial (sic) vision in both eyes is damaged, and will never return. I am having severe neck and jaw problems as well as numbness on the left side. I am now learning disabled as I no longer see things the way I did. My reading ability, memory, and comprehension skills have been severely affected. I have a Masters degree in Education and Learning Disabilities and am using my talents to teach myself to see things differently.

I know you are an awfully busy man and you don't read all the letters that are sent to you, but I hope this one gets by. My country tells me that I should be proud to be an American. I am proud. I have traveled to many countries and have always been proud and happy to say I am an American. It's been almost four months since the hijacking and I have not heard a word from you or anyone in your administration. I was shot in the head because I am an American. It's sometimes hard to be proud when the president of my country (whom I helped put in office) can't even pick up a phone or send a card to say "get well," "hang in there," or whatever. I am a survivor and I will survive the emotional and physical trauma this hijacking has done to me. It's not that I "needed" to hear from you, it just would have been nice and would have confirmed my proudness in being an American.

My husband and I had to leave our teaching positions and move back to the U.S. where I can get good medical care. I have to undergo brain surgery again next December. Right now, I am living one day at a time.

I am not asking anything of you. The comfort and the reassurance you could have given me then will no longer help me. It seems that in order to be recognized by you, one should be famous, in the military, or dead. I was never looked at as an individual.

You say we should trust in America and have trust in you. I don't look up to you like I did and probably never will. It will always be

in the back of my mind that the leader of America wasn't there when
I needed him.

Sincerely yours,
Jackie Nink Pflug

I mailed the letter and waited another week or two. There was no word.

I called the White House again. This time, the operator took down my social security number. I made twenty copies of my original letter—with my social security number on it—and mailed them all to the White House that same day.

A few weeks later, I was down in Houston visiting my parents. My mother and I were returning home from a shopping expedition at the local mall. Neither my mom nor I could drive, so we took a taxi.

As the taxi pulled into the driveway, my father ran out to meet us. Normally, my dad is a very low-key guy, not easily excited. So it was strange to hear him yelling. "Jackie! Jackie! The president called! He wants you to call him back!"

I was stunned. Yet, deep down in my heart, I expected his call. My Inner Voice told me we would connect.

I called the number my dad had written down and reached the White House switchboard. This time, the operator quickly patched me through to a White House aide who said, "Please hold for the president."

At that moment, the only thing on my mind was how frustrated I was about my financial situation. So I blurted out, "I really can't afford this phone call. Please tell him to call me back." I hung up the phone.

My parents were stunned. They couldn't believe what I'd just done—*hanging up on the president of the United States!* I was surprised at myself too. But I felt okay about it.

"Jackie," my dad said, "*we* can pay for the call."

"Thanks, Dad," I said, "but I need to pay my own bills. He'll call back."

A few seconds later, the phone rang. I picked it up and heard the same voice on the other end of the line, this time with irritation, I heard, "*Please* hold for the *president.*"

This time I took the call. "Okay," I said.

In a moment, I heard a calm, familiar, grandfatherly voice on the other end of the line. I was speaking directly to Ronald Reagan. He had read my letter and said it sounded bitter. I agreed it was. He apologized for the fact that Scott and I had slipped through the cracks. He said there were people on his staff assigned to contact people like myself. He was really sorry that they hadn't.

I asked the president if the government could offer me a low-interest loan to pay for rehabilitation and for my medical bills. I'd pay back the money—with interest—when I was able to go back to work.

He said the government didn't loan people money, but referred me to Project Hope, a nonprofit agency that helps Americans with special needs. We talked a few more minutes, and the president told me to call Anne Kelly, a woman on his staff, to work out the details with Project Hope. He also gave me a special address and phone number where he could always be contacted if I needed to reach him again.

On April 14, 1986, I flew to Washington, D.C. to testify before the grand jury. The FBI wanted to prepare an indictment against the hijacker if Malta didn't convict him.

I still lived with the constant fear of being attacked again—either on the ground or in the air. If a heard a door slam, I'd think it was a gunshot and instinctively brace myself for a bullet's impact. Flying was very scary. I devised a ritual to help me deal with my fear. When I first got on a plane, I'd pace up and down the aisles to check passengers for suspicious parcels that might contain guns or grenades.

One time, a man made a scene because he didn't want anyone to touch a box he was carrying. I asked the flight attendant to open the package anyway. There was a plant inside.

On the flight to Washington, I squeezed Scott's hand to help me feel safe. It was a lot easier to fly with someone along for support.

Frank Fleming, our lawyer, flew from New York to meet us in Washington. Cindy Carter was waiting to meet us at Washington National Airport.

I was excited to meet Carter. She was so reassuring and helpful on the phone. She is a short, well-built woman who looked to be about my age, and had dark hair flowing down to her shoulders. Carter had a slight accent and looked Spanish. She always seemed to smile and had a great laugh. She was married to a former FBI agent and had one child.

In Washington, D.C. Carter interviewed Patrick Baker and myself. She took detailed statements of everything we saw and heard, especially our identification of the men who shot us and the other passengers.

The next day, April 15, Carter drove us to a federal courthouse in Washington, D.C. Inside, I was ushered into a courtroom where a group of average American citizens were gathered to hear my testimony. A prosecutor asked me some questions and helped me stay on track as I told my story.

After testifying before the grand jury, Fleming took us out to lunch. We went to a very nice restaurant near the Capitol. I was relieved to be done telling the story again.

As we were eating, I kept hearing a voice in my head that said, "Call Anne Kelly. Call Anne Kelly." Anne Kelly was the White House aide whom Ronald Reagan had assigned to help me out.

It didn't make sense. *Why would I want to call Anne Kelly?* We'd been in touch over the past couple of months. She'd gotten Project Hope to help me out.

I was interested in meeting Kelly face-to-face, and wanted to personally thank her for all the hard work she had done on my case. Maybe that was it.

I got up from the table, went over to a pay phone, and dialed the White House switchboard.

"I'm so glad you called," Kelly said, above the clatter of dishes in the background. "I've been looking all over for you. The president really wants to see you."

Kelly told Scott and me to get over to the White House as fast as we could so the president could meet us at two o'clock. It was already one, so there was no time to waste.

This was no ordinary day in the nation's capital. It was the day after President Reagan ordered U.S. fighter pilots to bomb Libya in retaliation for state-sponsored terrorism against U.S. citizens and military installations abroad—most recently, the bombing of TWA Flight 840 from Rome to Athens and the bombing of a discotheque in Bonn, Germany.

All day long, stories about the bombing led television and radio reports. The U.S. government flatly denied that it was trying to hit Khaddafy's living quarters in the raid, yet reporters were skeptical.

The bombing was applauded by most U.S. allies, but denounced in some circles. In the United Nations Security Council, U.S. Ambassador Vernon Walters made a strong case for the U.S. action. Walters carefully listed the evidence that Libya was behind the most recent attacks and made an eloquent plea for united international cooperation to stop terrorism.

"The scourge of Libyan terrorism is not a problem for the United States alone," Walters said. "It threatens all members of the civilized world community. It challenges all members of this Council to give meaning to their commitment to uphold the principles of the Charter and to act in the common defense of those principles.

"Colonel Khaddafy's rhetoric and actions are not only anti-American, his support for terrorist violence is far-ranging and worldwide—his victims are of many nationalities. More than forty so-called Libyan diplomats have been expelled from Western Europe since 1983 for involvement in criminal activities. Terrorist attacks by Libyan henchmen have ranged from the bloody outrages at the Rome and Vienna airports *to the hijacking of an Egyptian airliner to Malta* [emphasis added]; to the streets of Bonn where two Germans were wounded during an attack on an anti-Khaddafy dissident; and to the murder of a British policewoman doing her duty outside the Libyan People's Bureau in London. . . ."

I was glad that something was finally being done to possibly stop the terrorism. I had mixed feelings, though: many innocent lives were lost in the bombing.

Scott felt stronger about it. "I'm glad they're going to get those bastards," he said.

While Walters was speaking at UN headquarters in New York City,

Scott and I were in a cab headed for 1600 Pennsylvania Avenue and the White House. The driver dropped us off right in front of the black metal gates surrounding the White House.

We got out and walked over to a security guard standing rigidly at the sentry station leading to the White House driveway. He looked extremely proper and official as he stood at attention. He was a young man, probably not more than twenty-four or twenty-five years old.

"I'm here to see President Reagan," I said.

The young guard laughed.

"No, I'm serious. I'm here to see President Reagan."

"What's your name?" he asked.

"Jackie Pflug."

The guard looked down his list and spotted my name.

"Wow, you must be a pretty important person," he said.

Another security guard escorted Scott and me inside the gate and into a White House entrance. We walked down a long corridor and then were met by Anne Kelly. She and another guard gave us a little tour as they walked us down another corridor towards the Oval Office.

"On our right is the Green Room, decorated by Dolly Madison during the War of 1812. . . . To your left is the President's Library. . . . "

We stopped in a small, modern, secure reception area just outside the Oval Office—one of the last barriers before reaching the president's inner sanctum.

"Wait here," Kelly said.

Twenty minutes went by.

I couldn't believe I was actually sitting outside the Oval Office in the White House, the supreme symbol of American power and strength. This was the same room where, the night before, President Reagan had explained the rationale behind the Libya bombing to the entire nation. I could practically feel the history around me: Franklin D. Roosevelt holding his famous fireside chats during the Great Depression; John F. Kennedy staring down the Soviet Union during the Cuban Missile Crisis; Richard Nixon uttering his famous expletives deleted during the Watergate Affair.

As we waited, important-looking people kept coming and going. We both felt like little kids waiting for Dad to see us.

After a while, the door opened and someone said, "Okay, we're ready for you."

We walked through the doors and into a room that was lit up with television camera lights. There was the fireplace that I'd always seen on television shots of the Oval Office. The high ceiling, emblazoned with the presidential seal, was brightly lit. President Reagan's desk was banked by a curving wall of windows facing out on the south lawn landscaping first sculpted by President Thomas Jefferson. There was a small bronze statue of a cowboy on a horse by American artist Frederic Remington. I was surprised by the size of the Oval Office: it was a little smaller than an average grade-school classroom.

The president's office was filled with newspaper reporters and other journalists. The room was buzzing with energy and commotion.

Above the fray, a very clear, refined, and strong voice—like that of a news anchor—announced our entrance.

"Mr. President . . . Mr. And Mrs. Scott Pflug."

President Reagan stepped forward, smiling, with his hand outstretched.

I couldn't believe it. He seemed so different from how he looked on television.

I threw my arms around President Reagan and gave him a big hug. He was caught a little off guard. I think I almost knocked him over!

Flashbulbs went off as our pictures were taken with Mr. Reagan.

He chatted with us a little bit. I thanked him for the help he'd given me in contacting Project Hope.

President Reagan explained to us that there were so many news cameras and recording instruments in the office because there is a public record of everything he did in the White House. Members of the public, historians, or researchers could later access those records.

Five months earlier, I was lying on an airport tarmac with a bullet in my head, waiting to die. Now, I was in the Oval Office chatting with the president of the United States.

What did it all mean?

A few weeks after our meeting in the White House, President Reagan sent me a poster based on the well-known poem "Footprints in the Sand."

The poem tells the story of a man who dreamed he was walking along a beach with God, reviewing his life. The man noticed there were two sets of footprints during much of his life, but at the saddest and most difficult times, there was only one set. He was troubled and asked God about it: "I don't understand why when I needed you most you would leave me." God responded, "My precious child, I love you and would never leave you during your times of suffering and trial. When you see only one set of footprints, it was then that I carried you."

Mr. Reagan was very influential in getting Project Hope to help us out. The charity paid off all the medical and therapy bills I'd accumulated to that point. The University of Minnesota Hospital agreed to cover 20 percent of my second brain surgery while 80 percent was covered by my insurance company.

CHAPTER 8

WHERE AM I GOING?

I FELT A SHORT PERIOD OF RELIEF after telling my story in court. But it didn't last long. Life started to get very difficult for me during this period. Everything was becoming an obstacle.

Even the littlest things, like taking out the garbage, became big struggles. It was hard because I still hadn't gotten used to coping with my vision problems. If I forgot to concentrate on looking up, down, and to the right, I'd still bump into things or have other minor accidents around the house.

One day, I pulled the garbage bag out from under the sink to wrap a twist tie around the top. I picked it up and started walking toward the door, then noticed something was wrong. There was blood all over the floor. Shards of broken glass poking through the bag had sliced a tendon in my right ankle. I must have dragged the sack across my bare foot and cut myself without realizing it. I looked in the plastic bag and saw a broken peanut butter jar. I forgot that I had put it in there. For six weeks, I wore a cast up to my knee, making it even harder to get around.

One day, while sitting in a hot bath with my cast hanging over the tub, I felt overwhelmed by all my grief and loss. The dam holding back my feelings had burst. Wave after wave of sadness, despair, and pain rolled through my body. I shook with grief as the feelings poured out. I sat in the bathtub and just sobbed and sobbed.

I'd stop for a while, then another wave would come crashing over me. I didn't seriously think about committing suicide, but I didn't feel much like living anymore, either. If there was a hell, I was in it.

In the midst of all my pain, I plunged into a deep depression. For several weeks, I could hardly get out of bed. I didn't feel excited about life or see a future that gave me hope.

What was going to become of me? Why were all these bad things happening to me? I couldn't make sense of it all, and was afraid I'd never adjust to my new life.

As a young girl, I'd suffered from low self-esteem. But I'd never really acknowledged or looked at that before. The whole time I was growing up, I was nagged by an inner fear that I just wasn't good enough. These feelings were especially intense during my junior and senior high school years.

Now, they were right back in my face. I couldn't rely on the old crutches I used to prop myself up with: filling up all my time with activities, losing myself in a relationship, or striving to be the best teacher I could be. Now, I was learning disabled and all my old fears came back to haunt me.

I could hardly read or drive or even take care of myself. I was stuck with myself, with nothing to distract me or gloss over my pain. I had to look at and feel what was inside me.

I thought back to the LD students I had taught over the years. I remembered what happened when I got mad or frustrated because they didn't seem to be listening or learning. I'd see their faces go blank. I'd see them withdrawing and feeling as though they just didn't measure up and maybe never would. I could tell they felt bad about disappointing me. I knew they wanted to do good, wanted to please their teachers and parents, but just couldn't. I remembered how, somewhere along the line, many stopped trying and gave up; they decided they were just too dumb.

I read the sadness and hurt in their faces, but couldn't know what they felt like inside.

Now, I did.

Now, I felt as if *I* was letting people down, disappointing them. I tried so hard, but I just couldn't measure up. I had a gnawing feeling that I wasn't good enough—maybe I never would be. Still, I was determined not to give up.

Jackie Nink Pflug, 1995

At home in Pasadena, Texas, a suburb outside of Houston, where I grew up with my two sisters. I'm the one who is standing in this picture, holding my grandmother's hand. My baby sister, Mary, is in Grandma Nink's lap, and my older sister, Gloria, is sharing the chair. My grandmother is a very influential part of my life. I learned a lot about what inner peace is from her, because she seemed so at peace with herself. She died at age ninety-three, four months before the hijacking.

Even at the age of fourteen, I dreamed of visiting strange, exotic lands and meeting interesting people. My parents took me on a lot of vacations in the United States, but I had a yearning to go abroad and see the world. Some people have a yearning for music or art or science. I had a yearning to travel.

Church played an important role in my life. Here's a picture of the Nink family on their way to church Easter Sunday. Standing in back at left is my mother Billie. Gloria is in front of my mother, with Mary in the middle. I'm standing in front of my father Eugene.

Egyptian people are very friendly and love to have their pictures taken, as this man did. He is selling his goods on the streets of Maadi, fifteen minutes outside Cairo. The man is wearing a gallabeyya, traditional Egyptian clothing.

I felt as though I was back in time, like Lawrence of Arabia, riding a camel near the great pyramids.

The hijacked EgyptAir plane at Luqa Airport in Valletta, Malta. I believe that the man squatting at the open front door of the aircraft is a hijacker; the man standing is a "helper," that is, a security person who was aboard the plane and was forced by the hijackers to help them out.

Four of the twenty-five Egyptian commandos who stormed the aircraft, and their two commanding officers (seated in front), are pictured here. I think the commandos had a well-intentioned rescue plan, but when they stormed the plane and saw the hijackers with grenades, they had to react quickly and lost control.

One of the real heroes of the tragedy is this man, Captain Hani Galal. A stray bullet probably grazed his head during the hijacking. Captain Galal landed the aircraft in Malta only by the lights of a plane on the ground.

Christmas 1985, a month after the hijacking. I'm posing for this picture outside of my in-laws' home in Hopkins, Minnesota. At the time, I was confused, hurt, and angry. I tried to live as if I had it all together, but I didn't. At the same time, I was in awe of the fact that I was seeing another Christmas. I was in awe that I looked OK. I didn't know what it all meant.

In January 1986, less than two months after the hijacking, I flew to Texas to visit friends and relatives. This picture was taken outside of Barb Wilson's house in Baytown, Texas. Barb had tied a yellow ribbon around the tree in her yard; the banner (at right) on the lawn reads WELCOME HOME JACKIE. I'm pictured in the middle; to my right are my dear friends Debbie and Kerry. To my left is another friend, Linda, and my sister Mary.

I'm pictured here with my long-time friend, Barb Wilson. Barb helped me get through a lot of hard times after the hijacking. She was an integral part of my support system.

Standing beside me is another good friend, Suki Fitzgerald, 1987, in Dallas, after my second brain operation. Suki is someone who is always there for a friend. She flew from Texas to Minnesota to visit me several times, and helped me through some hard times. Also pictured is Mike and Kathy.

Visiting my mom and dad in Pasadena, 1987. Though we lived far apart after the hijacking, my parents called me a lot and provided great support.

June and Greg ("Pops") Pflug. Scott and I lived with his parents for two months after we returned to the United States following the hijacking. June was of much help and made life easier for me. I could not see correctly, so she helped me get around the house. I had lost my short-term memory, so she helped me learn how to tell time and count money again. Just as important, she said things that made me feel better about myself. Pops could always make me laugh, even on some pretty dark days.

President Ronald Reagan, myself, and Scott Pflug in the Oval Office of the White House, April 15, 1987. It was the day after President Reagan ordered U.S. fighter pilots to bomb Libya in retaliation for state-sponsored terrorism against U.S. citizens and military installations abroad. Mr. Reagan was very influential in getting Project Hope to help me out. The charity paid off all the medical and therapy bills I'd accumulated up to that point.

A speaking engagement at the Northwest Mutual Life Annual Conference in Milwaukee, 1990. I was the closing keynote speaker. At first, speaking was a form of therapy for me. I got excited when people were listening and getting what I had to say, when the room was so quiet you could hear a pin drop.

At home in Minnesota, summer 2001, with husband, Jim and son, Tanner.

I took lots of baby steps on the way to becoming more independent. Going to the grocery store was very exciting for me. It gave me a feeling of independence, something I could do on my own. Before I could drive, Scott dropped me off at the grocery store.

Yet shopping was hard. Just writing a grocery list felt overwhelming. In the beginning, Scott helped me write down the items we needed, according to where they were in the grocery store.

I remember I'd ask Scott, "What comes first? The meat or the produce?"

"The produce is first," he'd say.

So then I'd write down all the produce items I needed that week: oranges, apples, lettuce, and so on.

"What's next?" One at a time, we went through the grocery store, department by department, and listed the items we needed in an average week.

I was able to write down the name of each item, but reading what I'd written was another matter. I had to really focus on one word at a time and cover the rest of the words with my hands to make any sense out of the jumble of letters and spaces in front of me. It was like trying to read words with my head underwater; letters were floating all over the place. My brain was confused by the bits and pieces appearing on the page.

This would be really tough to do in the grocery store. I had to think of a better way. I had an idea.

After writing my list, I read each item into a tape recorder. Then I rewound the tape, slipped it in my Walkman, and headed for the grocery store. In the grocery store, I put on my headphones and listened to the tape as I repeated each item on my list one by one. As I heard myself say each item—slowly!—I'd stop the recorder and go look for the item.

Sometimes, I'd hear myself say an item on the tape and start to go get it . . . then forget. I'd rewind the tape and listen again and again.

Reading continued to be a problem for me long after the hijacking. Even after the swelling in my brain went down and it returned to normal size, I still had trouble reading and understanding simple sentences. It was tedious work trying to understand every word and what it meant in the context of a sentence. Though the floating eventually went away, the loss of parts of my visual field was permanent.

I went to a neuro-ophthalmologist to have my vision checked. He gave me several vision tests. In one test, he put one red ball by my right eye and one by my left eye (where I could see) and asked, "What do they look like?"

"They're red," I said.

"Is there anything different about them?" he asked.

"Yeah, the one on the left side is awfully bright," I said.

He took them away and then showed them to me again. They were exactly the same color. He said, "We don't know why that happens, but sometimes it does with people, like yourself, who have had some brain trauma."

For some reason, red was a color that my brain connected with. This clicked with what the neuropsychologist had told me in Houston. The doctor suggested a technique that helps many learning disabled adults who have trouble moving their eyes from left to right while reading: take a red pen and go from left to right on a page, underlining each word, from the first letter to the last. This exercise would help my eyes to connect the letters that formed a word—and see them in the right order. He said the process might take a while, but with practice, I could do it.

I hadn't thought of it before, but I already knew how to do this exercise from my experience as a special education teacher. It was one exercise I taught kids who had problems with tracking—reading words from left to right. For some reason, red was a color that they could focus on. By following the red line under the words, they were training their eyes to move from left to right.

I might give them a list of letters like the following:

A D L H A C A P Q R

Some kids had a problem picking out a particular letter from this sequence. So I would tell them, "Every time you see the letter *A*, circle it and don't lift up your pen." It was a tracking exercise. When they got really good at that, and that problem with their vision improved, we'd move on to another exercise.

I sat down at the kitchen table in our apartment with a newspaper and tried to read. Let's say I wanted to read a simple word like *going*.

My eyes would automatically move to the end of the word and see the two letters *ng*. I knew that *ng* was not a word, so I put my fingers on the letter *g* and backed up, right to left. There was an *n*. I backed up another space and found an *i*, then *o*, and, finally, a *g*. Backing up one more time, I came to a space.

I always looked for the space, because the space marked the beginning of each new word. With my fingers, I traced over the word from left to right— *g-o-i-n-g*.

After I had identified each letter in the word, I'd go to the next space— end of word—and start over. Back up, back up, back up—space. Then read left to right.

After describing my reading method once, someone said, "Jackie, why don't you just look to the left side?"

"Don't you think I tried that?" I said with frustration.

My eyes wouldn't let me go over there. Before I was shot, I had the ability to go to the left side, just like anyone else. But I didn't have that ability anymore.

The exercise that really worked was the one that I used with my LD students and that had been recommended by my neuropsychologist. I took my red felt-tip pen and placed it on the first letter of a word. I made my eyes follow the pen as I underlined the first word from left to right.

My goal was not to read the newspaper, but to train my eyes to see the words from left to right. I used a newspaper instead of a book because I could throw it out every day and get a new one.

I put my red pen at the end of each word, then moved it from right to left until I found a space, the signal that I was at the beginning of the word.

Once I found the beginning of the word, I underlined it from left to right.

Red was the only color my eyes could stay focused on. If I used any other color my eyes would bounce right off the page.

After a few months of practice, I was able to read a simple story in the newspaper. As I practiced more and more, however, I gained proficiency and speed. My eyes and brain were beginning to learn how to read all over again.

As my brain went down to its normal size and the floating started to disappear, I began to think that maybe, just maybe, I might be able to drive again.

I wanted this so much because driving meant freedom. I wouldn't have to rely on others to shuttle me around. I thought driving would give me back a more normal life. As my memory improved, I felt ready to give it a try.

One clean, crisp Sunday morning in February 1986, Scott and I were driving through some back roads in our Ford Bronco. Since there wasn't much traffic, I thought it might be a good time to try driving.

"Are you sure about this, Jackie?" Scott asked.

"Yeah, I want to. I know I can do it. Let me just try a little."

"Okay," he agreed.

Scott pulled onto the shoulder so we could change places.

Scott didn't know if this was a good idea. He knew about my visual problems and thought it might be better for me to get used to sitting in the passenger seat of our truck.

It felt strange to be back in the driver's seat. I hadn't sat behind the wheel of a car or truck for nearly a year. In Cairo and Stavanger, I rarely drove. We mostly rode our bikes everywhere. The last time I'd been driving was when I was back in Houston before Scott and I got married. I felt a little like a teenager learning how to drive all over again.

I drove on the shoulder for a few feet, then stopped. It was too hard. I was too scared. "I can't do this," I said. "I can't see right."

I was exhausted by the effort it took to concentrate on the road and move my head back and forth and from side to side so that I could see where I was going. But I tried again.

At one point, we came to a stop sign. I thought I was very close to it—but stopped long before reaching it.

Scott didn't understand what was happening. He thought I just didn't pull up far enough. I kept going until, all of a sudden, a little boy appeared out of nowhere. In reality, I stopped quickly, before I was anywhere near the boy. But to me, he appeared very close to us. I was scared. "I can't do this anymore," I told Scott. "I don't belong here, behind the wheel."

My visual perception was still not healed. I was relieved to pull over and let Scott drive again.

Despite the mixed success on my first attempt, I was determined to drive again.

Scott wasn't thrilled by my continued eagerness to get behind the wheel. He saw that I sometimes had difficulty just walking without bumping into things.

Nevertheless, I wasn't going to give up. Affirmations and visualizations were important in achieving this goal. When I started praying to drive again, I didn't say, "I want to drive," or "I hope to drive," or "God, please let me drive." On a piece of paper, I wrote: "I drive today. I zip in and out of traffic today."

I stated my goal as if I had already attained it. I saw myself weaving through traffic on a busy freeway. Throughout the day, I repeated this statement to myself: "I drive today."

It took lots of work and practice to get to the point where I felt comfortable driving again. After I got my driving permit, I spent a lot of time practicing in parking lots and on side roads. My visual impairment created huge obstacles. It was more than a year after I first started driving before I felt confident behind the wheel. Eventually, I passed my written and behind-the-wheel driver's tests and got my license.

The technique I use to drive is basically the same one I use to read and to walk. I just put the vehicle by the white or yellow line and move my eyes down, ahead, and over to the left—all the places where my visual field is gone. Down, ahead, and over to the left.

In the late spring of 1987, a cultural festival was being held at the St. Paul Civic Center that I really wanted to go to. Scott didn't want to go, so I asked Mrs. Pflug if she would come with me.

She talks about what it was like being a passenger with me.

When I was ready to change lanes or take an exit ramp, I'd yell, "Okay, is there anybody coming?"

She'd yell back, "No!"

I'd ease into the lane and keep going. I needed her help to drive around. She said I was just going 55 miles an hour like nobody's business. She talks about how scared she was.

Again, I'd shout, "Well, is anybody coming?"

"No!" June Pflug yelled back.

And I'd change lanes again.

We made sure we came back from the cultural festival before it got dark.

In the beginning, I always drove with someone else in the car—just in case I got lost.

❦

In time, however, I wanted to venture out by myself. One of the first trips I made by myself was to the grocery store, just three blocks from our apartment.

I'll never forget that first trip. It was a beautiful day as I pulled out of the driveway and onto the main road. I took a left turn and stopped at the light.

Now what? Where am I? I couldn't remember what I was supposed to do next. *Take a right? A left? Or go straight?* I went straight. As I continued to drive, nothing looked familiar.

I got lost and arrived at the store an hour later.

I did my grocery shopping. At the checkout counter, the clerk rang up the bill. I was getting out my checkbook when the bag boy said something to me real fast.

"Paperorplastic?"

I just stared back at him with a blank face. "What did you say?" I asked.

"Paper or plastic?" he repeated.

I still didn't get it.

"One more time, please. Go slow."

"Pa-per or pla-stic?" the boy said.

He wanted to know what kind of bag to put my groceries in. I'd never been asked that before and, coming fast and out of context, it made no sense. I had to stop and think to myself, *What's paper? Okay, it's brown and I can use it again.* My response didn't come out automatically.

"Paper's fine," I finally said.

After loading my groceries in the back of the truck, I got back behind the wheel and started home. I got lost again. I couldn't remember how to get home! I felt terrible and started to panic.

I had to drive back to the grocery store again to call Scott. I felt so helpless. Through my tears, I told Scott that I didn't know how to get home and asked him to come get me.

When I first started driving, I got lost all the time. I'd get lost going to the doctor or the grocery store, or to meet someone for lunch. It didn't seem to matter if I'd been there twenty times before—I'd still get lost. Somehow, the repetition wasn't getting into my long-term memory. Something had to be healed in my brain before I could catch on.

I got very mad and upset when people didn't give me good directions or took for granted the little things I needed to focus on. I took everything so literally. I had to follow their directions to the T. If the directions were even slightly off, I'd be completely disoriented.

If people were depending on me, I'd get so frustrated, angry, and depressed when I got lost. Sometimes, I'd pull over to the side of the road and feel my attitude change immediately. I'd start crying, and think, *if I hadn't got shot, I sure wouldn't be here. I sure wouldn't be lost.* A few times I got lost on my way to a speaking engagement and had to call someone to drive me there.

One time I was driving from Minneapolis to our apartment in Minnetonka and ended up in St. Cloud—a city about fifty miles northwest of where I wanted to be! Time didn't mean anything to me back then. I just kept going and going. I was so focused on driving that I had little energy or attention left over to consider *where* I was going.

Sometimes, I'd call Barb Wilson in Texas and just cry, because I couldn't go down the street without getting lost. Something about my brain made it impossible for me to remember from one step to the next.

One weekend, I was invited to have dinner with some friends. I called to get directions, but managed to get lost anyway.

I was mad at myself for not being able to figure out where I was. I pulled over to check my map and, eventually, got back on the right road. But my exit came up surprisingly quick. I had to make a sudden lane change to make the exit. At the last moment, I pulled my car into the right lane and merged onto the ramp. There was a car not far behind me, so I waved to thank the driver for letting me in.

As soon as I pulled off, I realized I was in trouble. Looking back in my rearview mirror, I saw a very angry looking man right at my rear bumper. He gunned his car, pulled in front of me—then abruptly stopped on the ramp.

The man, about twenty-five or twenty-six years old, got out of his car and walked over to my car. I rolled down the window to see what he wanted. "You cut me off!" he yelled.

He started yelling a string of obscenities at me. "I'm sorry," I said softly, "I was having trouble with my directions and I'm on my way to a Thanksgiving dinner. . . ."

He kept yelling.

"I said, I'm sorry," I responded, even louder this time. He stopped yelling and left.

I was badly shaken by the incident. I'd never seen anyone so angry. His face was red with rage, the veins on his neck were popping out. I was afraid he might pull a gun and blast me right in my car. A week earlier, I'd heard a news story about a woman killed in traffic when a disgruntled driver got mad at her. It brought back memories of the hijacking.

Still shaking, I rolled up the window, pulled over to the side of the road, and sat in my car, sobbing.

This wouldn't have happened if I hadn't been hijacked! I thought to myself. I felt so miserable. *Why did this happen to me?*

❦

Just as I started to feel more comfortable driving, I suddenly had another problem to worry about—epileptic seizures. I had been warned that this delayed reaction was common for many people who suffer head injuries, trauma, or brain damage.

Seizures are caused by abnormal electrical activity in the brain. While most last only a few minutes, some continue for as long as thirty minutes. There are several different types of seizures, but two of the most common are *grand mal* and *petit mal*. A grand mal seizure is more severe and lasts longer than a petit mal seizure.

A grand mal seizure usually begins with shaking, convulsion, or muscle jerking. If the seizure victim is standing when a seizure strikes, he or she will suddenly collapse on the floor. Someone having a grand mal seizure may lose control of bladder and bowel functions, temporarily stop breathing, and bite his or her tongue or choke on anything in the mouth. During a seizure, people report experiencing a temporarily altered state of consciousness and perception. Seizures are typically followed by periods of confusion, distorted thinking, and memory loss.

Because seizures strike suddenly and affect motor control, a seizure could be deadly when I was driving. My doctor was also concerned because the shock caused by an epileptic seizure creates lasting neurological damage to the brain. My doctor explained that a little hole is created in the brain during a seizure. The brain "remembers" the seizure and may recreate it again—just because it remembers it. So doctors are eager to prevent seizures.

As a safeguard, I was put on Dilantin, a strong antiseizure medication. Since I took the pills regularly, I figured there was nothing to worry about.

❦

As I became more independent, I wanted to start exploring again. One thing I did to get out and meet people was to start going to Toastmasters, a group of mostly professional people, who get together to improve their public speaking skills. Most of the members had businesses of their own. My primary reason for going there was to meet people. I didn't have any friends at the time—none—and Scott's friends were *his* friends.

I also attended Toastmasters because I was starting to speak to church groups and other organizations, and I wanted to feel more comfortable as a public speaker.

One Saturday morning, I got in our new Ford Bronco and drove to a Toastmaster's breakfast meeting. As usual, I got lost along the way.

When I finally got to the meeting, I had a chance to meet some neat people, including a young woman named Heidi who was also a special education teacher. She worked with learning disabled students and people who were coming back from head injuries and accidents.

I was sitting at the table listening to a speech when, all of a sudden, something strange began happening to my eyes. A bright, rainbow light appeared in the left corner of my visual field. I shut my eyes and opened them again, figuring something was wrong with my contact lenses. The aura was still there. I took out my contacts, but that didn't help, either. I felt strange, confused. *What was happening to me?*

I leaned over to Heidi and told her what I saw. She told me I was about to have a seizure. Heidi quickly led me to a nearby ladies' room, moved away the trash can, and helped me lie down on the floor—and called 911.

I couldn't believe this was happening. I was taking my Dilantin regularly, so I thought I was safe. I told someone to go get the pills in my purse, hoping that more pills would stop the seizure.

By this time, the rainbow light had started moving to the middle of my vision field. Yet I was still able to talk to the people gathered around me. I couldn't see anything, but I could still talk.

I was just hysterical, because I didn't know what was going to happen to me. I'd never had a seizure before. I thought maybe I was going to die—that I wouldn't come back.

When a woman came back with my pill bottle, I told her to take out three pills. I got them in my mouth, but I never actually swallowed them. Luckily, I didn't choke. Pills wouldn't have worked then anyway.

Seconds later, I was having a full-blown grand mal seizure—the most serious kind.

I was still unconscious when the paramedics arrived twenty minutes later. I came to in the ambulance and saw that I was hooked up to a bunch of monitors.

"What's your name?" a paramedic asked.

"I don't know," I said.

"What were you doing when this happened?"

"I don't know," I repeated.

Everything that happened to me before the seizure was a blank. I didn't remember my name. I couldn't see very well.

The medics injected me with Valium, a tranquilizer, and more anti-seizure medication, and I went under. . . .

Having a seizure was an awfully scary thing. My whole body went into violent convulsions for about twenty minutes. In the grips of a seizure, I was totally unaware of what was happening to me or where I was. I could easily injure or bruise myself. I came out of them alive, but I lost some memory for a while and my head felt fuzzy. For days afterwards, I experienced a lot of mental confusion. My vision also got even worse for three or four days after a seizure.

Emotionally, I felt powerless and out of control. A seizure could strike at any time, with little warning. I could be eating in a restaurant, shopping at a mall, driving down a freeway, anywhere, when I'd suddenly see a rainbow-like aura signaling the onset of a grand mal seizure, equal in intensity to the electric jolts that psychiatric patients get in electroshock therapy.

When the rainbow light appeared, I had about three minutes to find a restroom, tell someone what to do, clear everything out of the way, and get down on the floor. As the rainbow light moved from the left side of my visual field to the middle, my body grew cold and prickly and I started to shake. Then everything went blank.

As the Valium wore off after a seizure, I felt overwhelmed by feelings of emptiness and helplessness. I felt terribly isolated and alone. I wouldn't talk to Scott about my feelings and didn't have any friends nearby.

The Dilantin slowed my ability to learn and recover from the hijacking. Mental confusion and dizziness are other common side effects of the drug. Emotionally, I also felt awful. I woke up every morning feeling anxious, irritable, tired, and depressed as if I were in a dark cave. I woke up to a world of fear and hate and anger. And I couldn't see any way out of it.

I often called Barbara to tell her how sad and miserable I was—or just to cry. Hearing her voice was a small comfort when the world around me seemed so cold and dead.

I was terrified by the prospect of having more seizures. I found myself constantly checking the left corner of my visual field, expecting to see the rainbow light at any time.

CHAPTER 9

AFTER THE RAINBOW

I WASN'T GOING TO LET SOMETHING as small as a seizure get me down. Not long after my first seizure, I started getting restless again. I was eager to get back into the world.

On Sunday mornings, I flipped through the "Help Wanted" section of the newspaper, looking for teaching positions. I applied for some, but didn't get any offers. The job market for teachers continued to be tight. Then, through a personal connection, I heard about an interesting opening.

My friend Suki Fitzgerald called one day to see how I was doing. Suki had just started working as an independent consultant for IBM. Her job sounded interesting; she flew all over the United States showing regular education teachers how to adapt IBM's existing education software so it could be used to teach LD kids.

IBM wanted to hire another independent consultant with special education teaching experience to learn their software and travel around the country showing teachers how to use it. The person hired would be responsible for covering a nine-state region.

I hadn't been out in the world much since the hijacking four months earlier, but I knew IBM computers. I'd used them often as a teacher. I would have to take only a few more classes to get more comfortable with them and learn some new software. *I could do that!* I thought. It didn't sound that hard.

Suki gave me the name of a contact person in Minnesota, and I decided to apply for the job. I didn't feel safe driving in downtown Minneapolis, where IBM had its offices, so Scott dropped me off for my first interview.

IBM's office was in a large, modern glass and steel tower in the heart of the Minneapolis business district. I walked in the building and saw busy men and women hurrying in and out. I was excited to be in the fast-paced, hustle and bustle world again!

I took an elevator up to the fifth floor, entered the IBM office, and gave my name to the receptionist. After a few minutes, a middle-aged man in a dark business suit came up and introduced himself. We walked back into his office and chatted a while.

"Are you sure you're ready to do this?" the interviewer asked me.

"Sure," I responded. "I'm ready to go back to work."

After I filled out some forms, the interviewer said I'd need to come back for another interview. I scheduled it for a week later.

The morning of my second interview, I put on a nice dress and heels and had Scott drop me off at a bus stop to catch a bus into downtown Minneapolis. I waited and waited, and the buses kept coming. But my bus was nowhere in sight.

Finally, I asked one of the bus drivers if I was standing in the right place. It turned out that I was on the wrong side of the freeway—going in the wrong direction!

I walked across the freeway. Bus number 23 finally came, but I let it go. I didn't see it correctly. To me, it looked like bus number 3.

I waited about an hour and finally another bus came. I asked the driver if I was in the right place, and he told me I was, but that bus 23 had just come and gone. He could take me downtown but not to the street I needed to be on.

The driver dropped me off in downtown Minneapolis. But since this was the first time I'd ever been downtown on my own, I was soon lost. I stopped to ask several people to help me find the street I was looking for. I didn't plan or think ahead at all. I didn't bring the phone number of the interviewer, so I couldn't call and explain my delay. I finally found the building and arrived at my interview two hours late.

The interviewer agreed to see me anyway, and we talked about the position. He thought I'd be a good fit, because of my special insight into the problems of LD children and teachers. I could speak intelligently about the main issues in special education—and I knew about LD.

He asked if I'd be willing to have another interview, and I said yes. For my third interview, I met with a very sweet woman. Again, I was asked if I thought I could do the job. I said yes.

The next day, she called and offered me the job. She knew I didn't have a strong computer background, but she was confident that I could learn about that. I thought I could too.

At that time, I hadn't been in any type of learning environment since the hijacking. I just assumed that I could learn the way I used to.

I was excited to go back to work. I was thrilled about working for a company with such an excellent reputation—and getting to travel again! The pay was good too: two hundred dollars per day. Yet I didn't know how my new learning disability would affect my job performance.

I spent the next couple of weeks in the field with Paula Lang, the woman who I was replacing. I wasn't required to do anything yet, because I hadn't gone through the formal training. My job was to watch and learn. I flew to meet her in different cities: New York, Boston, Atlanta. Paula always met me at the airport.

She showed me what schools she was working with and how she presented the existing IBM software to teachers. On one trip, I got to visit the Bronx. The kids and teachers were all assembled there. It was really fun.

I went down to Atlanta with another woman who worked for IBM out of Portland, Oregon. We met Paula in Atlanta, and the three of us rented a car and drove to a kidney dialysis camp about an hour outside of the city.

The summer camp was exclusively for kids with kidney problems. They had computers everywhere! The IBM consultants showed the kids how to use the computers. IBM was doing a study to see how the use of computers affected kids who were going through kidney dialysis treatment. Normally, kids going through treatment were sick a lot—they suffered from dizziness, vomiting, nausea, and so on. But IBM and the treatment staff were finding that kids who used computers were so happy that they weren't getting sick as much.

The kids were involved in a lot of other activities at the camp too: they were swimming and boating, and rehearsing a play to put on for their parents at the end of the week. The parents also watched their kids work on the computers.

I was very interested in what was going on, but the job was also very taxing. I tried to be easy on myself. But so much information was coming in that I felt as though I was constantly on overload. *Why was it so hard? Why wasn't this coming to me more easily?*

"Just take what you can take," I kept repeating to myself. I kept reminding myself that I was testing my limits. But how could I know how much I could do unless I really tried?

I tried not to let my co-workers and clients know how much I was struggling. I was afraid if they knew about the depth of my problem they might not want me.

I often got lost walking around the camp. One time I was walking from the barracks where I was staying to the warehouse that housed the computers. There were trees everywhere, and I was always paying close attention to them to make sure I didn't hit one.

I noticed a group of five or six young boys sitting in the grass alongside the path. They were whistling and they said something to me. I looked over to them, lost my concentration, and—Bam!—I smacked straight into a tree.

The boys started laughing. "Didn't you see the tree? Boy, are you stupid!" one of the boys shouted.

I looked over and said, "I was just shot in the head about four months ago and I lost a lot of my vision—*so I didn't see the tree.*"

I was embarrassed and mad.

"Oh, we're sorry, we're sorry," they apologized.

My head really hurt from walking into the tree, and I had a bunch of scratches. But the blow to my self-esteem hurt even more.

Traveling from city to city gave me a better idea of what my job was going to be like. Yet I still wasn't sure I could do it. It was hard for me to remember from day to day what I'd done just the day before. It was hard for me to make sense out of what was happening.

⚜

After about a month in the field, I was scheduled to take a special training course at IBM's headquarters in Thornwood, New York. I joined a large group of people who had the same job I did in different parts of the world. We all came together in Thornwood for further training. It was the first time IBM had done this type of training.

I was excited to learn that my friend Suki Fitzgerald was also scheduled to attend the training.

I flew to New York City to meet Paula Lang. She drove us into the city, where we parked and got out to walk to a restaurant for lunch. We stopped at a stoplight and waited for the light to change.

"Let's go!" Paula said.

The light changed and Paula was off and running. In blind faith, I obediently followed—then halted in my tracks.

I stood, bewildered, in the middle of a busy New York street. I looked around and saw jumbled-up pieces of cars—fragmented, broken, tangled-up images at odd angles—speeding straight for me. Their horns blared a rude warning. Somehow, I staggered to the median.

"Are you okay?" Paula asked, sensing my fear.

"Yes, but I want to get across the street."

"Let's go!" she said again.

This time, she went without me. I waited a few minutes to recover before venturing to cross again.

The mismatch between my enthusiasm for the job and my readiness to do it created a lot of stress. Four months after the hijacking, I was force-feeding my injured brain a ton of new information and jetting cross country with IBM executives. I was clearly in over my head.

What in the world am I doing here? I thought to myself.

I felt like a scared little girl. I knew people could quickly cross a busy street. But I'd forgotten how.

❧

The first morning in Thornwood, Suki and I both had some free time and decided to work out at IBM's beautiful corporate gym. We had the place to ourselves.

I always loved working out and being fit. I grew up playing softball and played on the softball and basketball teams in high school. In Cairo, Scott and I worked out at the Cairo American College. I'd worked up to running four miles a day and had really built up my legs.

I went over to the exercise bicycle and climbed on. It felt good to start pedaling. Then it happened. I saw the rainbow light that signaled an oncoming seizure, just like I'd seen at my Toastmaster's meeting a few months ago.

Oh, no! I said to myself. I was frantic and started panicking. I felt a surge of adrenaline rush through my body. I jumped off the bike and ran over to Suki who was jogging on a treadmill.

"I'm going to have a seizure," I said.

"What do I do?" she asked, coming to a dead stop.

We were both scared.

I told Suki to move things away the best she could and let me have a seizure. "You'll know when I'm finished, because I'll just collapse," I said. "When that happens, turn me over to my side so I don't choke."

I started feeling prickly, and my body started getting cold. In the meantime, the rainbow light continued its steady shift to the center of my visual field.

I could tell Suki was nervous. She isn't one to let on, but I could tell from the quaver in her voice. She found a phone and called 911.

The seizure rendered me unconscious and, the next thing I knew, I woke up in a hospital room. "Where am I?" I asked the nurse.

She explained that I was in a New York hospital. I called Scott and told him what happened. He offered to fly out to New York, but I didn't think it was necessary. That afternoon, a manager from IBM came to visit me. He was very kind and understanding. He arranged for IBM to fly me back home to recuperate. "Take some time off, Jackie," he said. "If you still want the job, it will be waiting for you when you're feeling better.

The grand mal seizure was over, but when I got back to Minnesota, my hands wouldn't stop trembling. There was something new and different about these tremors. My hands and arms were shaking, but I didn't see a white light or rainbow light.

I made an appointment with my neurosurgeon at the University of Minnesota Hospital to find out what was wrong. He came into my room and said he wanted me to see a Dr. Ilo Leppik a neurologist at the Comprehensive Epilepsy Program at the University of Minnesota.

My hands and leg were shaking when Dr. Leppik walked into the examining room. I was sure I was having another seizure.

Leppik had already reviewed my chart and started checking me out. First, he asked me to try walking a straight line—which I couldn't do. Then he asked me to hold my arms parallel to the floor and slowly bring my index fingers together to touch my nose at the same time. I couldn't do that either. I had problems with my balance.

"I don't think you're having a seizure," Dr. Leppik said. Before coming into my room, he carefully observed me from behind a one-way mirror, paying close attention to the nature of the shaking motion in my limbs.

The doctor put his hand on my hands and I stopped shaking. "I think this has to do with your emotional status right now," he said. "I'm going to change your medication so that you won't have any more grand mal seizures. What's happening is that your medication is not strong enough to keep the seizures from coming out in your body. We have to stop that. Those are real. But the tremors you're having right now have more to do with your emotional state."

I told Dr. Leppik about the depression I couldn't seem to shake. He said depression was a possible side effect of Dilantin, the antiseizure medication I was on, and that there were many other medication options we could try.

Dr. Leppik was more hopeful and positive about my future than other doctors had been. He was also very distinguished in his profession; he was an internationally renowned neurologist who traveled and spoke widely.

I liked Dr. Leppik right away. He understood what was going on with me and genuinely seemed to care. He was in his fifties, wore glasses, had dark blond hair, and seemed a little shy. "Tell me a little bit more about what's going on in your life right now," Dr. Leppik said, gently.

As I told him about my job with IBM, I saw his eyes widen. The look on his face said, "My God, woman, don't you realize you were just shot in the head!"

"Jackie," he shook his head, "you've got to slow down. I want you to take at least four months off."

I felt so good, as if somebody had finally given me permission to heal. For the first time, I began to realize the terrific pressure I'd been putting on myself to rush through my recovery and rehabilitation. Four months after being shot in the head at point-blank range, I'd taken a demanding professional job.

I was basing the most important decisions in my life on what I thought *other* people wanted or needed me to do—not on my own needs. I was relying on external authorities—doctors, Scott, my parents—to be my guides. I was acting as if I needed Scott's permission to take time off to heal. I was waiting for doctors to tell me how to heal.

It was obvious to Dr. Leppik that my strategy wasn't working, and it was becoming more obvious to me. I quit my training program with IBM and decided to stay home for a while.

Staying home was when the pain started to come. I'd been running to get away from the pain, so I wouldn't have to feel what was going on inside me. Now, I had nowhere to run. I had to give myself permission to heal.

There were many important milestones in my continued journey to find people and places that could help me heal. One of these was meeting Dr. Robert Maxwell, a doctor who filled in one time when my regular neurosurgeon was not able to keep a scheduled appointment in the summer of 1986. Dr. Maxwell was a tall man with dashing good looks and a kind, reassuring voice. He reminded me of a gentle, strong father figure.

I was having CAT scans often because the doctors were concerned about bone fragments still in my brain. The pieces had been left behind, because the surgeons couldn't get them all.

"Do they always get the pieces out?" I asked Dr. Maxwell. I certainly wasn't the first person shot in the head to have bone fragments left—I didn't want to be the only one. I sought some reassurance that my problem was "normal" and clearly understood.

"Sometimes we have to leave them in," Dr. Maxwell explained. "It would cause too much damage if we tried to take them all out."

He said doctors during World War II found that meticulously removing all the bone fragments sometimes caused people to wake up disabled.

"If the bones are too far in to get our fingers in, we just let them stay," Maxwell added. "We're keeping an eye on where the fragments are and making sure scar tissue develops properly." Doctors wanted to make sure the bone fragments didn't go in any deeper.

Dr. Maxwell showed me a copy of my CAT scan and pointed to the bone fragments and scar tissue forming over them. He took me by the hand, spent lots of time with me, and answered all my questions. I kept thinking, *Boy, doesn't he have another appointment?*

As I listened to Dr. Maxwell's caring voice and felt his reassuring hand on my shoulder, a light went on. *Ah, this is it,* I thought. *I've finally reached home. I finally got the doctor I wanted.*

Everything's so hard when you're healing from a head injury. If you have the right doctors, it's easier to ask questions and find answers. It took a lot of physical and emotional energy for me to get satisfying answers to my complex difficulties. Now that I knew I was being listened to, I could take time to heal other parts of myself.

Dr. Leppik referred me to a psychologist at the University of Minnesota's epilepsy center who worked with epileptic patients on an emotional level. My first visit was on December 16, 1986, a little over a year after the hijacking.

At that meeting, the counselor reviewed some memory strengthening exercises with me and encouraged me to slow down so I didn't set myself up for having a seizure. I was thinking about taking a university class, but the counselor suggested I consider taking a community education course to strengthen my memory. The counselor was very adamant about the notion that I needed to accept my long-term limitations and lower my expectations for myself. She saw me as refusing to accept these ideas.

"Jackie won't function normally for the rest of her life," the counselor told Scott and me during the ninety-minute counseling session. "You can forget about ever going back to teaching or working at a professional job. You may want to consider learning a trade."

Scott was angry.

"You can't tell Jackie that she can't go back to work," he said. "She is going to do whatever she wants to do. She can accomplish any goal she sets her mind to."

"Well," the counselor said, "I wouldn't get your hopes up."

I was hurt and angry. The counselor didn't know me; she hadn't seen the progress I was capable of the way Scott had. She didn't know the motivation and drive I had to overcome my disabilities.

On the drive home, Scott said, "Don't listen to anything she said, Jackie. It's a bunch of baloney. You know how people have come back from things. You're up and around and going downtown and things. Look how short a time it's been. Do you think you're going to be where you are right now five years from now? There's no way. You'll be five years better."

I wanted to stop seeing this counselor after hearing what she had to say. I wasn't ready to give up on my teaching career—or myself—that quick.

Yet I doubted myself too. *Maybe she was right. Maybe I should just learn to accept that I couldn't do the things I wanted anymore. I was brain injured after all, and the extent of the damage wasn't fully known. Was I just setting myself up for disappointment and pain?*

I'd always been a positive person, yet the meeting with this counselor took me down a notch. The counselor seemed to have such a limited view of my future. I was tempted not to go back again, but I wanted to learn more about epilepsy and how to let go of my fear of having more seizures.

I made another appointment for a week later.

Scott came with me to my second meeting. The focus of this ninety-minute session was on the status of my head injury one year after the hijacking. We also talked about my emotions and the post-traumatic stress syndrome reactions I experienced on the anniversary of the hijacking—and the possibility of a future recurrence.

The counselor told me to expect my recovery process to be much slower and to accept the fact that I had reached a "plateau." Basically, I should lower my expectations for the future. My goals would have to be "realistic," given my current limitations—seizures, need for medication, memory problems affecting my reading and math skills.

We also discussed issues of having a family. While my doctors said there were no medical reasons why we couldn't have children, the counselor pointed out some potential problems. These included the potential for increased seizure frequency during pregnancy, more frequent neurology visits, frequent monitoring of blood levels, potential need for increased medication doses, need for coordination of obstetric and neurological care, and planning for the specifics during labor and delivery.

I was frustrated and angry about having to make additional plans that other normal, healthy women didn't need to make in planning for a pregnancy. I didn't feel that the counselor was helping very much, so I decided to stop going after my second appointment.

My emotional ups and downs were hard on Scott. We'd be laughing and talking one minute; then the next minute I'd be crying without knowing why. I was dependent and needed his help a lot, yet at the same time I also resented this dependency—and him. I had to rely on him so much, and that bothered me. I felt trapped. Scott got the brunt of a lot of my anger.

One minute, I'd love and appreciate Scott's care and concern, and the next minute I was angry and resentful.

It was confusing to both of us.

"What in the hell's going on?" Scott often asked.

How could I tell him when I didn't know myself?

I often reacted by snapping at him or crying. One time I got so mad I chucked a plate at the wall. I was frustrated because I really couldn't explain what was going on. I didn't know. This only added to our mutual frustration.

The FBI was not able to pursue its own case against the surviving hijacker, Omar Mohammed Ali Rezaq. At the time, much of the evidence against him came from EgyptAir Capt. Hani Galal. His testimony was critical to the case, yet he and the other Egyptians were not cooperating with the United States. They were probably embarrassed because an Egyptian commando team was responsible for the botched raid. Without the Egyptians' testimony, the U.S. Justice Department prosecutors decided there was not enough evidence to prosecute. Since Malta was moving ahead with its prosecution of Rezaq, the U.S. government decided not to proceed further and to let the Maltese courts take over.

Malta did not charge the Palestinian specifically with hijacking, apparently because the plane was seized over Greece, not Malta. Rezaq was charged with sixteen counts of kidnapping, murder, and assault, to which he pleaded not guilty.

Prime Minister Carmelo Mifsud Bonnici refused Egypt's request for the extradition of Rezaq. Egypt was accusing Libya of ordering the Tripoli-based Abu Nidal Palestinian extremist group to seize our plane. Libyan leader Col. Moammar Khaddafy continued to deny the charges.

I often called the FBI to find out what was happening in the case. I wanted to make sure Rezaq got put away for good.

Sometimes, Scott just couldn't give me the support I needed to deal with the anger and hate I felt toward the hijackers. I needed to talk to someone who knew what it felt like to go through something so terrible as a hijacking. I called Patrick Baker, who was living in Alaska, to talk about what I was feeling.

I'd been excited to talk to Patrick. He had left Malta shortly after the hijacking, as he had no physical injuries that required sustained medical attention.

Yet Patrick didn't have much to say on the phone. He was very kind, but the hijacking didn't seem to have affected his life the way it did mine. It didn't cause him to change careers or make any other dramatic life changes. It was something that happened, and he wanted to move on.

Occasionally, I called Scarlett Rogencamp's mother to talk. The first time we talked, Mrs. Rogencamp wanted to know absolutely everything about the time I'd spent with her daughter—the last few hours on the plane before she was shot. This was very hard for me. Part of me wanted to hold some of the details back. I thought it might only add to Mrs. Rogencamp's grief to know that Scarlett had been so scared or that we'd prayed together.

But something inside me, my Inner Voice, told me that it was important not to hold anything back from Mrs. Rogencamp; she needed to know every detail of her daughter's last hours. I told her how Scarlett and I prayed together, how sad Scarlett was, and how she died.

Mrs. Rogencamp cried on the phone as I recounted her daughter's last few hours. So did I.

A month later, I called Mrs. Rogencamp again. I knew she was going through a difficult time, and I wanted to offer my support in her grief. This time, it was really hard for me to hear her pain. It brought it all back.

Eventually, I wanted to know the names of all the people who died on the plane. It haunted me. I needed to know who died so that I could have some peace. No one knew how to find the answer. I wrote to Egyptian President Hosni Mubarak, but never got a reply.

These were dark days. I felt myself withdrawing into a shell of my former self. I was shriveling and dying inside, and feeling powerless to stop my downward slide into despair.

One rainy Sunday afternoon, about a year after the hijacking—I'll never forget it—I felt completely worn out. I felt dumb. I was tired of the anger, tired of the bitterness, tired of the person I was becoming. I hated this new Jackie.

Why did this happen to me? I was crying all the time, feeling sorry for myself. My relationship with Scott was suffering immensely. Since I couldn't accept myself, I had a hard time accepting him and others in my life.

I felt utterly defeated, overwhelmed by despair—helpless, powerless, and hopeless. I went into a deep, deep depression. I felt as if I was sliding into a cold, dark abyss. It was as though I was losing my ability to cope and, perhaps, losing my sanity. This was a different kind of depression than the one I experienced right after the hijacking. It felt deeper and more threatening. I hit rock bottom.

At the same time, I also felt a sharp pain in my heart on realizing that I had wanted to live so badly during the hijacking. Now, I no longer cared.

To me, not wanting to live anymore didn't mean committing suicide. I saw suicide as a permanent solution to a temporary problem. Not wanting to live anymore meant not being excited about life, not valuing my life as the precious gift I'd always seen it as.

In my darkest hour, I did the only thing I could think of. It worked once before, so I decided to try it again. With my body shivering from fear and tears streaming down my face, I prayed.

I shut out the noise and clamor of the world and closed my eyes. I remembered how, in my loneliest hour on earth, I had found deep peace, serenity, and the courage to face death. If I could do that, couldn't I also face life? The answer was clear. I could. I knew God would listen.

I asked for help from my Higher Power, just as I did on the plane. I prayed as I've never prayed before. I wanted guidance. I wanted my inner peace back. I wanted direction.

Then and there, I made a commitment to Jackie. I made a commitment to health. I vowed to find healing, whatever it took. I was not going to remain a victim all my life.

CHAPTER 10

TODAY IS A BEAUTIFUL DAY

DURING MY "TIME OUT" I DECIDED to focus on healing. One of the first things I did was to join a health club. It felt good to regain some of the strength I'd lost after the hijacking. I could feel the muscles in my arms and legs growing stronger. I always feel better when I exercise.

I went to yoga classes at the club and signed up for relaxation classes at a local hospital. Both helped me learn to slow down and relax more.

To help deal with the social isolation I was feeling, I decided to volunteer to help others. My ears perked up when I heard someone talk about the Courage Center, a place that helps people with head and spinal cord injuries. It sounded like just the place for me. I called and offered to volunteer. I wanted to do volunteer work because I thought I had something to give, but when I got there, I realized I needed help just as much as the people I had come to serve.

Some of the people had more serious physical limitations than I had and were, for example, in wheelchairs. But some could talk better and understand things better than I could.

As I listened to some of the head-injured people talk about their experiences, my own feelings and frustrations made more sense. I could relate to so much of what they were going through. I learned that my mood swings—from giddy highs to fits of rage and depression—were normal. I also saw that I was better off than lots of head-injured people. I felt less sorry for myself.

Aside from the Courage Center, I learned more about the problems associated with head injuries by becoming a volunteer at the Minnesota Head Injury Association. I was mad that no one had referred me to a place like the Courage Center, or taught me about the process of recovering from a head injury.

One of the counselors at the Courage Center took me under her wing. I told her about my problems with reading and, one day, she brought me into a special room, the Courage Center's reading lab. She sat me down at a computer that had special software designed to help boost people's reading skills. She let me sit at the computer for hours, practicing with various programs.

A paragraph would flash on the screen, and I'd put my finger to the monitor and slowly read one word at a time. It didn't go fast; it let me go at my own speed. By the time I read the second or third sentence, I had to go back up to the top. I didn't remember what the beginning said.

After reading a small paragraph, questions appeared on the screen. I had to punch in the answers. It would say, "Yes! You're Right" or "Try Again!" I got a lot of "Try Agains." At the end of the test, the program totaled how many questions I'd answered correctly and incorrectly.

After spending a few hours on the computer, the Courage Center counselor offered a suggestion that might help me read better. "Some people with head injuries see better with certain colors on the screen," she said. The computer allowed you to adjust the colors of the letters and backgrounds.

The color of the screen made a big difference. I needed bright colors to see the words properly. A black-and-white screen was not good enough for me. I needed bright reds and oranges.

A few months earlier, Scott had planned an evening out with some of his friends. They gathered at our apartment and, before leaving, spent some time talking in the kitchen. I sat in a corner of the living room reading the magazine article about Barbara Mandrell.

One of Scott's friends came over to me and, gently, asked how I was doing. I'd never told anyone besides Scott and my family about the numbness I felt in my left side anytime I moved my head forward, but I had a feeling that I could tell this man. I also told him that my jaw sometimes locked.

Mark Lyso introduced himself and said he was a holistic chiropractor, someone who understood the healing connections between mind, body, and spirit. He started feeling my neck. He thought he might be able to help me and suggested that I make an appointment to see him at his office.

The next day, I followed up. I told Scott what I was planning to do. He was a little skeptical about the idea, but supported my decision.

I didn't know exactly what to expect. This would be the first time I was going to see a doctor who focused on healing—not just treating disease.

On my first visit to Mark's office, Mark explained more about the theory behind chiropractic medicine. Mostly, however, he and I spent a lot of time just talking about what happened in the hijacking and what my specific ailments were. These included the numbness in my neck, headaches, and some low back pain. He asked a series of questions to better understand how they might fit together physically, emotionally, nutritionally, and spiritually.

Mark did a series of x-rays and an orthopedic exam to determine if it was something that he could treat and, if so, how. Sprained ligaments in my neck, together with some misaligned vertebrae, were apparently causing the numbness when I bent my head forward. Based on my personal history and the x ray results, Mark and I developed a treatment plan designed to help heal my mind, body, and spirit. Part of this involved muscle tissue work and chiropractic manipulation to help gain movement into the vertebrae and relieve some pressure on the nerve root that was causing the numbness.

Another part of the treatment process involved relaxing on a table in Mark's office and using visualizations as he worked on the areas of my back and neck that were injured. As he treated these areas, I would visualize blue-white lights coming from his hands and fingertips and flowing into my neck and body.

In the next few weeks, I could tell the treatments were making a difference. Someone was finally helping me! My neck was getting better. My jaw was starting to loosen up.

Mark was my chiropractor, but he did much more than just help me with the physical problems with my neck. He was a very interesting and spiritual man. He shared many helpful thoughts and insights about healing and spirituality. I enjoyed asking him questions. I'd finally met someone who understood the journey I was on! As I trusted him more, I shared some of the dreams, fears, and frustrations that I was having.

"Imagine taking a little eyedropper and transferring five or six drops of water from the ocean to a glass jar," he told me one time. "The jar would contain elements of the ocean—but is not the ocean itself. In a similar way, each of us has the elements of God within us. We are not God, but contain little droplets of God inside us."

After five weeks of working with Mark, the numbness was completely gone. He helped me change my diet, and I started taking vitamins and drinking lots of water with lemon. In a short time, my jaw no longer locked.

Seeing Mark was really a rite of passage for me. It opened me up to a whole new world of alternative medicine that I had never known about or experienced before. In the process, I gave myself permission to be vulnerable with my feelings. I felt safer to seek out answers to the many questions I was having. I was beginning to see a connection between mental, physical, and emotional healing.

Though Mark played such an important part in my healing process, I was learning to take more and more responsibility for my own healing and to reach out in new directions. I was slowly moving away from the limits that other people set for me—about how much I could heal or what I could do after the hijacking. I was starting to discover that there were people on my path who *could* help me get better.

Mark was also involved with a group called "Executive Futures" [the name has since been changed to "Unlimited Futures"]. This organization offered motivational training and personal growth seminars. Mark told me that Executive Futures specialized in helping people erase limits and discover their greatness.

I decided to check out the group for myself. I was drawn to Mark's philosophy and felt the group could help me learn and understand more about what had happened to me and why. I wanted to grow as a person and process all the spiritual insights I'd been having after the hijacking—the sense that there was something much more to life and that I had a purpose to fulfill.

Executive Futures gave me an opportunity to associate myself with people of like mind and energy. Here I found a group of people who were on a journey similar to mine and who supported me without judgment. The program also provided a helpful structure for me. It linked the physical, mental and spiritual aspects of healing that I was learning about with techniques for setting goals and overcoming limitations.

When I first started trying to figure out what *I* wanted in my life, I tried to quiet my mind. It was not easy. I was so used to going, going, going that all these thoughts were buzzing through my head. . . . Thoughts about my responsibilities. . . . Thoughts about conversations I had with people that day. . . . My thoughts drifted back to my life when I was a special education teacher in Baytown, Texas.

I had worked with several kids who were diagnosed as LD—yet were extremely gifted intellectually. I remember one fifth-grader, in particular, whose name was Bill. He scored in the superior range on IQ tests but was reading at the fourth-grade level. Usually, students don't qualify as LD if they are reading just one grade level lower. But when you had someone with superior intelligence—who should be reading at a much higher level than fifth-grade—it was a big deal.

Bill was a very different student. He had a very hard time focusing and paying attention. I could tell he was really frustrated. He was almost in another world. Bill came to me for help with learning difficulties. He was having a hard time weeding things out and focusing on what people were saying to him, and he would get upset for no apparent reason.

I thought Bill needed some help in learning to relax and slow down, so he and I listened to a relaxation tape together. We'd move the chairs out of the way and lay on the floor side by side as I turned the tape on. There was some soothing music on the tape, as the speaker guided listeners through a series of breathing and relaxation exercises.

"Relax your arms. . . . Relax your legs. . . . Relax your toes."

The tape seemed to work. Bill never fell asleep as he listened.

I saw a real difference in Bill when he left the classroom. I thought he would benefit by listening to the tape on a daily basis, but his regular teacher wouldn't let him come every day because it wasn't reading or math. Bill still came in to listen to the tape after lunch, sometimes just for five minutes at a time.

I remembered how well relaxation had worked for Bill. Could it work for me? Many of the books I was reading and people I was meeting spoke of the healing effects of meditation and relaxation. I decided to give it a try.

I found a safe, quiet room in my apartment, shut the door, closed the blinds, and sat down in a comfortable chair. Slowly, I felt myself letting go of my anxieties and worries. I felt my body relaxing and my breathing becoming deeper, slower, more even and regular.

A few more minutes went by, and I felt my muscles relax. I felt peaceful and quiet inside.

I asked myself a question: *What do I need in my life today?*

The first thing that came to me was *Joy.*

I relaxed and thought more about joy. I saw what joy would look like and how I would feel if I had joy in my life.

After a few more minutes, I opened my eyes. I wrote some thoughts down on a pad of paper.

Boy, did I ever need joy in my life!

Though I had trouble reading, I turned to books for support and encouragement during those dark days. One of my favorites was a book called *Affirmations*, by Stuart Wilde. It was simple and easy to understand. I underlined the sections that struck me as being true.

In the book, Wilde says,

> *It is important that an affirmation have emotional force behind it and that it means something to you. Emotions harness the energy. It puts you in flow. . . . The words do not really matter: it is your feelings that count.*

I underlined other sections of Wilde's book that gave me strength and comfort, such as

> *Each time the individual faces adversity he brings to that adversity his ability to transcend. His ability to be creative and to adapt is dominated by his experience of life so far, whatever that might be. And these confrontations, or trials in consciousness, more or less set down the quality of events the individual will experience for the rest of his life.*

And, every morning before starting my day, I'd repeat the following affirmations:

> *May the freshness of this new day vitalize and heal my body. May there be balance and power in this day.*
>
> *In this day, I express love to each person I meet, for I know that I am truly lovable.*
>
> *The universe is abundant, therefore I feel abundant. All my needs are met.*

I found passages that meant a lot to me in other meditation books too. I underlined and put stars by them in the books so I could return to them again and again. I wrote down a list of affirmations and started saying them to myself every day. Some of them were

> *I am loving and lovable.*
>
> *Today is a beautiful, loving, and fun day.*
>
> *I am honest to whoever comes across my path.*
>
> *I relax and am patient.*
>
> *Good things happen to me today.*

I didn't rush through my affirmations, but put my heart into each one. As I said each meditation, I visualized what it looked like. I used the affirmations along with the visualizations to set goals and achieve them.

Shakti Gawain was another author whose books helped me walk through my depression. One of the passages in her book *Living in the Light*, a book about personal growth and transformation, really hit home for me. Gawain writes about our need to develop healthier relationships with ourselves, others, and the earth itself, because the old ways don't work anymore.

> *It's as if we've been in school our entire lives, receiving an education that teaches the exact opposite of the way the universe actually functions. We try to make things work as we've been taught, and we may even enjoy some degree of success, but for most of us things never seem to work out as well as we had hoped. . . .*
>
> *Thus, our first task in building the new world is to admit that our "life education" has not necessarily taught us a satisfying way to live.* We must return to kindergarten and start to learn a way of life that is completely opposite of the way we approached things before [emphasis added]. *This may not be easy for us, and it will take time, commitment, and courage. Therefore, it's very important to be compassionate with ourselves, to continually remind ourselves how tremendous this task is that we are undertaking.*

Wow! I thought, this woman is great. She was speaking to me. I was learning to love the new Jackie—and I was learning to heal some of the old Jackie's emotional wounds too.

I started thinking more about what the epilepsy center counselor had told me about my limitations. It didn't sound right to me. I recalled a similar episode from earlier in my life that put her predictions in perspective.

In my senior year of high school, I started thinking about my plans after graduation. I thought about working for a while but decided that what I really wanted to do was go to college. No one in my parents' families had ever been to college, but education was a top priority in our home.

I made an appointment to talk about my plans with the high school guidance counselor, as all graduating seniors were required to do. Mr. Jenkins was a tall, imposing figure of a man.

"I'm thinking about college, but I need a scholarship to pay part of it," I told him.

Mr. Jenkins stared across his desk at me with a sad, sympathetic look on his face. It was hard to break the bad news, his eyes seemed to say, but someone had to do it. "I really don't think you're college material, Jackie," he said. "Just look at your grades (I had mostly B's and C's). I think you'd be a lot better off doing something else. Have you thought about a vocational-technical school?"

He urged me to learn a trade. I left his office feeling disturbed and confused. Somehow, it didn't feel right.

There has to be a better way, I thought to myself.

I went ahead and applied to college anyway—and tried for one scholarship. Three months later, I got two letters in the mail. I was accepted at a junior college *and* awarded a scholarship by the Deer Park Cafeteria Workers Scholarship Fund! It wasn't a lot of money—$120 for one year—but it was something.

At the beginning of my junior year at Sam Houston State, I declared myself a sociology major. Taking an education class was one of the requirements. I wasn't thrilled about it, but I signed up.

Was I in for a surprise! A whole new world opened up to me. I was finally in a class where I was getting it. I decided to switch my major from sociology to education. I amazed myself by making all A's. My self-esteem shot up and I finally felt that I belonged in school. My grade point average went from a C to an A. After that, I made the dean's list every semester.

I started thinking about becoming a teacher. Then the doubts crept in. I'd have to study and work harder to graduate on time. *Who did I think I was? Me, a teacher?* I saw teachers as being leaders, role models, the "good" students. In my mind, I didn't fit the bill.

I went to my academic advisor and asked, "Do you think I could be a teacher?" And he said, "Yeah, I think you could."

C H A P T E R   1 1

EXORCISING DEMONS

THE U.S. ARMY PSYCHIATRIST I saw in Germany had hinted that I might have a delayed reaction to the tragedy. At the time, however, I didn't really believe him. *Me have a problem with anger? No way.* I wasn't ready to give up the image of myself as a happy, "together" person. I wanted to get to the other side of my pain without actually going through it. Going through it meant giving myself permission to feel all of my feelings, especially the ones I wasn't "supposed" to have.

Throughout the hijacking, I remember feeling very angry. I was furious that the hijackers had taken away my power to make decisions. I had worked so hard to take responsibility for my life and my choices, and now that was all yanked away from me with no questions asked.

For the first time in my life, I felt powerless over the most basic aspect of my existence: whether I lived or died.

Now that I was finally starting to slow down a year after the hijacking, the pain started coming out. I felt survivor's guilt for a long time. I kept thinking, *If I had taken the middle seat on the plane, Scarlett would have lived.* The bullet in the gun that shot Scarlett was more powerful than mine. As for the children, I tortured myself with thoughts such as *If I'd only kicked the gun out of the hijacker's hands, maybe the troops wouldn't have needed to storm the plane and the children would not have died.* I had to really own and accept that Scarlett had died, that the children had died.

❦

I decided to call Brenda Schaeffer, a local psychotherapist who had been rec-ommended by my chiropractor, to see if she could help me cope with the fear, pain, and rage I was feeling.

Scott wanted us to go together to my first therapy appointment. Understandably, he was concerned about whom I might be opening up my life to. The therapy process was going to affect his life too. Yet I also sensed that Scott might be tempted to exercise a little too much control over my choice of a therapist. So I made the ground rules clear. He could come with me to check her out, but if I liked her, I was going to go.

We both went to her office in Golden Valley. I felt safe with the coun-selor right away and sensed her authenticity. I knew she could help me heal and grow. I was learning to trust my intuition and feelings about people and situations. In addition to her private practice, Brenda was the best-selling author of several books.

During the hijacking, I had to freeze my emotions in order to cope with the horror of what was happening around me. I numbed out. Now, to sur-vive emotionally, I had to start thawing out.

Psychotherapy helped me get in touch with all my anger toward the hijackers that I had stuffed. After I'd been in therapy a while, Brenda used a Gestalt method to help me get my feelings out. She had me sit in one chair and imagine the hijacker who shot me was sitting in another. She'd point to the other chair and say, "Jackie, why don't you talk to the hijacker."

At first, I was a little embarrassed about talking to a chair. Brenda sug-gested that I not think of it as a chair but rather really imagine the hijacker. I'd start talking and saying what I felt. As I did, I got angrier and angrier. The rage started pouring out.

After saying what I wanted to say, I'd sit in the other chair and become the hijacker. Now I'd be looking over at Jackie, from the hijacker's point of view. I'd tell Jackie why I did it, everything I wanted to tell her but couldn't.

I kept going back and forth, taking turns being myself and the hijacker. It was so powerful. My blocked emotions were flowing again. It helped me—not to forgive, because I wasn't ready for that yet—but to start to grieve.

Grieving was hard work but, together, we were working through my pain.

With Brenda's help, I did a lot of visualization. I imagined my hatred, bitterness, and anger as a black cloud inside my body. Then, I released the cloud and replaced it with bright, healing energy. I saw healing light and energy flowing through my body, from the top of my head to the tips of my toes. As I breathed in, I continued to pull in white, healing light. As I exhaled, I breathed out the black cloud inside me.

About three months after starting therapy, Brenda and I both sensed the positive changes taking place inside me. I don't remember exactly when or how it happened, but I knew that much of the depression, bitterness, and anger had lifted.

At the end of a therapy session, Brenda asked how I felt about completely reliving the hijacking from beginning to end. In therapy, we were always talking about the hijacking, but we hadn't gone through it step by terrifying step. Brenda thought doing this "body work" would help release more feelings and allow me to move forward. She knew another psychologist who worked with Vietnam veterans suffering from post-traumatic stress disorder who could be there to help.

I said yes.

I wanted to do it, but at the same time I was scared to go through the hijacking again. I called Barbara for support. "I'm really scared, Barb. I don't know what it's going to be like."

"I know, honey," Barb said. "But you're going to be okay. Wayne and I are praying for you. We both love you."

I felt stronger after talking to Barb. I was ready.

At 9 A.M. one Saturday morning I pulled into Brenda Schaeffer's driveway. Inside her office, I met Brenda's colleague. We went into a room and Brenda had me lie down on a mattress so I wouldn't get hurt as I replayed the hijacking. Brenda and the other counselor positioned themselves at either end of the mattress.

I didn't know what to expect. *Would I freak out and start yelling and screaming?* I didn't know.

I shut my eyes and Brenda slowly guided me back in time to the day of the hijacking. She talked me through the process of packing my suitcases at the hotel, hailing a cab to the airport, checking my bags, and waiting to board the plane.

"What do you see now?" Brenda asked.

"I'm talking to a Canadian woman who is traveling with her baby. I'm offering to carry her baby carriage down the stairs to where we're boarding the plane."

"What are you doing now?" Brenda continued.

"Well, I'm getting on the plane."

"Okay, look around the plane. Who's there?"

"I see the flight attendants. . . . There's a man standing in the aisle. . . ." I rattled off all the people I'd seen.

Slowly but surely, I described talking to the Egyptian man sitting next to me, offering him some caramels, smelling the deli sandwiches being served for dinner. Then I got to the point where the curly-haired man suddenly stood up, holding a gun and a grenade. I felt the two sharp blows on my head and heard him say, "Are you scared, lady?"

"Do what you'd want to have done if you could have done it," Brenda said.

I got up and started yelling at him, and I knocked the gun and grenade out of his hand. I slapped him around for a while and yelled at him, *"What are you doing?"*

I didn't really hurt anyone, but I brought blood. I brought blood to those hijackers.

Then Brenda came to the midair gun battle, the forced landing in Malta, and the torture of waiting to die. Brenda encouraged me to talk back to the hijackers, to say and do all the things I wanted to do at the time but couldn't because my hands were tied behind my back and I had a gun to my head.

This time when the hijackers came to me, I fought back. I slapped and punched and tore at them until they bled. I took the gun of the man who shot me and pistol-whipped him with a kind of savage glee. I described what I would gladly do to the men who had hurt me. I screamed and yelled and cussed up a storm that morning.

I left Brenda's office five hours later. The time had gone so fast! I thought I'd been inside for maybe an hour. As I walked to my car, I was a new woman.

I felt lighter. I cleaned a lot of anger out of my system. I knew my life would never be the same.

After that session, the terrorists never showed up in my mind again. I was in control, so they vanished.

Now that I'd actually felt and expressed so much of my anger and rage toward the hijackers—really for the first time—I felt ready for the next step: forgiving them for what they'd done to me and the people who died on the plane. *But how could I forgive people who had done such terrible things?* It didn't really seem possible. *Was it realistic? Did they even deserve to be forgiven?*

Forgiving wouldn't be easy, but it seemed like the only way I'd ever be able to get on with my life. To truly forgive the hijackers, I had to really *want* to forgive. And it couldn't be for fear of being a bad person or going to hell if I didn't.

As long as I held on to bitterness and hatred, I wouldn't heal. If I didn't forgive, I'd continue to be angry and bitter for the rest of my life. And the bitterness and resentment would slowly eat me alive. If I held on to hatred, I'd remain a victim of my attackers for the rest of my life. To be a free person, I had to forgive.

The choice was mine.

As my feelings were released, I began to more clearly understand and heal other parts of my life too.

When I first went into therapy, I thought I was there to deal with the hijacking. To an extent, that was certainly true. But the hijacking soon became a catalyst to work on other parts of my life—including relationships with my parents, with Scott, and with myself. I began to deal with years of accumulated feelings that I'd never named or expressed.

I was learning how to be a whole person. I was learning that it's okay to say no; it's okay to speak my mind; it's okay to do what I want in life. I needed the reminder.

After years of stuffing my dreams, I'd finally found the courage to go after them by getting jobs in Norway and Egypt. Now, I felt a pull to shrink back into a more fearful stance toward life. Plenty of people in my life encouraged that.

It was never said exactly this way, but I got the message from some people that I got what I asked for by choosing to live in Egypt. If I'd only stayed home, like my sisters and others in my small town, this never would have happened. In a way, I was to blame.

With my therapist's help, I sat imaginary people in chairs in front of me and explained to them how important it was to be myself and follow my own guidance.

Brenda and I dug deep into my past to explore the messages I'd internalized in childhood. I was in for some surprises.

I'd never realized it before, but feelings were rarely talked about or expressed at home. I believed that everything that happened in the family was supposed to stay in the family. I thought I was not supposed to talk about our problems or feelings with outsiders. I grew up thinking that all families were that way, that that's how families were supposed to be.

This insight helped me begin to understand why I had stuffed so many feelings about the hijackers.

As a child, I learned to repress anger, sadness, and depression. The messages I heard were "Be strong. Don't cry. Don't ask for help. You can do it by yourself." If I cried or was angry, I learned to push it down. I became invested in maintaining my good-little-girl image and learned not to have angry thoughts, and when I did, I sure kept them to myself.

I was the one in our family who took care of everyone else's pain. People came to me for advice and it was my job to please. I remember when my parents bought me a game called *Sorry* and how that became my friend's favorite nickname for me, because I was always saying, "I'm sorry, I'm sorry." As an adult, I kept saying "I'm sorry." I often said this to Scott, because I thought I was always screwing up.

To win my parents' love and friends' admiration, I thought I needed to make them proud. I knocked myself out playing softball, basketball, trying to get on the main line of the drill team—whether I wanted to be involved in these activities or not. I loved softball and the drill team, but the motivation for many of my actions was a strong need to win other people's approval.

Opening up emotionally was a completely new experience for me. Most of my life, I'd carefully hidden feelings of pain, sadness, anger, and fear. I got much of my identity and self-esteem from being the strong one, taking care of everyone else's feelings. I feared that if I took off my mask of caretaking and competence, people would think I was bad, selfish, or weak and wouldn't love me anymore. Revealing my own human frailty and vulnerability was a big blow to my ego. These feelings and fears surprised me. *What was going on? How did I get this way? Why was I so hard on myself?*

Brenda helped me see how important it is to stop caretaking, to let people take care of themselves, even as I continue to love and care about them. Even though I have an effect on people, I learned that I am not responsible for other people's feelings or lives, that I am only responsible for my own choices and behaviors. I learned new skills and techniques to express the real Jackie, not a cardboard cutout of what other people expect. I was learning to speak my mind and go for what I want in life—even if I don't always get it and even if it doesn't fit into what people expect of me.

My work with Brenda was creating some exciting new possibilities. As I became more emotionally healthy, I had the guts and passion to stand up for myself, to change the rules, to say "yes" to my life and my healing. One of the affirmations I used to help me cope with the strains in my life was "I have joy and happiness in my life today." I didn't have it at the time, but I wrote the goal as if I already did. It took a while, but I noticed that I did start to feel better.

I noticed something else too. As I started to act as if I had joy in my life, some of my "friends" stopped calling. I started to realize that I had chosen some very negative relationships in my life. Before I was shot, *I* was very negative. I had to let go of old beliefs and unhealthy relationships to make room for the new. *But how?*

It all happened slowly, one day at a time.

As I felt stronger and more in control, I looked forward to the exciting possibilities in my life.

Dr. Leppik had changed my seizure medication from Dilantin to Tegretol, and it seemed to be working. Months went by without having a seizure and I felt less depressed than when I was on Dilantin.

I continued seeing Mark Lyso three times a week and felt major relief from my symptoms. My neck was getting better; my jaw was starting to loosen up. He was fixing what other doctors said could never be fixed.

My spirits lifted, and I became tired of lying around the house. I felt ready to get out and start living again.

I wanted to go back to work. But this time, I decided to look for a teaching job. It seemed more my style than the big-shot corporate job with IBM. Mike Pflug, my brother-in-law, saw an ad in the local paper for a part-time special education teacher at an elementary school in Wayzata. I called to set up an interview with the school's principal.

The principal, Louis Benko, was sitting behind his desk, reading my résumé, when I walked into his office. As he began asking questions, I could tell he was impressed with my education and teaching background.

But was it all a lie?

The person on my résumé didn't exist anymore. I could never have earned a bachelors degree—much less a masters—with the learning disability I now had. I was reading at about a third-grade level.

What should I say? I had already toyed with the idea of shading the truth about my medical history and faking my way through job interviews. I'd probably stand a better chance of getting hired. But what about my seizures? How honest did I want to be? Should I admit that, if I had a seizure, I'd need downtime to recover? Wouldn't it be smarter to say, "I haven't had a seizure in a long time, and if I do, I just bounce back on my feet again"?

The application form asked for a description of any health problems that might affect job performance. *What should I write?*

During the interview, the principal explained that he wanted to hire someone who could stay in the position for a while. Four or five teachers had been hired for that job in the past year, and the high turnover undermined the stability the children needed. He looked down at my application, then shot straight to the point: "How would your seizures affect your ability to stay in the job?"

All I heard from my Inner Voice was "tell the truth."

"They are under control as far as I know," I said. "But if something happens, if I have a seizure, I'll need to be off for three or four days. It takes that long to get my memory back and to get back on my feet again."

"Well, we really need someone who can be here all the time," Benko stressed. "We really need stability."

What do I do now? Minimize the possibility of having a seizure, or the time it takes to recover? Or? . . .

"It's better that these kids know me, because I have a lot to offer," I countered, "especially with the understanding of learning disabilities I have today. It's better that these kids know me than that they not know me at all. If I have to be off, I'll be off. But I'll come back, and I'll be ready to teach them again."

We shook hands and I left. I didn't expect to hear back.

Later that evening, the phone rang at our house. It was the principal calling to say the job was mine!

It felt great to be back in the classroom. I quickly established a special rapport with a tough group of kids: learning disabled boys in grades four through six, the kind with a lot of behavioral problems. They were wonderful. I could really relate to them, because I was one of them.

I had a hard time reading. I knew how hard it is to be thought of as lazy because our brains don't allow us to focus. I knew what it was like to feel as though you can't keep up with what people are saying. I felt the frustration of looking normal and having people get mad at me because I didn't experience the world the same way they did.

The new job gave me the chance to share what I knew and was learning about learning disabilities.

It was a perfect fit for me in other ways too. It allowed me to ease my way back into the worlds of work and teaching. The part-time position gave me the time and flexibility I needed to stay focused on my recovery and rehabilitation.

I was excited about going back to work. I'd always had a special place in my heart for kids who had a harder time than the rest.

After my first year of teaching in Baytown, Texas, I'd decided to focus on teaching kids with learning disabilities. Looking back on those years, I remembered the excitement I felt from seeing my first- and second-grade students' progress. There were also frustrations. They often tested my patience. It took a lot of energy, patience, persistence, creativity, determination—and love—to reach these students. I racked my brains to invent specific, concrete ways to teach the kids how to write and say their ABCs.

If we were working on the letter *B*, for example, we'd all make *B* sounds and write the letter *B* in different colored crayons or markers. Together, we'd repeat different words that started with *B*. I'd bring red and black licorice to school and, together, we'd form it into letters. One time, I brought in a box of sand for the students to write their letters in. We'd bake cookies in the shape of *B*s. We'd all curl our bodies into *B* shapes and pretend we were *B*s.

When we were done, I'd say, "Okay, what's the letter for the day?"

"B! B! B!" the kids sang out in a happy chorus.

Before shifting gears to work on another subject—such as math—I'd tell the kids, "Okay, in about an hour we're going to come back, and I'm going to ask you what this letter is."

Just to refresh their memories, I'd make the *B* sound again: "Buh"—as in the word *Be*, and the word *Bat*, and the word *Boy*. And they'd say, "B! B! B!" and laugh.

An hour later, we'd come back to our letters and I'd ask the kids, "What's the letter for the day?"

Their faces went completely blank. If I was lucky, one child might hesitatingly say, "B?" Everyone else would chime in and say, "B! B! B!" But the only reason most of them got it was because they heard what the one child had remembered.

"We just *did* this," I'd say. "*Don't you remember?* We made the cookie in the shape of a *B*. What else did we do with the letter *B*?"

No one remembered what we did with the *B*. No one remembered that we all became Bs by forming our bodies into the shape of a *B*.

Why wasn't I getting through to them?

Then it hit me: we've got twenty-four more letters to go!

Sometimes, I took my students' learning problems personally—as if I had failed as a teacher. At those times, I grew frustrated and impatient. "Why aren't you listening?" I'd ask. "Why aren't you paying attention to what I'm saying?"

They hung their heads in shame. They felt terrible about disappointing me.

Parents of my LD students also became frustrated with their kids, because they didn't understand their child's problem. I remember one father who was so frustrated because his little boy couldn't follow simple instructions around the house. "We ask Timmy to go clean up his room and, a few minutes later, he'll come back and say it's clean," the father reported. "But when we go to check, the place is still a mess. I don't get it. Is he *trying* to drive us crazy?"

I understood his bewilderment. "You have to keep your directions very simple," I explained. "If you want him to take care of his bedroom, you can't say, 'Clean up your bedroom and when you're finished with that, I want you to go wash your hands, and then I want you to come down for lunch.' You just can't do that."

I told parents that their LD kids didn't know what they meant by a "clean bedroom." It was too abstract. The parents had to show them, in a concrete and specific way, what constituted a "clean bedroom." To a child, it might mean just putting his or her shoes in the closet.

The parents would have to say just one thing at a time and actually show their children how to do each task—"This is where your gym shoes go. This is where you hang up your jacket. Your socks go in this drawer," and so on. As parents, or teachers, we couldn't take anything for granted.

I encouraged parents to stay with their children and watch them pick up the room—to make sure they had actually learned. Only then could they be expected to clean their room.

I often wrote down information on learning disabilities and handed it out to parents to help them understand what they were dealing with.

Some children followed a behavior modification program to help them stay focused and responsible at home and school. I suggested that parents make a list of the chores that the kids were supposed to do and put it in a prominent place like the refrigerator. After finishing each task, the kids would then put a sticker or a check mark by the task to show that they had done it. This helped kids see their accomplishments and feel good about them.

Sometimes, the teaching stuck and sometimes it didn't. In the beginning, I wasn't very good at predicting what would work. It was neat to see the progress of my students even though it was always very slow.

At first, speaking publically about the hijacking was a form of therapy for me. It was a way for me to make some sense out of a terrible tragedy, and, hopefully, encourage others to persevere through hard times.

Though I had no public speaking experience before the hijacking, I was discovering a new gift: the ability to hold a crowd in rapt attention. I got a high from seeing people sitting on the edge of their chairs, so interested in what I was saying that they couldn't take their eyes off me. I got excited when people were listening and getting what I had to say, when the room was so quiet you could hear a pin drop.

When I first started speaking, I wrote my speech on thirty-two large note cards. I used a red ink pen, because red was the easiest color for me to read.

In Toastmasters, I learned it was important to use audiovisual materials to illustrate the points I made in my speeches. I started using video news clips from the hijacking.

I was also learning that my speaking style had to come from inside me. Lots of people were giving me advice on what to say, how to say it, how to stand—you name it. I tried to remember what they were all saying, but my memory was too weak. I found that I couldn't listen to what they were saying and stay focused on my speech. I had to find my own voice as a speaker.

Finding my own voice improved my speeches. People were very interested in what I had to say, and were particularly curious about the hijacking. "Do you think they should have stormed the plane?" a man asked me one time.

"I have to be real careful not to be judgmental about things after the fact," I said. "There were a lot of lives lost during that action. . . ."

Although my speeches centered around my experience in the hijacking, my focus was really on what the hijacking taught me about life, about what's really important, about survival.

During the question and answer period following one speech, I talked about the importance of meditation and getting centered in my life.

A woman in the audience raised her hand. "I feel like God is standing up there in a red dress," she said.

I was wearing a red dress that day.

She continued, "How do you get that feeling that you're talking about? How do you get to that point?"

"I get into a deep meditative state," I said. "When I come out, I feel energized. I feel that I'm tapping a power that has always been there. When I reach that, I feel that I'm becoming stronger. Sometimes, I ask questions when I'm in that state. I'm always asking God questions."

I enjoyed so many touching and sometimes humorous moments with the people I shared my story with. After speaking to a church congregation one time, the pastor announced that, after my speech, coffee and cookies would be served. "This will give Jackie a twenty minute 'headstart' to get off the highways before the rest of us have to be on the same roads," he said.

We all laughed.

NO TURNING BACK

SHORTLY BEFORE THE 1987–88 SCHOOL YEAR STARTED, I went in to see Dr. Maxwell, my neurosurgeon, for one of my regular checkups. When I first started seeing Dr. Maxwell, I went in once a month. As my condition stabilized, my appointments tapered off to once every six months.

On this particular visit, Dr. Maxwell announced, "I don't think you need to come in anymore. Your condition is pretty good. You should continue to see Dr. Leppik, but I don't think we need to worry about the bone fragments still in your head. There has been no change for the past year, and the scar tissue seems to have developed nicely."

The news felt good. But I still had a problem—namely, a huge soft spot in my head. "What are we going to do about my caved-in head?" I asked. "It limits me from being able to play softball and ski hard, from doing all the fun things I want to do."

"Jackie, there's a lot of people in this world running around with caved-in heads," he said.

"That's fine," I said, "but I don't want to be one of them anymore. I'm tired of having a hole in my head."

"Okay," he said, "then let me tell you about the surgery."

He explained the risk involved from the anesthesia. Dr. Maxwell would shave my head, lift up the skin covering my brain, then use a drill to attach a plastic mesh to my skull. Then he would take some putty and lay it over the mesh—to hold it in place. Finally, he'd shape the putty to blend in with the rest of my skull. When the putty hardened, the doctors would put the skin flap back over the wound and stitch me back up.

I had the surgery and was still bald when school started that fall. I wore a turban or a scarf over my head. You could tell I didn't have any hair, because a scarf over hair looks different from a scarf over baldness—it lay flat against my head.

The kids probably knew that I didn't have any hair, but none ever said anything about it to me. Until one day.

I got to school early one hot, muggy morning, and I had to run a bunch of errands. The scarf felt hot and uncomfortable, so I decided to take it off until the kids arrived.

One little special education boy came into the room and saw my bald head. "You're bald!" he pointed at me and started to laugh.

This little boy had emotional problems, and I knew he didn't mean to hurt me, but I still felt bad. It didn't feel good to have someone making fun of me.

I was getting another good lesson in humility, in what it was like to be handicapped, in what it was like to look different. It reminded me of how hard it is for kids. When adults saw me bald, they would do a double take. But it's different when a child sees you bald. They make fun or point.

In the 1987–88 school year I was teaching full time. I was still teaching learning disabled children in the mornings, but I was now teaching a mainstream first-grade class in the afternoons. I shared the first-grade class with Marcia Behring, and the two of us soon became close friends. I enjoyed talking and laughing with Marcia.

She was such a big help to me at work. When parents wrote me letters about their kids, Marcia read them to me—it would take me forever to get through them. Sometimes, when I got lost on my way to school and was late for a staff meeting, I called Marcia and asked her to let the other teachers know that I was on my way. Marcia and I got together outside the classroom too. She and her husband, Bill, were both very supportive of what I was doing in my life.

I enjoyed teaching my two different groups, yet I was having a difficult time of it. It was a lot harder working full time than I had remembered. By the end of each day I felt really drained. Attending meetings, doing paperwork, and preparing lesson plans took a lot of mental and emotional energy for me. I loved working with the kids, but all these other duties were taxing.

In some ways, the counselor I saw at the Minnesota Center for Epilepsy was right. My expectations did need to change. Teaching was much harder than I imagined it would be.

When I worked as a teacher before the hijacking, I'd always gotten "A" ratings. I was a good teacher. But now my evaluations were not so positive. A teacher evaluation specialist spent a lot of time in the back of my classroom, to make sure I was doing a good job. She often gave me ideas on things to do with my students. Before the hijacking, I never needed other teachers to give me ideas. I was always coming up with them on my own. People came to *me* for ideas.

It made me feel even more frustrated and unsure of myself. I knew something was wrong with my brain that blocked me from coming up with ideas or even remembering those I had used before. I was struggling just to do the basics. I was gaining a new appreciation for how hard it is to be a teacher, always having to think and make decisions.

I also understood why LD kids didn't like surprises. As a teacher, I learned not to change things on them suddenly, but to keep a regular and predictable classroom. They needed to stay at an even keel. If I changed or interrupted their schedule in any way—say by canceling a physical education class one morning to go on a field trip—it threw off my LD kids.

Now, I felt the same need for order and predictability in my life and routine. If my principal announced any kind of change or added something extra to our jobs as teachers, I got mad and frustrated. I'd think, *My God, now how am I going to do this? Now I have to learn something else! I'm having a hard enough time as it is.* Before the accident, I could go with the flow so easily— with no whining or complaining. Now my brain didn't have the ability to change gears all the time.

Discipline was another difficult thing for me. I had to think hard about how to manage kids' behavior in the classroom. I had to really concentrate when two kids started fighting. *What do I do now? How do I handle this?* Before the hijacking, my responses came naturally. I didn't need to think through every situation.

Fortunately, Scott was there to give me some support when I came home, exhausted, with stacks of papers to grade. He often helped out by grading papers. If I had some new assignments from the principal, Scott read them to me.

❦

In time, I calmed down and adjusted to my new job. It became easier. I felt more comfortable in the classroom.

Yet deep down, I knew I didn't belong in the classroom anymore. My heart was no longer in teaching. Every morning when the alarm went off, all I could think was *I don't want to go to work.* My body was rebelling too. I got sick more often, had a lot of sore throats, and was eating a lot. I used up all my sick days. I needed to move on.

I thought about how two months after the hijacking, I'd given my first speech about what happened on the plane and on the tarmac to a congregation at my church in Baytown. In the following months, I received speaking requests from church groups and schools that had read about my story in newspapers or seen the hijacking on television.

Early on, speaking was something I needed to do to heal, a way to make meaning out of my painful experiences in recovery. I also genuinely loved speaking to people.

Now, I kept hearing, *I've taken you this far in the world and given you life, now share your story with the world.*

I was answering back, *No way, Jose.*

I just kept stuffing and stuffing that message. I'd never taken a speech class or had any formal speech training, but I just kept getting messages that speaking was where I needed to be. Becoming a public speaker and sharing the details of my personal life with thousands of strangers was the last thing I ever imagined myself doing.

Then one day, I came home exhausted after a taxing day in the class-room. My Inner Voice kept saying, *Share your story. Share your story.*

I sat down in a chair, closed my eyes, and asked, *How do I share my story? Television,* my Inner Voice said.

Television? What did that mean? Then, I remembered. Right after the hijacking, I was swamped with interview requests for talk and news shows. I turned them all down, because I didn't feel like I had anything to say at the time. Yet Scott and I made a list of everyone who called.

A year and a half later, I pulled out the list and scanned it from top to bottom. I stopped by *Philadelphia P.M.,* a talk show in Philadelphia. I wanted to go somewhere far from Texas and Minnesota, where no one would recognize me. I dialed the number and spoke to *P.M.*'s producer. I told him who I was and explained that I was ready to share my story and that I could promise them an exclusive interview: it would be the first time I had shared my story on television. The producer remembered my story and booked me for the show.

I had a great time doing the show in Philadelphia. As I told my story to the host, I felt my body responding. I felt really good again: my posture was better; I felt my old glow coming back.

I had more than a hijacking story to tell now; I also had a message that could help people. It was a message about weathering adversity, going for dreams and goals, and not giving up. The talk show host opened the show to callers wanting to ask me questions. One woman called in to ask me all sorts of questions about my life and about the hijacking.

After that broadcast, I went to get my coat and head over to the hotel with Scott. As I was leaving the station, the receptionist said, "Our phone lines have just been jammed. Everyone wants to talk to you!"

It was hard for me to believe that so many people wanted to hear what I had to say. It also felt great! It gave me the feeling that I was making a posi-tive contribution, that sharing my story and message could actually inspire and help people.

When I got back home to Minnesota, interview and speaking requests began to trickle in. I accepted all the offers because I wanted to use my expe-rience to help others if there was any way it could. I never expected money for any of these appearances. I spoke for free during this first year, sharing my story with whoever wanted to listen. In time, people started insisting on paying me. At first it was twenty-five dollars, and then gradually it grew to one hundred dollars.

❦

One of my early goals as a speaker was to leave the podium. Speakers who didn't use a podium seemed to be more powerful and have a better grasp of their audiences. There wasn't a wall between them and the audience.

Yet the idea of leaving the podium was scary. I felt more exposed. People could see my body and how I moved it. I couldn't hide my nervousness behind the podium. If my hands shook, I couldn't put them underneath the podium.

To accomplish my goal, I'd have to memorize my speech. I read the speech into a tape recorder and listened to it while I was driving, taking a bath, or doing household chores. I also watched videos of my speeches so I could see my gestures.

There was another problem: I couldn't see the stage underneath me unless I looked down. At first, I couldn't take the chance of moving around a lot. I couldn't see the end of the stage or gaps or cracks in the stage. One time my heel got caught in a gap and I almost fell off the stage. I was able to pull it out in time, but people noticed it.

I wouldn't be vulnerable to falling or tripping if I stayed behind the podium or if I kept looking down. But if I looked down, I would lose my contact with the audience. Neither option was acceptable. I wanted to move around on stage and maintain my contact with the audience so that my presentations were smooth and professional.

It took about a year and a half before I had the courage to leave the podium and trust that I knew my speech well enough to give it without my notes. I found that by keeping the podium on my left, I could center myself on stage and reduce the risk of falling.

When I first left the podium, I often looked and felt awkward. I leaned forward and made exaggerated gestures with my hands. In time, I gained more confidence as a speaker. I was able to stand up straight and concentrate more on what I was saying.

⟆

There were other challenges to telling my story.

After one talk show appearance in which I talked about the bitter feelings I had after the hijacking—how I'd felt abandoned by the U.S. government—I got an angry phone call at home.

"What right do you have to be bitter!" the woman practically screamed in my ear. "You have no right to complain or whine about what happened to you. You knew it was dangerous to be in the Middle East when all that terrorism was going on. And you chose to be there. So stop complaining!"

My God! I thought. *All I'd done was to express my feelings honestly.* I explained how owning my own bitter feelings was an important part of my healing process, how getting these painful feelings out and accepting them allowed me to move past them. But the caller couldn't understand. She hung up in the middle of my sentence.

I called the phone company and got an unlisted number. From then on, I never discussed my angry feelings in public.

Sometimes people challenged me when I talked about the lessons I'd learned through the hijacking. "I believe we live forever," I said in one of my speeches. "I also believe in reincarnation. This is not the only body that I've been in. My spirit is learning lessons, and each time that I come back, I come to a higher level of understanding. I get excited about traveling, doing new things, following what my heart needs. That's something I don't ignore anymore. I made a commitment that I won't stuff God anymore. I'll let God come out in me."

I was often challenged when I talked about what I believed—especially when I spoke at some churches. If I didn't say what they believed, I wasn't right—or people would think I was in la-la land.

After the question and answer period, some people would come up and try to push the Bible on me. They quoted different biblical verses to prove that I was wrong about the lessons I'd learned through my own experience!

I could tell they were angry about some of the things I said.

I was very puzzled about how to communicate my beliefs and experiences to people who felt threatened by me. I kept trying to think, *How can I convince them that I'm on their side? That we believe the same thing but we're saying it in different ways?* I looked for language that could bring us together.

I found a wonderful meditation guide called *The Daily Word.* It contained thoughts such as "I walk in the newness of life for God is my life and I am well" and "Whenever a friend or loved one experiences a health challenge, I continue to hold that dear one in thoughts of wholeness and wellness." I read that quote at a time when one of my girlfriends was having problems with her child. Each day during my prayer and meditation time, I held her in the light.

I started reading *The Daily Word* along with my goals and affirmations every day. I found a lot in the guide that I could read in my speech that would make sense to churchgoers and to me. I also drew strength and inspiration from other readings by many different authors. A whole new world was opening up to me as I searched for answers to help me make sense of my new life—and attempted to share the meaning of my experience with others.

Along the way, I felt affirmed many times by the books I read and by the many people in my life who loved and supported me unconditionally. Slowly, I gained more confidence in my ability to talk about my journey in a way that was both meaningful to me and to the audiences I wanted to reach.

I felt honored when a friend asked me to be a reader at his wedding. Not only that, but he trusted me to select the reading myself. I chose this beautiful passage from Kahlil Gibran's book *The Prophet*, an inspiring collection of poems that meant a lot to me.

> *Then Almitra spoke again and said, And what of Marriage, master?*
> *And he answered, saying:*
> *You were born together, and together you shall be forevermore.*
> *You shall be together when the white wings of death scatter your days.*
> *Ay, you shall be together even in the silent memory of God.*
> *But let there be spaces in your togetherness,*
> *And let the winds of the heavens dance between you.*

Love one another, but make not a bond of love:

Let it rather be a moving sea between the shores of your souls.

Fill each other's cup but drink not from one cup.

Give one another your bread but eat not from the same loaf.

Sing and dance together and be joyous, but let each one of you be alone,

Even as the strings of a lute are alone though they quiver with the same music.

Give your hearts, but not into each other's keeping.

For only the hand of Life can contain your hearts.

And stand together yet not too near together:

For the pillars of the temple stand apart,

And the oak tree and the cypress grow not in each other's shadow.

CHAPTER 13

ON A MISSION

THOUGH I WAS CONSTANTLY BEING INVITED to share my story with large and small groups across the country, I still hadn't quit teaching. Mostly, I spoke during my time off—on weekends or evenings during the week.

As more and more speaking requests continued to pour in, however, I began to seriously think about becoming a full-time speaker. The tremendous response I received after appearing on the television show in Philadelphia gave me hope that I could do it.

Scott supported the idea. "I think you can do this," he said. "Don't worry about it. We can get by." His early encouragement and reassurance were so important to me. I knew that, even if things didn't work out with my speaking career, he would be there to back me up. Though our marriage wasn't going well, I never even considered that we wouldn't work things out.

Still, I was worried about whether I could make enough for us to live on. I was making twenty-seven thousand dollars a year as a teacher, and it would be tough to give up my steady paycheck.

I'd also have to give up the medical benefits I received as a full-time teacher. I called several private insurance companies to ask about individual coverage for Scott and me. I was eventually turned down by every single one: none would cover me due to my "preexisting condition"—the gunshot wound in my head from the hijacking.

Finally, Blue Cross/Blue Shield of Minnesota agreed to write a policy for me, if I agreed to two major conditions: 1. None of my treatments relating to wounds suffered in the hijacking (neurological exams, x-rays, physical or emotional therapy, seizure medication, and so on) would be covered—I'd have to pay all of these expenses out of pocket; and 2. My policy would have a thousand dollar deductible.

I wrestled with other fears about my future too. I'd spent a lot of time and money earning undergraduate and graduate degrees in education. Though the link seems obvious to me now, I asked myself, *What does public speaking have to do with my training as a teacher? If I quit teaching, wasn't I throwing all that hard work away?*

Yet my Inner Voice kept talking to me. I heard, *Trust and it will be okay.* And I also heard, *I have taken you this far—share your story.*

One morning. I shared my goal of speaking full time with my teaching partner, Marcia Behring. Marcia was very supportive. She said she would talk to her husband, Bill, about my idea. He was a director of marketing and sales for a local corporation and might give me some support. He eventually offered to help me polish my existing speech, and both he and Marcia acted as my agents in booking speaking engagements.

In March 1988, I went in and talked to Louis Benko, the principal at Greenwood Elementary School, the man who had taken a chance in hiring me. I told him that I was interested in taking a two-year leave of absence. I didn't want to quit my job outright because it seemed smarter to give myself some flexibility. I still didn't totally trust the messages I'd been hearing.

I had one or two speaking contracts lined up, paying about one hundred dollars each. It wasn't much. And I had three more months of pay coming in from my teaching job.

Not long after I went on the show in Philadelphia, while I was still teaching, I got a phone call from the producers of the *Donahue* show. Phil Donahue was planning a show about people with near death experiences (NDE) and wanted me to share my story with his audience of three million viewers.

Impressed with the uniqueness of my story, Donahue asked me to be the lead guest on the program.

A few years earlier I would have been reluctant to appear. For more than a year after the hijacking, I was afraid to tell people what happened to me on the tarmac. I was afraid they'd think I was crazy, making up the story, or hallucinating. I waited several years before going public with my story, telling only a few close friends about my near death experience.

People often asked, "Are you sure that really happened? Could you have been dreaming?"

It happened.

I was excited—and a bit scared—to appear on the show.

"May I bring a companion?" I asked the producer.

"Yes. Uh, who did you have in mind?" he inquired.

"My mother," I said.

I asked my mother because she had always wanted to meet Donahue. She flew from Houston and I from Minneapolis, and we met in New York City. We stayed at a hotel in the city. In the morning, *Donahue* sent a limousine to pick us up.

Unfortunately, Mom wasn't allowed to be in the audience of the show. *Donahue* has a policy of not allowing relatives of guests to sit in the audience; it can be too distracting. So Mom watched the show on a television screen backstage. She was so disappointed.

Before going on the show, I got a chance to talk with the show's six other guests. I felt a strong connection with several of the people. Their stories sounded a lot like mine. I felt a bit nervous as the makeup people primped my hair and face before we went out on stage. But I really got a kick out of being inside the glamorous world of big-time television.

One of the show's producers showed us where to sit and gave us a brief idea of what the broadcast would be like.

I had a good feeling about Phil Donahue, the man. He seemed to have a genuine personal interest in the show's topic and was well-prepared to ask questions about our near death experiences.

Phil opened up the show by talking to me about my experience. I was impressed that he'd read up on my story and had good questions to ask. After briefly going through the hijacking, I gave a detailed description of what I thought and felt during the precious moments I spent with my grandmother in the light.

I was fascinated by the stories of the other guests and the many similarities between their stories of being in the light and my own.

Melissa, one of three women on the show, "died" on an operating table during surgery to remove a diseased kidney. Her heart stopped beating for twenty minutes, and the doctors declared her legally dead. During her twenty-minute trip to the other side, Melissa had the wonderful experience of being in the light. In the white light, she saw several relatives who had died, including a brother. "That part didn't make sense," Melissa reported. "I didn't have a baby brother on earth. Yet I *had* seen him."

Melissa eventually returned to her body and made a full recovery. She started telling people about the experience, including the encounter with a baby brother. She got a lot of flak from family members and friends. "But you don't have a baby brother," they challenged.

One day, Melissa's father took her aside. "I'm sorry," he said. "Your mother and I never told you this, but she had a baby boy who died during a miscarriage."

Melissa had a baby brother after all!

I felt especially close to the man who followed my story, a man named Tom Sawyer (yes, his real name!). A heavy equipment operator and mechanic by trade, Tom had been pinned underneath a two-ton truck for over fifteen minutes when the ground underneath him shifted. The pressure of the truck lying on his chest forced all the air out of his body, and he was unable to breathe during that entire time. His heart stopped. Miraculously, rescuers managed to lift the truck and pull Tom to safety.

Though he couldn't communicate by sound during the ordeal, Tom was totally aware of all that was happening around him. "I have all of the conversations that took place around me memorized," he said. "There were about thirty-two people who gathered around within just a minute or so—the neighbors. This happened at my house."

Tom's and Melissa's stories were very similar to mine and others who have had NDEs. Tom told the *Donahue* audience that he, too, felt tremendous peace, joy, and love as he drifted towards a shining white light, which he later called Christ. There was something else he said that really caught my attention.

"I actually think it's a little comical," Tom said, "because I fervently believe that if I didn't get pinned under that truck, something else like that would have happened to me. Because I believe that at that time in my life, I needed to have a thing called a near death experience. I feel as though it was necessary. . . ."

When I heard that, I thought, *Wow! This guy is great!* Tom felt the same way I did, that in some mysterious way, my spirit needed the same thing.

It was obvious that the NDE had dramatically changed Tom's perspective on life and death, as it had mine. "I had a very profound, direct communication with this light," Tom continued. "And, of course, what I'm talking about is the essence of God; it was heaven. I communicated with that in a telepathic way. And I coined a phrase that's very accurate—superluminal telepathic communication. It was a communication, telepathic, that functions at the speed of light, conceivably faster."

Tom was thirty-three years old when the incident occurred. "I would have to describe myself as an agnostic at the time," he said. "I thought religion was fine for the religious-type people—it did more good than harm—but as far as I was concerned, it just had nothing at all to do with me. I didn't totally dismiss the possibility of God, but I certainly didn't believe in it. I do now. I know that there's not only God, but that there is a Christ."

Like many people who have NDEs, Tom was at first reluctant to share his story with others. "As a result of my experience, I started realizing things that were above and beyond my comprehension scholastically," he said. "I started talking about quantum physics, wave functions, religious matters. I just barely have a high school education, but from that experience I instantly came to know many, many things that are extraordinary—people have told me they are extraordinary."

I was amazed by the many positive reactions of people who saw us on *Donahue*. Many told me about similar experiences they'd had and kept to themselves for fear of being misunderstood, ridiculed, or called crazy.

After the show, I talked to Raymond Moody, best-selling author of *Life After Life* and the nation's leading expert and author on near death experiences. I said I wanted to read his book about near death experiences and learn more about them.

"You don't need to read it," Moody said. "You already know more about near death experiences than I do. You've had one."

❧

In the next few months, I was on numerous local and national television talk shows, including *Oprah!* In addition to being on talk shows, *People* magazine did a profile of me, as did *Redbook, Family Circle, Woman's World,* the *Chicago Tribune, St. Paul Pioneer Press, Minneapolis Star Tribune,* and numerous other publications.

I eventually formed a partnership with Bill and Marcia Behring. Together, we developed a series of presentations for business, educational, and religious organizations. It was an exciting time. A whole new world of possibilities was opening up to me. I hadn't felt this excited about life since I first left home to teach in Norway.

❧

At the same time, it became more and more clear to me that there was a price to be paid for my new growth. My career horizons were expanding, and I was feeling better about myself, but my marriage was foundering. Scott and I continued to grow further apart and, eventually, we separated and later divorced.

Out of respect for the privacy of those involved, I choose not to disclose or describe the intimate details of our relationship after the hijacking, or the specific events that led to the end of our marriage. That story is beyond the scope and purpose of this book.

Scott and I were young and had only been married for three months when the hijacking occurred. Under the best of circumstances, we still had a lot of work ahead of us to build a solid foundation for our future together.

The hijacking only made the task harder. In the aftermath, as I struggled to cope with my physical and emotional wounds and accept the "new" Jackie, our paths diverged. In different ways, the tragedy served as a catalyst for dramatic change in both our lives.

I remain very thankful for all that Scott and his family did to help me after the hijacking. I don't think anyone could have been more understanding or patient with me through all my emotional ups and downs and confusion about who I was and where I was going. I learned a great deal about myself—my strengths and weaknesses—during our three-and-a-half-year marriage. Most important, I learned to be true to myself, take care of myself, and really listen to my heart.

Working through the painful feelings that followed the end of my marriage was just as hard as coping with the anger, sadness, and resentment I felt after the hijacking. Knowing it was something that I wanted and knew had to be done didn't make it any easier.

Yet I knew in my heart that I was growing. My eyes were being opened. Deep in my spirit, I knew that, for me, there was no going back.

I was getting a lot of encouragement to keep sharing my story. As I gained proficiency as a speaker and traveled more, I got cards and letters from many people all over the United States and Canada who heard me speak and identified with what happened to me. After seeing a Canadian television documentary about my life story, a young man in prison began writing to me.

Some of the people wanted to know what I thought about what they were going through. Others wanted to know if I could suggest a doctor who could help them or help their daughter or son. One writer said, "My mother had a stroke, and she has been having the same kinds of memory problems that you struggled with. I didn't understand before."

I got a call from a woman whose son recently went blind from a hereditary eye disease. Although he still had his peripheral vision, his straight-ahead vision had been destroyed. The woman's friend had heard me speak in

Montreal, so she called me and said that I was talking about the same thing that her son Martin had been telling them. Martin's mother was very upset and was crying. I really didn't know what to say other than just be there for support.

I used to think that I had to have all the answers, because I wanted to help and was a caretaker. That's still part of my personality, but it's not so strong anymore. I was learning to let go of caretaking and let people take care of their own lives.

I received hundreds of letters from people who had experienced great hardships and pain, yet they were healing and my story seemed to help them. Teachers, coaches, housewives, secretaries, salespeople, executives, and managers wrote to thank me for some inspiring or comforting word or thought they had taken away from one of my speeches. No matter what issue or problem they were dealing with, they identified with the same issues and struggles I had gone through in my healing journey.

I was encouraged and inspired that I was touching so many lives through my speaking. I felt like I was a teacher again, only this time I was working with adults, helping them deal with the problems and challenges in their lives. A woman recovering from brain surgery and the death of a close friend wrote to thank me for telling my story. "You do have an effect on people," she said. "You did on me."

❦

As I opened my eyes and ears more and more, unexpected gifts started flowing into my life. I was listening more and more to my Inner Voice, and things were happening. I was excited about the many changes I was making—and needed to make—in my life.

It was an exhilarating and exciting period of growth and healing. The blinders over my eyes were being lifted, revealing a world more beautiful than I'd ever imagined.

When I healed from the pain of leaving my dog Spike with Scott, I got a new dog, a bichon frise that I named Oliver. When Oliver was very young, he barked and ran around my apartment a lot. He was extremely nervous and excitable. In time, he settled down and became a very important part of my life.

I was also gaining confidence that I actually had something worthwhile to say to people. I started seeing how my speech could help inspire people to work and live better, to reach beyond their limitations and fears to become the best they can be. I was gaining a new faith and confidence that I would have a life after teaching. I'd been sharing my story with people in churches and schools. Now, the business world was warming to my message.

I really enjoyed getting to know people in the new world that was opening up to me. In December 1989, I was invited to be a guest on the television show *Twin Cities Live* to talk about healing from post-traumatic stress disorder. Being on that show once again reminded me of how far I'd come.

I felt sad about the other guests on the show. Their bodies were slumped in their chairs, and I could see the sadness in their faces. I could hear the anger in their voices. And they said they had already worked through their pain! They seemed to think that all they had to do to work through their pain was to talk about it.

I was happy that I'd gone through the hijacking, but the other guests on the show continued to hate the people who had hurt them. It made me realize that many people don't find a way to work through their issues—they just end up being lost.

Somewhere I read a study done by a national trauma research center that found that one-third of people who live through a traumatic event experience psychological deterioration afterwards, another third stay the same, and the final third actually use the trauma as a springboard for personal growth and development.

What makes the difference? Being open to new things, new people, and new ideas was so important to me. I committed myself to doing whatever it takes to be whole again. Sometimes, I needed to be open to ideas or thoughts that other people saw as "far out." I tried everything, because I thought I had no other choice. I wanted to be happy again, and I needed to do whatever it took to be happy. I knew that happiness was down the road, but I had to work at it.

Steve Edelman and Sharon Anderson, hosts of the former Twin Cities talk show *Good Company*, decided to do a show on healing through mental imagery. They invited me to appear with Shakti Gawain, a noted author and speaker whose books meant so much in my healing process. It was so exciting to be on the show with someone I admired and respected so much. I saw Shakti as one of my spiritual guides and teachers. It was such a thrill for me, as a student, to meet my teacher face-to-face!

☙

I was excited to be touching so many people's lives with my story. While the vast majority of questions people had for me were loving and supportive, I was also learning to better handle the few hostile reactions that came up.

The Wisconsin Teacher's Association invited me to deliver the keynote address at their conference in Eau Claire, Wisconsin. After my speech, there was a question and answer period. An elderly woman raised her hand. "I want to know more about your faith," she said with a challenge in her voice. "I want to know more about your religious beliefs."

I stiffened for a moment, fearing the wrath and suspicion of an angry fundamentalist. The question brought back unpleasant memories of people coming up to argue and push the Bible on me. They were angry about how I described my relationship with God. I could tell some people were uncomfortable when I talked about my near death experience and the lessons I learned in my recovery.

At first, I was confused. Their response didn't make any sense to me. Then it slowly dawned on me: They might be scared. How could I be so positive and have healed so much if I didn't believe exactly as they did?

"I believe that each of us has to live and seek the truth that is within us," I told the woman. "You can call this the search for God, a Higher Power, the Christ Within, or our Inner Voice. It is a power beyond our limited human understanding, but it leads us in the direction of our destiny if we just tune in."

The questioner abruptly got up and left. To those who remained, I said more: "You need to choose whatever or whoever it is that you need to get where you want to go. I can't tell you there is only one way, because I don't know what that is. I only know what the way is for me today.

"I believe everything that happens in our lives happens for a reason," I continued. "Events or situations that first appear as tragedies are really opportunities to learn more about ourselves and what life is really about."

In December 1990, I decided to make an audio tape of my speech. I wanted to be able to reach more people with my story and was continually getting requests to put it on tape.

Yet I was having a hard time working on it. The old self-doubts were creeping in—the old self-limiting beliefs that said I really didn't have anything worthwhile to say. This was happening despite the fact that I shared my story all over the United States, had been on national talk shows, and written up in national magazines, and even had a Canadian television documentary made about my life.

I used affirmations to encourage myself to go forward with the project:

My motivational tape is very popular and loved by all.

I am safe to work on my tape.

I am capable to produce a powerful, uplifting tape.

Making the tape was a necessary and important step in my career as a professional speaker, one that would allow me to reach more people with my message and story.

In my mind, I'd visualize myself working on my tape, being happy in it, smiling. But I was still having a hard time seeing the final product. I focused on doing the part I could see myself doing: producing it and working on it.

Later that spring, I sat in a recording studio, preparing to make a tape of my speech. (A generous friend had given me the studio time as a gift.) Doing the speech one more time, with no one watching or listening but me and the engineer, should be a piece of cake. I'd spoken to thousands of men and women around the United States and Canada.

I hit a brick wall. "I can't do this," I said. "I don't have a degree in this. I've never made a recording before. What makes me think I'd be good at doing this?"

I sat in the studio for another ten minutes, staring blankly at the microphone. This was too hard. I couldn't do it. I got up and walked out the door.

A year later, I had another chance to make my tape. This time, I was smarter. I asked for help long before driving to the recording studio. I remembered listening to a tape by James Robinson, a well-known motivational speaker. I decide to play it again before going to the studio.

On the tape, Robinson asked his listeners to recall a time when they pulled back from something their heart wanted to do because they were afraid. He was certainly speaking to me. First, Robinson had me close my eyes and picture a goal or a dream I really wanted to achieve. That part was easy: I wanted to make the tape.

"Now," Robinson instructed, "close your eyes and see yourself a year from now and you haven't done what you wanted to do."

I shut my eyes and saw a lot of disappointed people. During my speeches, I had told my audience that I was making a tape, when it would be ready, and how they could order it. I had a long list of people who wanted to buy my tape, but it was a year later and they still hadn't heard from me. My body started to slump down.

"See yourself five years from now," Robinson continued, "and you still haven't done it."

I was getting a headache. I was disappointed in myself because I knew I could make the tape. I was smart enough, but I still hadn't acted.

"See yourself ten years from now and you still haven't done what you wanted to do," Robinson said.

My body was aching now. My back hurt.

"Now pull yourself out," Robinson said.

I was relieved, but I also felt sick.

According to Robinson, the main reason people don't get what they want is that they fear the pain involved. In this exercise, he wanted us to see that there's even more pain involved in *not* following our dreams.

Before doing this exercise, I spent a year and a half procrastinating about making the tape. A week and a half after listening to Robinson, my speech, "Choosing Your Road to Success," was in polished tape form.

BE MORE THANKFUL

I LOVE SPEAKING TO CHILDREN OF ALL AGES in schools across the United States and Canada. They are always on the edge of their seats when I recount the story of the hijacking and my long recovery. Their eyes completely focus on mine.

Talking to kids is special to me because they are so direct, real, and honest about their feelings, especially young children. They are so full of hopes and dreams and the spark of life.

They also ask me great questions, such as "Do you dream half or whole?" and "How do you put on your makeup?"

To the first, I answer; "I don't usually remember my dreams, but when I do, I remember thoughts, not visual images."

To the second question, about putting on makeup, I say, "Very carefully." I have to be very patient when I put on my eyeliner. I can only see half of my eyes, so I have to put on a little bit, then move it slowly to the next section and the next. I do the same with face powder. I put on a little bit, then move on to another section and cover a little bit more of my face. I have to hope that, somehow, it all connects and I don't end up with blotches of eyeliner or gaps of face powder.

The two subjects kids are most interested in are my divorce and my out-of-body experience.

About my divorce, I say, "You have to be truly, truly committed in a relationship. You have to always try new things to make it work out. Whenever one person isn't truly committed, it kind of breaks down. My ex-husband and I just started to go our separate ways and do things separately and, before we knew it, we had grown far apart. To tell you the whole story of what really went on, I'd need three and a half years, because that's how long it lasted."

Sometimes, kids follow me to my car after I've spoken to their class. They want to ask me more questions: "Do I have any kids? How did the guns get on the plane?"

Some of them just want to stand by me, be with me.

❧

Kids are more direct than adults about their fears as well as their curiosities. Most adults, for example, live in denial of their own mortality. Kids, on the other hand are more interested and open to talking about death. They haven't yet learned to fear it the way most adults have.

On one of my *Good Company* appearances, I talked about my near death experience. My friend Sandy's young son, Anthony, came with me to the studio. He was puzzled and curious about death. How could I see my grandmother who was dead?

How could I explain it to him? Then I remembered watching a television movie a few years ago. Richard Thomas, the actor who played John Boy on the *Waltons,* starred as the father of a young boy dying of AIDS. In a very moving scene, Thomas tries to explain to his son, William, what will happen when he dies.

The father takes an ordinary glove and dances it around, saying, "This is your body." He holds his other hand up in the air and says, "This is your spirit. When you are up in Heaven, your spirit comes down and goes into a body."

Then the father puts his hand in the glove.

"It's a little bit restricted," he continues, "but your body gets you around here on earth. So, here you are, your name is William and now William has AIDS and he has to leave his body."

The father removes the glove and leaves it on the boy's bed. "Your body goes to the graveyard," he tells the boy, "but here is your spirit—it goes back up to Heaven. *Your spirit is who you really are.*"

My message to kids, and adults, is that death is not the real tragedy in life. The real tragedy is not living while we can here on earth. It happens when we withhold our gifts and talents from others, and never feel the excitement, peace, and joy that comes from sharing our deepest selves.

The message I give to kids is the same message I give to grown-ups in suits and ties, and business outfits working in major corporations, to teachers, medical personnel, insurance executives, salespeople, secretaries, nurses, and physical therapists: "You can be and do anything that your heart desires—if you believe you can. *Attitude is all.*"

The power of belief, attitude, and expectation always amazes me. With belief, I've seen people accomplish things they never thought possible. I remember one experience from my first year of teaching first grade students that made me begin to appreciate the huge impact teachers can have in shaping a young person's life. I learned that if I truly cared about my students, I'd have to look deeper inside myself and be willing to learn from them. It had to be a two-way street.

As a student of psychology and learning, I was especially interested in how our expectations affect our relationships. I was aware of studies showing that we make our first judgments of people seconds after first meeting them. But that was something *other people* did. I was far too educated to be guilty of that kind of shallowness. I never saw myself as a person who prejudged others.

One student's mother set me straight. Her son John was a shy, skinny little boy. His classmates shunned him and didn't invite him to play in their games. He didn't know his ABCs. John was very quiet and withdrawn, the kind of child who often gets lost in the classroom shuffle. I had to spend more time and attention on kids with more obvious, disruptive behavioral problems. I cared about John, but my concern wasn't translating into action. I mostly saw him as hard to teach.

School had been open for about two weeks when, one day after school, John's mother walked up to my desk.

"John has been coming home every day for these last two weeks saying that he hates school," she announced. "He doesn't want to be in school anymore. None of my kids hated school. Why does he hate school?"

Something inside me clicked. I knew why John hated school, and I played a part in it. "Let's see what we can do," I told his mother.

The next day, I spent more time talking and relating to John. I became more aware of his classroom participation. I started giving him pats on the back and hugs. That led to another positive change: I began paying more attention to all my students, including others I had prematurely judged. After a few weeks, my classroom was filled with happy, alive kids.

John's mother noticed a change too. She called to report on John's progress. "Whatever you're doing, keep doing it," she enthused. "John just loves school. He doesn't want to go to bed at night because he's so excited to start school in the morning!"

When the other kids saw me moving toward John, paying attention to him, caring about him, they caught on. They decided, "John must be okay. Miss Nink likes John, so let's like John too."

John turned out to be a happy, smiling little boy. He was still a slow learner, but I loved him. And so did the other kids.

We make a tremendous, positive impact on people when we choose to love them just as they are, without judgment, without limiting or labeling them, or expecting them to live up to our vision of who they should be. Thank you, John, for teaching me that!

In my travels, I've had great opportunities to meet people and hear their stories. I'm always impressed that, no matter what one's station in life, people struggle with the same problems.

As a guest speaker at the International Platform Association meeting in August 1993, I flew to Washington, D.C. to speak on the same podium with Gen. Colin Powell, Anita Hill, and Ross Perot. I was especially curious to talk to Anita Hill. Like the rest of the country, I'd seen her testify before the U.S. Senate Judiciary Committee's confirmation hearings on the appointment of

Justice Clarence Thomas to the U.S. Supreme Court. I was impressed by her courage and stamina and wanted to know how she had gotten through this difficult time in her life.

I went up to her hotel room and knocked on her door. Hill opened the door and welcomed me in. We sat on her bed and talked a little.

"How did you get through such a hard time?" I asked her.

"Well, I leaned on my friends a lot," Hill said. "They gave me a lot of support."

"How did you discover what your purpose is?" I'm often asked by people who hear me speak.

There isn't anything magical or mysterious about it. The most important thing is to quiet down and slow down enough so that we can listen to our Inner Voice. When I started doing this, I asked my Higher Power what my purpose was. The first answers I received were to share my love with others. *To share my love with others? What did that mean? I could do that with almost anything*, I thought.

In time, my Inner Voice taught me more. I share my love with others through teaching but, even more basically, by just being in every moment. What does that look like in practice?

I might be driving down the highway and someone is in the left lane going only 40 miles per hour in a 55 mile zone. I say to myself, "I'm going to be in this moment. I'm going to learn all I can from this moment. I'm going to be relaxed in this moment. I'm being in the moment." Instead of screaming and using obscenities, I'll just smile and wave. I don't always do this, but I'm always trying to get to that point.

There's an important difference between our purpose and how we live it out. I believe our purpose is constant and never changes. Hopefully, as we go through life, our purpose becomes clearer and clearer. How we live out our purpose may take many different forms. Earlier in my life, I lived out my purpose by teaching. At this writing, I'm living out my purpose by speaking and doing this book.

When we start meditating and relaxing, and asking what our purpose is, thoughts will come to us. It's good to have a pen and paper handy so we can write down whatever pops up. These are all glimpses of our purpose. For some people, it comes in a grand, shining vision. For most of us, however, it comes in bits and pieces. Don't worry; your Inner Voice will show or tell you your purpose in the way that is best for you.

A few years ago, I saw a film called *City Slickers,* starring Billy Crystal. It's the story of three men from New York City going through a midlife crisis. Inspired to seek the meaning of their own lives and break from their world-weary days, they sign up for a two-week "adventure" vacation on a Wyoming dude ranch.

The film made me laugh, but I also liked its message. Crystal is intrigued by a crusty, old cowboy played by Jack Palance. Palance is the classic cowboy type, completely independent and unfazed by the problems of city dwellers like Crystal and his friends. Hoping for enlightenment, Crystal asks Palance, "What's the meaning of life?"

Palance raises one finger in the air.

"Okay, what is it?" Crystal asks.

"One thing," Palance answers gruffly.

"What?"

"One thing," Palance repeats. "It's up to you to find out what it is."

I believe we're all on a journey to find our way back home, to the deep inner core of who we are. Intuitively, we know that finding the "one thing" is the key to unleashing our personal passion and purpose—the things that make life truly worth living. The "one thing" is the guiding principle that keeps our social, emotional, physical, and spiritual lives in a harmonic balance with others, with the world, and with God as we understand God. Discovering our purpose on earth and then living it out is one of the most exciting experiences we can ever have.

Living a life of integrity, based on personally chosen and internalized values, is, in my opinion, the only way to find the "one thing." It's never an easy journey. There are many distractions and temptations along the way. It's about living the truth that will set you free.

In my experience, truth can never be boiled down to a single phrase or idea. There aren't any simple formulas. The truth is too vast. The best I can do is to share my sliver of truth with you, the truth of my own experience.

I believe we have everything we need to live a more fulfilling, satisfying life here and now. The kingdom of God has come and lies within each and every one of us. There is greatness inside us all, waiting to be tapped and expressed. The challenge we all face is how to unleash the wonderful gifts we *already* have.

Finding our purpose takes a commitment to growing and changing, expanding our maps of reality, and developing the disciplines needed to support us on our journey. It takes determination and the willingness and ability to focus on what we want. It's hard work, but it yields the treasures of our heart.

I use the following list as a transparency in my speeches when I get to the part about motivation and goal setting. It gives people a chance to see the world as I do, vision damage and all. Not only are letters missing for me— but also the top, left, and bottom part of each letter is missing. After giving people a look through my eyes, I show how the same words appear to someone with normal vision.

ɛɛ 's ┠ ɛss

1.   inɡ —
     ɛɛ   ans ᴜ   irvɛ
        ᴜr   a ls.

2.   ɛnɛɛ —
        rd   inɡ   suit,   ɛn
     n hɛ   ɛɛ ┠   ɛlɛs.

3.   ivɛ   lf-   aɡɛ —
        linɡ kɛ a   nɛr,   yinɡ
     "   an ᴜ t; l   ll ᴜ t."

Three P's of Success

1. Planning —
   Set plans to achieve
   your goals.

2. Persistence —
   Hard working pursuit, even
   in the face of obstacles.

3. Positive Self-Image —
   Feeling like a winner, saying
   "I can do it; I will do it."

I can always tell when people are serious about going for what they want. They are focused on something and determined to get it. They see themselves as worthy and capable of having already attained their goal. They have a "nothing-can-stop-me" attitude. If you don't, something will stop you. It always does.

Reaching for our goals and dreams is necessary if we want to enjoy life to the fullest. It's the most exciting, energizing, worthwhile thing we can ever do. People who have a goal, or are engaged in a cause, crusade, hobby, or relationship that deeply matters to them are healthier, happier, more resilient, joyful, and alive. Going for our dreams means going with our natural flow, unleashing the energy, talents, abilities, vision, and initiative inside us. Living our purpose gives us greater satisfaction and success in life.

It's so easy to get sidetracked, isn't it? As we make the commitment to living our dreams, it's important to become more aware of how that happens.

One way to stay focused on what's really important to us—on our top priorities, values, and goals—is to write a personal mission or vision statement. It's a concrete expression of the vision we have for our life. A vision statement is a personal road map we can use to stay focused on the things that really count in life. In the midst of the chaos and confusion that can easily overtake us—if we let it—a vision statement gives us guidance and direction. No matter how crazy life gets, we can always return to it to get our bearings. Like a wise teacher, the vision statement reminds us, again, and again, of what we already know to be true.

Here's mine:

Jackie's Vision Statement
- Always tell the truth
- Do what it takes to feel at one with God; inner peace
- Always keep promises and commitments
- Smile a lot
- Find the good in everyone and everything
- Take time every day to meditate and be silent
- Seek first to understand, then be understood
- Take time to be with nature
- Always ask my Higher Power for guidance
- Listen to my heart and act on it
- Exercise every day
- Set goals and take action to achieve them
- Give thanks for what I have and who I am
- Take several vacations each year
- Surround myself with loving, supportive people
- Communicate from my heart
- Maintain a positive attitude
- Laugh often
- Live in the moment
- Accept and love others just as they are
- Have fun with life

Always Tell the Truth

People usually think about telling the truth in obvious terms. I shouldn't tell you I'm going to the movies unless I really am. If you ask me what I did yesterday, and I spent three hours reading, I should tell you that's what I did. But there's more to it. If I ask you if you smoke, and you do but don't want me to know, telling the truth means being honest about it.

Perhaps you say to me, "Jackie, let's go to dinner tomorrow night. I haven't seen you in three weeks, and I need to get together with you." Let's say, however, that I've already made plans. It's been a tough week and I've been working really hard. My plans for tomorrow night are to cook myself dinner and then take a bath and go to bed. But I don't want to disappoint you. I want you to be my friend. So I will say, "Sure." I'll go to dinner with you, but all the while I'm thinking, *I don't want to be here.* So I'm not really present. Neither of us is well served when I'm not true to myself.

Always telling the truth is about saying "yes" when you really mean yes and saying "no" when you really mean no. It takes a certain kind of courage. A lot of people have a problem doing this because so many people were brought up to please others. Telling the truth is about taking care of yourself and trusting that people who care about you will understand. It could mean simply saying, "I want to get together with you, but I can't do it tonight. Here's my schedule."

Do What It Takes to Feel at One with God; Inner Peace

The Bible says we are created in the image and likeness of God. I believe when we slow down and become quiet, we can more easily tap into the divine part of ourselves. I always seek to be open to any messages that my Inner Voice, or God, is trying to send me. The messages come in many forms. I might receive a card or letter in the mail and feel led to call or write someone. I might become aware of needing to make an appointment with my doctor to check something out. The message could come in the form of a feeling: perhaps I'm feeling some stress and need to go work out at the club. I need to constantly pay attention to these messages if I want to maintain the peace and serenity I've worked so hard to attain.

Always Keep Promises and Commitments

I learned about keeping promises and commitments from Stephen Covey's book *The Seven Habits of Highly Effective People.* He says that if you break a promise, you need to go to that person and apologize from your heart—and not just say, "I said I'm sorry!"

As human beings, however, there are times when we have to break commitments. Circumstances can make it impossible for us to keep previous commitments. In these situations, it's important to apologize from the heart.

The best way to consistently keep promises and commitments is to take them seriously. I don't make a commitment unless I know I'm going to follow through on it. I don't make promises unless I know I want to make a promise. It's about being true to myself. It takes a lot of conscious effort to do this. If I'm confused about what I want, I give myself the time I need to decide.

Smile a Lot

I do smile a lot. Sometimes, I don't want to smile. If I'm not feeling good, for example. If I don't want to smile, it's usually because I don't feel good about something in one of my relationships. There's something I need to do to get right with someone. There's something I haven't taken care of. It's about taking care of something that I'm not happy with—so that I can smile again. It's not about the fakey smile, because people can see right through that. Do what it takes so you can smile every day.

Find the Good in Everyone and Everything

I work hard not to judge people but, despite my best efforts, I sometimes do. When I catch myself judging someone or focusing on some negative trait, I ask myself, *Why am I judging?* If I'm having a conflict with someone, I try to hold on to the good parts of that person. The conflict is still there and it needs to be worked out, but finding the good in someone stops me from getting so wrapped up in the conflict.

Take Time Every Day to Meditate and Be Silent

Meditation is also very important for me. To me, *meditation* is just a fancy word for getting away from the world. I do this in a variety of ways. I get away from the world about twenty minutes in the morning and twenty minutes in the evening. I go into a room where I won't be disturbed. I shut the windows and blinds, close the door, and sit in a chair with my hands in my lap. With my feet on the floor and my eyes closed, I focus on my breathing. It's important to breathe in deeply and slowly exhale. If I'm distracted by thoughts or worries, I let them drift past. Sometimes, I listen to guided meditation tapes. These can be very soothing and relaxing, taking me to a mountain retreat or a beach by the ocean.

There are different levels of meditation. The level I try to reach is the alpha level—the level right before you go to sleep. I tell my audiences that if you actually fall asleep, you've gone too far. At the alpha level, the inner peace stays longer. If distracting thoughts come, and they will, just let them go. It takes time and patience, but if you're committed to slowing down and getting quiet, you can more easily hear your Inner Voice talk to you during the day.

My attitude improves when I meditate, and if something negative appears to me, I can handle it more calmly and confidently. I don't get thrown off guard as easily.

Seek First to Understand, Then Be Understood

Stephen Covey talks about the notion of seeking first to understand, then be understood in his book *The Seven Habits of Highly Successful People.* I believe some of the most uncomfortable and painful experiences people have in life come from being misunderstood. Misunderstandings often create confusion, distrust, suspicion, and fear in our relationships. In our deep desire to be understood, we can easily forget that other people also want to be understood.

But there's a problem. Each of us has a slightly different point of view. The way we understand things is based on our very different life experiences. This is where misunderstandings often start.

To truly understand another, we have to be willing to suspend our own point of view and try to look at a situation or event from someone else's standpoint. We have to be willing, for a moment at least, to accept the possibility that our point of view is incomplete or possibly even incorrect. This is hard for many of us to admit or practice. If we want to have deeper relationships, based on honesty and acceptance of our differences, we must make this leap.

I work very hard on doing this in my own life. When a conflict or misunderstanding arises, I do my best to try and see the situation from the other person's point of view before reacting. Doing this helps me have more empathy for other people and broadens my horizons. When I seek first to understand people, I don't waste time defending my point of view and am able to learn from others.

Take Time to Be with Nature

Being out in nature leaves me feeling refreshed and rejuvenated. Taking time to enjoy the many miracles of creation renews my spirit in so many ways. I really enjoy going on camping trips or just taking a long drive in the country. I feel more at one with God when I meditate or pray, or spend time with nature. I love taking my dog, Oliver, out for his daily walk in my neighborhood. I do it for him, because he loves it, but I also do it for me: it helps me slow down.

Always Ask My Higher Power for Guidance

Is it going to be easy to bring our gifts into the light of day? No. There is no simple formula, no guarantee of success. One thing I do know is that we can't fulfill our purpose in life all by ourselves. We need to reach out for help.

The Bible says, "Ask and ye shall receive." I believe this is true. I also believe that the Kingdom of God lies within us. If we don't know where we are going or what step to take next, it's important to ask our Higher Power or Inner Voice for guidance. When we slow down long enough, our Inner Voice may reveal dreams, hopes, insights, or awareness that have long been covered over. One person might decide to start a business or start looking for another job; another may feel led to go back to school or take up a musical instrument or other hobby. Only you and your Higher Power—working together—know what new vistas you may choose to explore!

Listen to My Heart and Act on It

At first, it can be scary to start listening to our hearts. Once we start to get in touch with our hopes and dreams, we have to start dealing with the many obstacles that are blocking us from acting on them. We may have to look at some painful realities, revisit some decision we made a long time ago. Many of us will have to deal with the reality that our dreams were not encouraged by relationships and social systems which pushed us to conform rather than express our unique creativity and purpose.

What do we do once we become aware of our dreams and the barriers to reaching them? Choosing to follow our dreams involves reclaiming and proclaiming that we are truly responsible for our own lives. We are responsible for making the choices we need to make to live out our purpose. It's an excit-ing—and daunting—responsibility! If we want to unleash our full potential, blaming forces beyond our control won't cut it anymore.

Listening to our hearts is about making a place for passion in our lives. Without passion, I don't think we can move past the edge of our fears. The passion which comes from listening to our hearts and saying "yes" to our dreams emboldens us to energetically follow our purpose.

Exercise Every Day

I do some form of exercise every day. I do heavy exercising five days a week for an hour. During this time, I do aerobics or the StairMaster or exercise bike at my health club. The other two days I walk around the mall, some form of exercise to get my heart pumping. I play softball, basketball, golf. I also walk my dog every day. Even ten or twenty minutes a day is good. This helps me deal with stress and is a way of being good to my body.

Set Goals and Take Action to Achieve Them

Setting goals is about deciding what your dreams are and what you want. I was talking to a woman the other day and she said, "I never set goals." My thought was *if you don't do that, if you never really decide what you want and take action, you may never get what you want.* Just because you have a dream doesn't mean it's going to come true. You have to do something about it. I think it's important to write them down as if you already have them. You don't have to decide how you're going to get them.

The action step is important. If I have a dream of going to Hawaii, it's important to take the action steps needed to realize the goal: find out how much it costs, save the money, and so on. So many people start off by mak-ing excuses for why they can't do it.

I believe that, if your goal or dream is for your higher good, God provides the path to your dream, the opportunity to take you where you need to go. And you can take them or not: the choice is yours. Maybe a job will come up in which you can make enough money to realize your dream of a Hawaiian vacation. I believe that if we're doing what we're sup-posed to be doing in life—living our purpose—we will always be provided with what we need to help us along. I've seen this principle work in every area of my life.

Give Thanks for What I Have and Who I Am

I'm constantly giving thanks for the people and things in my life. Some people may think it's going overboard, but I even thank my material possessions. I talk to things and thank them for letting me use them. People say I always have good luck with the vehicles I buy, and I wonder if it isn't because I'm always talking to my cars and thanking them for safely transporting me where I want or need to go. I tell my cars how pretty they look. I also thank my dog for being in my life. I think it's important to give thanks during the good times and the bad times. It makes me feel good to thank and acknowledge the things around me and not take them for granted. I give thanks for who I am in many ways.

Take Several Vacations Each Year

This isn't necessarily about spending money. It's about getting away and exploring new people, places, and experiences. I like to do this with people I love. It doesn't have to be a quiet vacation, either. I like spending time with people, so my vacations are full of people. It could be going camping, taking a cruise, or whatever. The important thing is to get away from your routine so you can come back refreshed, with a new perspective on the environment you're in every day. I get to do this a lot because my job requires a lot of travel. When I go off on trips, I get that time away.

Surround Myself with Loving, Supportive People

I'm very careful about whom I spend my time with. In planning my daily activities, I always try to ask myself, *Is this person or situation going to give me energy or take away energy?* It could be something as simple as listening to the radio. Is that going to fill me with energy, or drain energy from me? If I'm thinking about meeting with someone, I ask the same question. If it turns out that I think meeting with a particular person is going to drain me of energy, that doesn't mean I don't go ahead and meet with him or her. Some people I love take energy from me. It just means that after I meet with someone like that, I have to give myself time to rejuvenate. I do try to limit the amount of time I spend with people who are negative. If we spend too much time with negative people, their negativity starts to rub off on us.

Communicate from My Heart

For me, communicating from my heart is about being real, about being true to myself with others. I do this in many ways. When I talk to someone, I do my best to give him or her my full attention. I try hard to listen to what the other person is saying instead of distractedly thinking about my response. I also watch the words that come out of my mouth. For example, if I am having a conflict with someone, I don't go around bad-mouthing that person behind his or her back. I always try to be as direct as possible in my communications with others. Sometimes, I succeed better than other times. When I slip and get a message that I need to put things right, I will contact that person and talk it through.

Maintain a Positive Attitude

Gratitude has a lot to do with maintaining a positive attitude. It's about not getting up in the morning and saying, "Oh, look, it's cloudy or rainy out—I'm going to have a bad day." I try not to judge even things like the weather.

When I go to sleep at night, I have already thought about what I'm going to do the next day. I've looked at it in a positive way. Some things I may not want to do, but I try looking at them in a positive way. For example, it's been hard for me to read through the many drafts of this book prior to publication. Reading is so hard for me. When I saw that I was starting to get down about this, I worked on changing my attitude about the reading. I told myself, "I bet I'm going to find some positive things when I'm reading."

Instead of looking at the bad of things, I constantly try to look at the good of things. If I'm still dreading something, I work to find out why. *How do I feel about it?* Usually, some kind of fear is involved.

Laugh Often

Finding the humor in situations or events is such an important part of maintaining a positive attitude. More than that, it's really one of the most effective ways I know of coping with life's ups and downs. If we get too serious, life can start to close in on us. We can end up letting little things get us down because we exaggerate their importance. When I lighten up and take myself a little less seriously, I find that most problems are not as bad as I might imagine or fear.

I try to watch funny movies, spend time around people who have a good sense of humor, and like to laugh out loud.

Live in the Moment

Most of us spend a lot of time in our heads, listening to the tapes that endlessly remind us of our responsibilities, worries, fears, duties, and obligations. Usually, we're rehashing some painful or uncomfortable experience from the past, or imagining some dreaded event in the future. It's hard to just live in the moment, yet that's really the only place we can fully experience life. The present is where we experience the closest thing to Heaven. As the author C. S. Lewis once wrote, "The past is fixed, and has already happened; the future is an illusion."

Living in the moment means appreciating and accepting who we are and where we are right now. For example, if we are at work and are worrying about making a phone call at four o'clock, my advice would be to go make the call—and then come right back. When we don't live in the moment, we miss out on the many wonderful things and opportunities that happen right in front of us. If we're in a long, slow-moving line, it's so easy to get all frustrated and mad because we have to wait. As someone once said, "Life is what happens when you're waiting for something else!"

I've learned that life flows much more smoothly when I make a choice to just stand there and wait my turn. I stop and look around, maybe watch some kids go by. When I'm living in the moment, I have time to be curious about other people. I am often wonderfully surprised by the unexpected people who come into my life when I choose to live in the present.

Accept and Love Others Just as They Are

Accepting and loving others just as they are has been hard for me, probably because it's taken a lot of work to accept and love myself just as I am. I discovered that it's often hardest for me to accept and love the people who are closest to me. I get angry with them more easily when they don't act as I want or expect them to. Usually, my anger or frustration comes when I decide that the person isn't acting or behaving as a boyfriend or parent *should*. If that person doesn't fit in my little mold, I might get mad. At times like these, I try to stop and reflect on what's going on. In some cases, I may have to end a relationship. In others, I have to change my expectations. In either case, the goal is to accept people as they are and not try to change them.

Have Fun with Life

Having fun with life is what it's all about. When I plan my day, I always make sure to include some fun things. It might be something as simple as talking to a neighbor, going to a movie, or taking a relaxing hot bath. If I don't put something fun into my day, I usually feel more stressed.

I always plan my days ahead. For a few minutes before going to bed, I visualize the day ahead. First, I see myself having a restful, peaceful sleep. Then I see myself getting up in the morning and feeling great. I see myself laughing through the day, meeting and talking to people. I see myself doing things such as exercising or walking Oliver. I don't see myself as being on automatic pilot, drudging along from one obligation to the next. I see myself as happy during the day.

Even though I've done a lot of healing since the hijacking, I still see my neurologist, Dr. Leppik, about every six months. The check-ups are needed to make sure the seizure activity in my brain is under control. In August 1993, I had one of these appointments. Nothing abnormal showed up, but on my way out the door of his office, Dr. Leppik stopped me.

"It's been a while, Jackie, and I'd like to get a new electroencephalogram (EEG) done on you, just to make sure everything's okay," he said.

I wasn't worried about what he was going to find on the EEG, a test used to measure electrical impulses in the brain. Quite the contrary.

The last time I'd had an EEG done was in Germany, shortly after the hijacking. Doing another test would allow Dr. Leppik to see how my brain was doing. If the results were positive, I might be able to reduce the amount of medication I was taking to control my seizures.

It seemed like a great idea. I was excited to compare the results of tests before and after all of my healing. I was feeling really cocky, certain that the test results would just blow my doctor away. Dr. Leppik is a speaker who travels around the world. I was sure he'd be so impressed with the progress of his prize patient that he'd want to tell everyone who I was and what I did to get better.

I went in for the test on a Friday. I remember getting into a meditative state. The nurse in the waiting room asked if I wanted to listen to music or read a book or magazine, and I said no. I wanted my mind to be completely relaxed during the test. I shut my eyes and quieted my mind. I became mindful of my breathing, taking a long slow breath in and slowly letting it out. I entered a state of deep relaxation. About an hour later, when the test was over, I pulled out of my meditative state and left the office.

For a few weeks, I forgot all about the EEG. Dr. Leppik never called and I didn't call him back. I figured everything must be okay and he'd just call me when he was ready.

A few weeks later, I was traveling to give a speech and had a brief layover at the Minneapolis-St. Paul Airport. I'd been on the road for a few days, so I called home to check the messages on my answering machine. I was excited to hear a message from Dr. Leppik.

I just knew he was going to say, "Jackie, I checked your EEG, and I was just amazed. It was so great, you wouldn't believe it. I can't wait to show it to you."

As I listened, however, I noticed that Dr. Leppik's voice was calm and measured. He didn't sound like someone eager to report a medical miracle.

"I checked your EEG, Jackie, and there is still seizure activity in your brain," Dr. Leppik said in his message. "Stay on your medication. Do not get off your medication. If you need anything, call me."

Then he hung up.

I just went crazy. Seizure activity in my brain? How could that be? I'd come so far, done so much healing. How could it be that I wasn't aware of what was going on in my body? It seemed like all the work I'd done over the past several years was for nothing. I cried and cried until tears were streaming down my face.

I needed to talk to somebody right away. I desperately needed reassurance. I dumped all the quarters from my little change purse onto the pay phone counter and started popping one after another into the slot. With anxiety bordering on panic, I dialed five or six numbers. No one was home. Finally, one of my friends picked up. I told her what the doctor said and how frightened I was.

She was so gently reassuring. She said so many wonderful things about me—that I was such a good person, that I wasn't going to have a seizure, that I was taking enough medication and the doctor said I was taking enough medication. She was as encouraging and compassionate as anyone could be. It helped, but not enough.

When I hung up, I was still fearful and shaking. Was I going to have a seizure right here in the airport? I got on the plane and tears filled my eyes as we were taking off. I felt so scared and alone. What did this all mean? I didn't know what to do. I closed my eyes and I asked what was I to learn from this situation. Whenever something troubles me or I am in the midst of any type of conflict, I always get quiet and ask myself, *What am I to learn from this?*

The answer that I got was *Be more thankful.*

What? I knew better than to argue with a divine response, but I argued anyway. Then I got mad. How could I be more thankful? I'm always full of thanks. When I'm in the car, I thank God for a wonderful day. I thank God for allowing me to live through the hijacking, for allowing me to have all these wonderful gifts. I thank God for Jim, my partner. I'm always thanking God. I thank God for being able to see butterflies.

Be more thankful? I didn't get it. I was still afraid. But I kept hearing *Be more thankful, be more thankful.* It didn't make sense—or did it?

Then it came to me. I'd forgotten to thank myself! I'd forgotten to thank myself for all the hard work I'd put into my recovery. Most of all, I'd forgotten to thank my brain.

Sitting on the plane, I put my hands over the top of my head and I held on to it and just hugged it. For a good fifteen minutes, I told my brain how much I loved it. I just held it as the tears started to flow. These were tears of sadness—not fear. I felt sad that I'd let so many years go by without thanking the part of me that did some of the hardest work in my recovery. I'd forgotten to thank my brain, the part of me that was most damaged in the hijacking.

To this day, whether I'm in the shower or relaxing in the living room, I remember to thank my brain. I hold on to it and hug it and tell it how much I love it. I'm amazed and very thankful that the brain can heal so quickly after suffering such trauma. The brain is remarkably resilient. My memory is much stronger than it was during the first few years after the hijacking. I've trained myself to compensate for my vision impairment by putting bits and pieces together to form whole objects.

When we're going through tough times, gratitude is often the last thing on our minds. When we're overwhelmed by painful thoughts and feelings, it's easy to lose perspective, to focus only on the hardships immediately in front of us. That's when I need to give thanks for the good things in my life—for the progress I've made, for friends, a warm bed, or a hot meal.

CHAPTER 15

WHAT DOES IT MEAN TO HEAL?

IN JANUARY 1993, THE FBI LEARNED that Malta planned to release Rezaq from prison for "good behavior" in February, after he'd served seven years. There was speculation that Malta felt pressure from Libya to release the hijacker. No notice of these plans was given to the U.S. government or other interested nations.

The U.S. State Department declared that it was "shocked and angered" by Malta's action. In 1986, the U.S. House Foreign Affairs Subcommittee on international security had called Rezaq a suspected member of the Abu Nidal organization, a PLO terrorist group. The panel said that Malta had assured the United States that Rezaq would remain in prison for a long, long time.

I thought the case was closed too. In November 1988, the hijacker had pleaded guilty to killing Scarlett Rogencamp and Nitzan Mendelson, and attempting to kill Patrick Scott Baker, Tamar Artzi, and myself. A Maltese judge had sentenced him to twenty-five years in prison.

The U.S. Justice Department, along with the governments of the other countries whose citizens were killed, urged Malta to keep the hijacker in custody. At the same time, Washington also began proceedings to extradite the hijacker to face additional charges in the United States. On February 12, 1993, the U.S. District Court for the District of Columbia issued a warrant for Rezaq's arrest, but Malta released him before an arrest could be made. On learning of Rezaq's release, U.S. Rep. Tom Lantos introduced a resolution strongly condemning Malta for the action and requesting international cooperation in prosecuting him in the United States.

On July 16, 1993, FBI Special Agent Cindy Carter, now assigned to national security, called to let me know that the FBI had captured Rezaq in Nigeria and, at that very moment, were flying him to Washington, D.C.

Details of the arrest were sketchy. After Malta granted Rezaq amnesty, he was permitted to fly under an assumed name to Accra, Ghana on February 25, 1993. Again, Malta reportedly did not inform the United States of Rezaq's departure or travel plans. After the FBI agents found Rezaq, they bundled him aboard a jet to Washington, D.C. where he appeared before U.S. District Court Judge Royce Lamberth. Since he'd already been convicted of murder and attempted murder, he would now be indicted on a single charge of air piracy. At the arraignment, prosecuters agreed not to ask for the death penalty. News reports speculated that this was done in exchange for the cooperation of several nations who assisted the United States in Rezaq's capture. If convicted of air piracy, he faces a possible sentence of twenty years to life.

Sandra Sonenberg, Rezaq's court-appointed lawyer, refused to enter a plea. The defendant is "not acceding to the court's jurisdiction" because Rezaq was seized abroad, she told the *New York Times*. Judge Lamberth entered a not-guilty plea in his behalf.

Rezaq, wearing orange prison overalls, listened closely at the defense table as an interpreter whispered a translation of the bail proceedings into his right ear.

Prosecutors said a fingerprint lifted from the inside of the cockpit window matches Rezaq's.

The arrest of Rezaq marked only the second time in history that the U.S. government acted under the provisions of a law passed by Congress in April 1986. There was a definite need to change the law as it was written. Terrorists knew that most countries, even those friendly to the United States, did not regard attacks on U.S. citizens abroad as a major problem.

After several presidential and congressional proposals, Congress passed a series of measures to try to deal with the problem. Two of the measures in particular, the Act for the Prevention and Punishment of the Crime of Hostage Taking ("Hostage Taking Act") and the Act for Prosecution of

Terrorist Acts Abroad against United States Nationals ("Terrorist Prosecution Act"), extended federal criminal jurisdiction to foreigners abroad who took hostage or killed a U.S. national.

Before the new laws were passed, the FBI had authority to seize individuals involved in terrorist acts against U.S. citizens only if the victims were high-ranking government officials. The new legislation expanded that power to protect all U. S. citizens living or traveling abroad.

On August 2, 1993, Rezaq appeared in Judge Lamberth's courtroom for another pretrial hearing. Sandra Sonenberg, Rezaq's lawyer, told the court that she planned to file a motion to have the government's case dismissed. She argued that U.S. courts had no jurisdiction to hear the case and that Rezaq was essentially being tried twice for the same crime. She asked for more time to do "legal research and documentary investigation" to support her motion for dismissal of all criminal charges against her client. The judge granted her five weeks to prepare her case.

U.S. Justice Department prosecutors described Rezaq in court papers as "a terrorist and a cold-blooded killer who attempted to systematically execute five persons simply because" they were Americans and Israelis, noting that he "hummed and sang" as he pulled the trigger. "He had previously demonstrated his hatred for Americans and attempted to murder every American he came into contact with on EgyptAir Flight 648." During the siege, court papers continued, Rezaq "made various demands, and, to emphasize them, attempted systematically to murder all of the Israeli and American passengers on board the airplane by shooting them in the head at pointblank range."

Assistant U.S. Attorney Joseph Valder said Rezaq should be denied bail because he has confessed to committing a violent crime and is likely to flee the country if freed. Lamberth granted the motion.

In October 1993, Rezaq appeared in court again to enter a plea of not guilty to a charge of air piracy. The proceeding was held in a special courtroom equipped with bulletproof glass in front of the spectators' section, and people entering had to pass through metal detectors. Pending a criminal trial, Rezaq is being held under heavy guard at an undisclosed location by the U.S. Marshals Service in Washington, D.C.

I had mixed feelings on hearing the news of the hijacker's release and capture. I was shocked that he could be released so soon. He personally murdered two women in cold blood, and his actions indirectly led to the deaths of fifty-eight additional men, women, and children. The hijacking really shook my basic trust in life. It forced me to confront the darkest side of human nature. For many years, I feared being attacked again.

Yet I also felt a strange detachment from his fate. Strange as it may sound, I don't hate him anymore. Though I feel he should be held legally responsible for his actions, I don't even wish him harm.

After years of bouncing back and forth between holding on to my pain and anger and letting it go, I've managed to truly forgive the hijackers. It took a lot of work for me to grieve the many losses I suffered from the hijacking. But I've let go of my bitterness and pain and moved on with my life. I've chosen to focus on the good things that came from the hijacking. God gave me many wonderful gifts as I became willing to walk through the pain of rebuilding my life.

I don't see myself as a victim anymore.

Reaching out to help others by sharing my story helped me a lot. At the beginning of all my speeches, I show a videotape that includes footage from the hijacking. I've seen it so many times over the past ten years, that I sometimes forget the terror of those grim hours on the tarmac.

Rezaq's trial in the United States was originally scheduled for January 1994. The month before, I remember feeling especially fearful. It was during a period when local television and newspaper reporters were devoting a lot of coverage to a string of rapes, muggings, and murders in the Minneapolis area. I had a gnawing fear of being raped or hurt.

The trial and crime wave reopened many of my feelings and wounds all over again. One day, in the process of writing this book, I went back and looked at some of the newspaper stories published right after the hijacking in *The Times*, a newspaper published in Valletta, Malta.

The stark black and white photos: a Greek man with bandages over both eyes; the grieving young man whose mother and sister—the Mexican actresses Guadelupe Palla de Ortiz De Pinedo, junior and senior—both died in the storming of the plane; a thin, gaunt Patrick Baker, shaken, but glad to be alive; and a truck loaded with coffins bound for St. Luke's Hospital. The photos were grim reminders of the tragedy.

The trial was delayed. In November 1994, I got another call from the prosecutors on the case. They wanted to fly Patrick Baker, Tony Lyons (an Australian businessman who survived the storming of the plane), and myself to Washington to identify the hijacker in a lineup. Prosecutors also wanted to talk to me more about the statements I had given when I was in Malta and since then.

I was nervous and a little scared. Over the years, I had identified the hijacker two or three times with pictures. But it had been about five years since I had last seen his picture. In the past, I had identified him from the FBI pictures by his eyes. So I thought, maybe I could still identify him by his eyes.

Days before leaving for Washington, I was really nervous. *Would I be able to pick Rezaq out? If I didn't pick him out, how would that damage the case?* The FBI kept saying that it doesn't matter if I picked him out. They reassured me that it was all going to be okay, but I knew that they wanted me to identify him.

The Sunday morning before flying to Washington, I met with my women's group. I told them about my upcoming trip and how nervous I was. They all agreed to pray for me during the time period when I was to be identifying the hijacker.

I flew to Washington the following Tuesday. An FBI agent picked me up at Washington National Airport and drove me to my hotel for an exciting reunion with Patrick Baker. I was most looking forward to this part of my trip. Though Patrick and I had talked on the phone several times over the years, I hadn't seen him since the hijacking—since sitting next to him on the plane, waiting to be shot.

That evening, I had dinner with Patrick. We shared what had taken place in our lives since the hijacking. Patrick said he came back from the hijacking and was able to get on with his life. I don't think it affected him like it affected me. However, he did say that he couldn't talk right and was shaking a lot for three months.

The next day, the FBI agents picked us up at the hotel and drove us to the federal building. For several hours, we went over a lot of things that I had already stated in Malta nine years earlier. They wanted to update me and refresh my memory.

Thursday was the lineup. In the morning we went to the federal building and met with Tony Lyons. We were just like little kids, we were so excited about our reunion. We barely knew each other, but there was a special bond between us because we had gone through such a terrible ordeal together. We shared an experience that is difficult or impossible to communicate to anyone who has not gone through something similar.

At the federal building, we went through a three-hour preparation period. We were told what to expect, and we went into the room where the lineup was scheduled. We would see the lineup through a one-way mirror.

Once the lineup started, we were placed in a hallway near the room. Patrick was called first. It didn't take Patrick long. He just went in, picked Rezaq out, and left. A minute later I was called to view the lineup.

FBI agents and police officers were standing in the back of the room, along with the hijacker's attorney and the prosecutors. Through the glass, I looked out on ten men standing in a long row, staring straight ahead. Each of the men had a number pinned to his chest. It was just like in the movies.

The men were similar looking. They were about the same height and had the same tone of olive skin and Arabic features. They were trying to fool us. I quickly scanned them, one by one, looking at their faces, their hair. Then I went back for another pass—and stopped.

I knew who he was right off the bat. I knew by those eyes. When we were hijacked, he went into the cockpit immediately. When he came out, he had a mask over his face—but I could still see his eyes through the holes.

In the lineup he was wearing a baggy, khaki outfit with a yellowish tint. His hair was shaven much shorter than when we were hijacked. There was just a little on top.

At one point when I was looking at him in the lineup, he looked right at me. He didn't know he was looking at me—right at me, in my eyes. I was taken aback.

It was strange staring at the man who had caused so much pain, knowing that I could see him, but he couldn't see me. I realized that this was a wonderful opportunity—in such a safe environment. My Inner Voice said, *Just stay here. Stay here.* And I looked at him and as I kept staring at him and staring at his eyes, all the memories from the hijacking came. When he stood up and went into the cockpit, and when he came out. When he kept looking at Scarlett and me. All the events quickly flashed in front of me.

I stood there, listening to my body and paying attention. And I realized, I had forgiven this man. It felt so good. There were no angry feelings as I looked at him. There was sadness because of what had happened—so many people had lost their lives. But I didn't have any anger toward him anymore. He was just a man. That was the value in doing the lineup: I needed to realize the hijacker was only a human.

After about five minutes of looking at the hijacker, one of the police officers said, "Do you know who he is?"

"Yes," I said. "And I knew who he was right when I walked in. But I may never see this man who shot me in the head ever again. And I wanted to take this time. He's number 10."

When I left the room, I started to cry again. I ended up crying and crying on one of the FBI agent's shoulders. A police officer said, "Come on into this room." I don't think he wanted me to sit out in the hallway and cry.

I said, "No. I just need to let this out real quick."

The FBI agent just kept holding on to me. I know that about myself. If something comes up, I just have to let it out real quick and then it'll be over with. So then we went to this room and it was okay.

Some of the FBI agents took Patrick, Tony, and me to lunch. When it was time to go home, Patrick and I shared a cab to the airport. We were talking about the lineup and I told him that I had picked out the man wearing the number 10.

"Number 10!" Patrick said. "No, it was number 2!"

I said, "No, he was number 10."

Again Patrick insisted, "No, he was number 2!"

Had I picked the wrong person?

Then I remembered what the FBI agents told us: After each of us made our pick, the agents randomly shuffled the numbers the men were wearing. This was done to make sure that our selections were not biased by a particular number or position in which the man was standing. Patrick and I laughed on realizing that we were both right!

When I got home, the emotions hit me. For a few days afterwards, I found myself suddenly crying for no apparent reason. I thought, *If I've forgiven, why am I still sad?* I wondered, *Am I lying to myself and others that I have forgiven?*

Then I realized you can forgive and still feel sad. Especially when you're pulled back into the pain.

After returning home I made a point not to schedule anything for days. I stayed home. I was moving at the time, so I packed boxes and processed the events in Washington, D.C.

A few days after returning home, I got a Christmas card from Patrick Baker. In the card, he said that after the lineup, he felt greatly affected also.

A few years ago, I was in Houston for my twentieth high school reunion. While I was at Hobby Airport waiting for my flight, I went to the rest room to wash my hands. I just happened to look up and saw something behind me in the mirror that didn't belong in a women's rest room, namely, a urinal!

What is that thing doing in a women's rest room? I wondered.

When I got outside, I realized what had just happened. I'd gone into the wrong rest room by mistake. With my vision loss, the signs "Men's" and "Women's" look like " n's" and " en's." If I don't stop and really look at the signs, I can easily mix them up.

It's a lot easier for me when I see " ies" (Ladies) or if there are silhouettes of a man in pants and a woman in a dress. If there's a skirt on the right, I can safely assume there's a skirt on the left.

I still play a lot of memory games—even today—to keep my memory sharp. During my busy months, I'm in about three or four states a week. I'm going through one airport and I'm always going back through that same airport. So when I get off the plane, I pay attention to who picks me up at the airport—what color hair they have, what dress they're wearing, what color tie they have on. I pay attention when I'm walking through the airport—everything on the left has to be on the right when I come back. I'm always paying attention wherever I go. This has strengthened my memory—so my memory is strong today.

As far as reading, if the letters are small or short, I do pretty good. I do pretty good with the newspaper, for example. I go left to right with my eyes without even using my fingers. But if the letters are a little bit bigger, I see more gaps—and I need to use my fingers to trace the shape of the letters.

If I'm ordering food at a restaurant, and the menu has pretty big letters, I have to use my fingers to read. Using my fingers helps me stay grounded on the page.

It's still hard for me to decipher the meaning of big or difficult words. When I'm on an airplane and they have signs that say "vacant" and "occupied" on the rest room doors, it takes me time to figure out what these words mean. For people like me, I wish they would just say "empty" and "full."

When I see *vacant*, I have to think, *What does vacant mean? What is vacant?* It's a big, abstract word and the thought process is hard for me. I have to go into a different part of my memory to retrieve the meaning of the word, whereas I understand *empty* right away.

After four or five seconds, the meaning of *vacant* comes to me. But it's not automatic. Though I can read at about the eighth-grade level, my comprehension is still only about fifth grade.

There are other problems. When I speak, I still have to ask people not to take my picture. I allow them to take photos during the question and answer period, because then I don't have to rely on my memory or focus on what I'm saying. If someone suddenly comes up and takes a picture during my speech, I can get off track very easily. I used to be afraid to tell people this. Usually, I'm always looking around for cameras before I speak. If I see one, I'll go up and very politely, say, "Are you planning to take a picture of the speaker?" If they say yes, I'll say, "Well, I'm the speaker and I would like it if you could take it during my questions and answers." Usually, people are very under-standing about this when they know it's a problem.

I've gotten better at seeing people's faces. But I don't see people's hair, their right sides—which is my left side—or their lips. Yet I have learned to hold images in place longer so that I get a pretty good picture of people's appearance.

I could always move my eyes from your hair to your right side and down to your lips. But as soon as I took my eyes off your hair, it was as if your hair never existed. I couldn't remember what color it was, what texture, what shape. Now, because my memory is so strong, I move my eyes up to your hair, down to your right side, and down to your lips. And in my mind's eye I get a whole picture of what I think you look like.

I've learned to compensate for my visual perception problems in other ways too. In my house, for example, I have a small television. Because the screen is small, I don't see large gaps in the picture that I would on a larger screen.

My learning disabilities and head injury still cause some problems in my rela-tionships. For the most part, I'm not as hard on myself as I used to be. But I still can get frustrated or mad at myself when I get lost or have trouble doing a simple task.

The people I choose to have relationships with are generally very sup-portive and understanding of my disabilities. But even close friends some-times lose patience with me. During a recent lunch, my dear friend Cheryl expressed the difficulty she sometimes has in communicating with me. "I get real frustrated and aggravated sometimes, Jackie. Sometimes, I feel like you're not listening to what I'm saying. When you repeat what I just said, it comes out all mixed up. It makes me feel like I haven't been heard. Then I feel bad about how *I'm* feeling. I have to stop and remind myself that you were shot in the head."

As we were talking, tears were coming to my eyes. It was the first time in a long time that someone was telling me that they were sorry. I'm always apologizing for misunderstanding people or for not understanding them right away.

When people get frustrated with me, I often have to remind them of my learning disabilities. It's not that I had a head injury—I still *have* one. What this means is that people can't take certain things for granted in communicating with me. They often have to spell out very clearly and concretely what they need from me. It takes work. Otherwise, I may not get what they are trying to tell me.

Back when I first started teaching learning disabled children in Texas, I didn't know how to help their frustrated parents cope with kids that could often be so frustrating. I had lots of techniques, of course. I knew all the "book answers" I'd been taught in graduate school. But I was still missing something.

Now that I am like one of the kids I used to teach, I've had to learn how to cope with the frustration felt by the learning disabled and those who care about them. And I've tried to pass the message on.

When I speak to parents, I tell them to try not to get upset when their kids don't remember something—just love them and accept them and say it's going to be okay. Their kids will get through it all.

The simple things make all the difference.

Letting go of our biases, preconceptions, and prejudices to truly love and accept someone who thinks or looks differently than us is never easy. It takes a willingness and spiritual maturity that many of us lack. But if we could only move toward love and peace, and stop insisting that other people think, speak, and act as we do, the world would be a much better place.

I've lived in countries with sizable Jewish, Buddhist, Muslim, and Christian populations. No single religion or creed has cornered the market on truth. It's available to anyone, anywhere. It can be found in the great religions and spiritual teachings of many different societies, cultures, and traditions. It can be found in the core principles taught by enlightened psychologists, philosophers, teachers, and wise parents and grandparents.

Truth is equally available to the wise and the foolish, the rich and the poor, people of all shapes, sizes, and colors. I believe that the differences between us matter less than our common humanity and identity as children of God.

About a year ago, I attended a traditional worship service at a church near my home. This particular Sunday, the minister was talking about the need for Christians to patiently wait for Christ's return to earth, for the Second Coming.

My interpretation of the Bible is different. When I heard the minister's sermon, I kept thinking, *He's already come. The kingdom is already here.*

Through the hijacking and years of recovery, I pulled God out of Heaven. I no longer believe God is up in Heaven and the devil is down in hell—that good and evil are "out there" somewhere. God gives us the free will to choose to live in Heaven or hell. I believe Heaven and hell are not actual physical places, but states of mind, attitude, and being we can all experience here on earth. As Jesus said, "I have come to bring the kingdom. The kingdom is here now."

I also believe God is inside us all, that our souls are connected to the very essence of God—the creator and sustainer of the universe. When I think of God, I think of a light flowing down from the heavens. I visualize that light before each of my speeches. I see the light flowing through my body and shining out from me to my audience.

I can touch the power of that light every day. Prayer, meditation, reading, getting in touch with nature are just a few ways I stay in touch with the light. By choosing to reconnect myself with God every day, I actually can have Heaven here on earth. I can also choose to have hell on earth. But God never forces Himself on us; we always have to open our hearts and ask God to come in.

"Letting go, and letting God" doesn't come naturally or easily to many of us. In our culture, we are taught to control situations and people. There is so much emphasis on material things that few of us are encouraged to develop or nurture our inner life or spiritual core. It's almost as if we didn't exist as spiritual beings. We learn to behave like machines stamped out on an assembly line. We learn to judge ourselves as "functional" or "dysfunctional" units, instead of seeing ourselves as the unique, exceptional people we are.

I believe we're all born with an Inner Voice, that that's what it means when the Bible says we are created in the image of God. Our Inner Voice is constantly leading us to health, wholeness, and fulfillment.

People call our Inner Voice by a number of different names: God, the Intuitive Self, a Higher Power, or the Christ Within. What you call it is up to you. At different points in your journey, you may use different names. *That* you call on this Inner Voice matters more than *what* you call it.

Our Inner Voice is directly connected to God and is, therefore, the truest expression of our deepest selves. Our Inner Voice usually signals us in quick flashes. It speaks to us in dreams, in sudden bursts of insight, in intuitive hunches which guide us toward our destiny.

Many of us are not aware of our Inner Voice. There may be so much chatter and static in our lives that messages from our Inner Voice are drowned out or ignored. We may dismiss what we hear because it sounds silly or too risky. Are we willing to stop and listen? Do we dare not to?

Listening to our Inner Voice is the key to unlocking our creative potential, to find purpose and meaning in our lives and to enjoy fulfilling relationships with ourselves and others. Our Inner Voice is constantly providing clues to our values, goals, mission, talents, and passions. The challenge we all face is how to unleash the love, energy, motivation, and creativity inside us. Tuning in is a discipline that anyone can develop.

To grow and develop into the people we were meant to be, we need to listen very carefully to our Inner Voice. It knows us better than we do. It knows the lessons our spirits need to learn. That's what our life on earth is about, listening and learning what we need to learn. That's why our Inner Voice is so important. Only by paying close attention can we learn what we need to learn, and thereby fulfill our purpose on earth.

When confronted by challenges or problems, it's important to get a sense of what resources you can draw upon to deal with them. The Inner Voice is directly connected to our Higher Power. When we tune in, we can access the supernatural strength, serenity, healing, and insight our Higher Power wants to give us. Our Higher Power is always looking out for our best interests and the best interests of those we love. But we have to do our part. Our part is to listen to our Inner Voice and follow where it leads. We need to obey our Inner Voice in the truest sense. The root of the Latin word *obedience* means "to listen."

Slowing down and listening to my Inner Voice didn't come naturally to me. I was always in a rush to get from one thing to the next, never stopping to reflect on the experience I just had before rushing headlong into the next one. I was a *do*er. My life was always filled with activities and people, but I didn't make conscious choices about how I spent my time. Much of my energy was focused on doing things for the wrong reasons—on doing things to please others, not me. I was afraid of displeasing my mother, or a teacher, or a supervisor, or a friend, or, when I was married, my husband. My life was defined by external expectations—not by what my heart wanted. I was often out of balance.

I could also be very impatient. I always wanted things to happen on my timetable. I cared deeply about my learning disabled students, but I expected them to learn as fast as I could teach.

Fear is the biggest reason many of us don't slow down and listen. We're afraid to feel the pain inside us, afraid to make changes in our lives. It seems safer to stuff down our feelings and awareness. When we don't listen to our bodies and spirits, however, we build up resentment and anger. We push people away and isolate ourselves from others, stifle the Inner Voice and our own true selves.

When I speak of the need to slow down, I recognize that many of us are very busy. Yet we don't have to radically change our lifestyle to gain the benefits of slowing down. It could mean something as simple as taking a few minutes during the day to breathe deeply or listen to some relaxing music. I have to consciously stop and think before I do anything. Because of my head injury, I can't take simple things for granted.

After the hijacking, I started slowing down. I started to become more aware of my thoughts. I noticed that I would often say things to myself like, "I'm no good at that" or "I don't look good" or "If only it weren't raining." As I became more aware of these thoughts and beliefs, I started to change what I said and thought about myself.

People and situations had been sending me signals to do that long before the hijacking. But, because of all my distractions, I never paid attention. I just kept doing things the way I was programmed, never stopping to pause or reflect on the why's or wherefore's. The only way life was going to get Jackie Pflug's attention was by hitting her over the head. That's what I think happened. The hijacking forced me to deal with a reality that I would have postponed until my dying day.

Yet we don't need to be in a hijacking or suffer some other huge tragedy to change our ways. We can tune in to the many messages our Inner Voice is sending us every day. Today, if I get a headache, I don't run to get some aspirin. The first thing I try to do is sit down, close my eyes, and relax. Usually, the headache is trying to tell me something. Most of the time, it's telling me I'm stressed. It's a signal I need to do something good to take care of myself.

We live in an increasingly violent world. How do we respond to that violence? With more violence? More hatred? With more rounds of retaliation and revictimization? What are the alternatives?

I believe there is a way, through reconciliation, love, acceptance, and understanding that each of us—individually and collectively—can truly make a difference in the world. We can reach out and stop the cycle of violence, hatred, and more violence.

We are really powerless over many of the forces that shape our lives. Yet we do have power over how we respond to those situations and events.

Listening to one another is such an important part of that reconciliation process—really seeking to understand, instead of seeking to be understood. This would help so much in resolving the conflicts we have with others. If we could just pay close enough attention to really hear what another person is saying—to work through all the feelings that may stir up in us. Because when we really listen, we're going to hear anger and pain. To be present to that takes hard work.

What difference would it make if we listened and were present to our loved ones and to other human beings? What difference would it make if we committed ourselves to forgiving others and to healing the hurts in our relationships? What difference would it make in our lives and in our children's lives if we all prayed for, expected, and gave thanks for the everyday miracles we see all around us?

I often wonder.

BIBLIOGRAPHY

Covey, Stephen. *The Seven Habits of Highly Effective People*. New York: Simon and Schuster, 1990.

Gawain, Shakti. *Living in the Light*. Mill Valley, Calif.: Whatever Publishing, 1986.

———. *Creative Visualization*. Mill Valley, Calif.: Whatever Publishing, 1978.

Lavoie, Richard D. *How Difficult Can This Be?: Understanding Learning Disabilities*. Produced by Peter Rosen Productions, PBS video distributor, Alexandria, Va. for F.A.T. City Workshop. Eagle Hill School Outreach, 1991.

Moody, Raymond. *Life After Life: The Investigation of a Phenomenon—Survival of Bodily Death*. New York: Bantam Books, 1975.

Robinson, James. *Personal Power: A Thirty-Day Program for Personal Success*. Irwindale, Calif.: Robbins Research International; produced by Guthy-Renker Corporation, 1989.

Schaeffer, Brenda. *Loving Me, Loving You*. Center City, Minn.: Hazelden, 1991.

———. *Is It Love or Is It Addiction?* Center City, Minn.: Hazelden, 1987.

Unity School of Christianity. *The Daily Word*. Unity Church monthly publication. Unity Village, Mo.: Unity School of Christianity.

Walters, Vernon A., and Herbert S. Okun. *Security Council Considers U.S. Self-Defense Exercise*. Department of State Bulletin, vol. 86 (June 1986).

Wilde, Stuart. *Affirmations*. Taos, N. Mex.: White Dove International, 1987.

INDEX

Achille Lauro hijacking, 9-10, 11, 53, 91
Acropol Hotel, 8-9
Act for Prosecution of Terrorist Acts
    Abroad against United States
    Nationals ("Terrorist Prosecution
    Act"), 210-11
Act for the Prevention and Punishment
    of the Crime of Hostage Taking
    ("Hostage Taking Act"), 210-11
Affirmations, 117, 144-46, 155, 170,
    183
Alternative medicine, 142
American embassy (Athens), 44-46, 48-49
Americans, xiii, 19-20, 24, 211
Andrews Air Force Base, 68, 102
Anger, 70, 100-4, 120-21, 124, 135-36,
    137-38, 149-51, 152-53, 212, 215
Artzi, Tamar, 22-23, 50-51, 209
Athens, 2, 4, 6-8, 11-12, 19
Athens American School, 6
Attitude, xiv-xv, 189-90, 194, 197,
    202-3, 219-24
Audio tape, 183-85

Bahi-El-Din, Imad, 16
Baker, Patrick Scott, 24-26, 50, 106,
    136-37, 209, 213-16
Beffel, Edwin, 44
Behring, Bill, 178
Behring, Marcia, 164, 178
Benko, Louis, 156, 174
Blue Cross/Blue Shield of Minnesota,
    173-74
Bonnici, Carmelo Mifsud, 20, 136
Business presentations, 178, 181

Cairo, 1-5, 6, 11-14, 95
Cairo American College (CAC), 2, 13,
    95, 100
Carter, Cindy, 90-91, 105-6, 210
Chiropractic care, 141-42

Comprehensive Epilepsy Program, 131,
    133-35
Courage Center, 139-40

DeLaet, Alfons, 19-20, 23
Delta Force, 22, 49
Depression, xiv, 111-12, 123-24, 131-32,
    135-36, 137-38, 146, 151
Donahue, Phil, 174-78
Driving, 77, 116-21

Egypt, xiii, 1-5, 9, 86-87, 89-90, 100,
    136-37
Egypt Revolution, The, 5, 16
Emotional changes, xiv, 58-60, 61-63,
    70, 75-76, 83-84, 85-86, 92-93,
    111-12, 123-24, 131-36, 137-38,
    139-40, 142-46, 149-55, 180-82,
    205-7, 212, 215-16, 221-24
Epileptic seizures. *See* Seizures
Executive Futures, 142-43

Faith and spirituality, 26-27, 84-85,
    137-38, 142, 169-71, 177,
    182-83, 188-89, 193, 196, 199,
    206, 219-24
FBI "Disaster Squad," 90
Federal Aviation Administration (FAA),
    11
Federal Bureau of Investigation (FBI),
    49, 90-94, 105, 136, 210-11,
    213-16
Fitzgerald, Suki, 87, 129-30
Fleming, Frank, 96, 105-6
Forgiveness, 153, 212, 215-16
Frankfurt, 58

Galal, Hani, 16, 18, 23, 28, 34, 51, 136
Gestalt method, 150
Goal setting, 194, 200-201
Good Company, 181-82, 188

227

ABOUT THE AUTHORS

Jackie Nink Pflug was born and raised in Pasadena, Texas. She received a B.S. in education from Sam Houston State University in Huntsville, Texas; and an M.S. in education and diagnostics from the University of Houston at Clear Lake. Jackie is a full-time motivational speaker, traveling throughout the United States and Canada. She lives in a suburb of Minneapolis, Minnesota.

Peter Kizilos received a B.A. in psychology and philosophy from Yale University; and an M.A. in Russian and East European studies from the University of Michigan. Peter is an award-winning freelance writer and communications consultant. He lives in a suburb of Minneapolis, Minnesota.